Also available at all good book stores

9781785316302

9781785315329

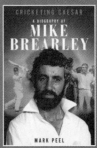

9781785316623

9781785316630

9781785316395

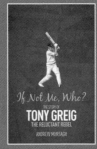

9781785316418

9781785315053

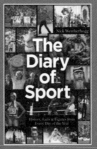

9781785316289

9781785316197

BARBED WIRE

WIRE

AND CUCUMBER SANDWICHES

BARBED WIRE

AND CUCUMBER SANDWICHES

The Controversial South Africa
Cricket Tour of 1970

COLIN SHINDLER

FOREWORD BY SIR MICHAEL PARKINSON CBE

First published by Pitch Publishing, 2020

Pitch Publishing
A2 Yeoman Gate
Yeoman Way
Worthing
Sussex
BN13 3QZ
www.pitchpublishing.co.uk
info@pitchpublishing.co.uk

ISBN 978 1 78531 634 0

Typesetting and origination by Pitch Publishing
Printed and bound in India by Replika Press Pvt. Ltd.

Contents

DEDICATION

This book is for Tony and Ruth
for so many years of hospitality,
advice and great kindness.

ACKNOWLEDGEMENTS

M Y first thank you is to Malcolm Lorrimer, the publisher of my Bob Barber biography, who gave me the idea for this book sitting in the sun at Old Trafford cricket ground. My second is to Jane Camillin at Pitch Publishing who gave me a commitment 24 hours after I sent them the first chapter. Previously, it had taken six months to get precisely nowhere and I was in danger of missing the start date to enable the book to be published on the 50th anniversary of the cancellation. Their speed of decision and unwavering support has made the writing of this book a pleasure. My thanks also to Graham Hales whose diligent aid with photographs and final editing was gratefully received.

I am grateful of course to the many people who spoke to me recalling the events of 1970. Among them are Lord Peter Hain, Mike Brearley, Peter Baxter, John Woodcock, Robin Marlar, Raymond Illingworth, Keith Fletcher, Peter Lever, Ken Shuttleworth, David Brown, Farokh Engineer, Jonathan Agnew, Mike Atherton, Bob Barber, Jim Cumbes and Jack Simmons.

Robert Curphey and his staff at the MCC Library at Lord's could not have been more helpful in providing the original documents of the Cricket Council. Working there is like being locked up in a sweet shop when you're seven – or seventy. This is the first book I have written in which I have been unable to read contemporary newspapers at the much loved British Newspaper Library in Colindale. Everything is now available at the British Library and accessible at the click of a mouse but I can't help pining for that old Art Deco building and the enormous leather-bound volumes delivered to your seat by workers in brown overalls. It gave a much better sense of working in an archive and digging for buried treasure. Key work too was done at the Cambridge University Library, a vital resource for me for 50 years.

Conversations which proved helpful at various times during research and writing were conducted with Stephen Chalke, Lawrence Booth, Lee Stribling, Michael Parkinson, Jon Holmes, Katherine Fisher and Michael Henderson. All mistakes, factual and analytical, are of my own making.

FOREWORD

T HE controversial campaign to stop the 1970 tour by an all-white South Africa cricket team was one to which I fully subscribed at the time.

Looking back at the period covered by this book is to remember a different country. I believe *Barbed Wire and Cucumber Sandwiches* is an important document with a reach far beyond the boundaries of the game and the consequences profoundly affecting the way people regarded multi-racial sport. To be reminded of the stupidity of the executive, cricket and political, not to mention 21 million viewers watching *The Black & White Minstrel Show* is to be thankful that cricket has helped change things for the better in more ways than its being simply a contest of 22 'flannelled fools'.

Since 1992 South Africa has been gladly welcomed back into the community of cricket-playing nations but the painful struggle she endured in order to get there is a story that should never be forgotten. This book is a powerful reminder of those turbulent times.

Sir Michael Parkinson CBE

PREFACE

THE narrative of this book describes in detail the events leading up to the cancellation of the scheduled tour of England by South African cricketers in the summer of 1970. Hastily, after the MCC withdrew its invitation to the South African Cricket Association barely ten days before the tour was due to begin, it was further announced from Lord's that England would instead play a series of five Test matches against a Rest of the World XI which, ironically, included five of the key players who would have arrived as part of the South African side (Graeme and Peter Pollock, Mike Procter, Barry Richards and Eddie Barlow). The matches turned out to be an absorbing affair. Perhaps they weren't on the same level as the Ashes series of 2005 but after a decade of turgid, attritional Test cricket they were a breath of fresh air. England lost the series 4-1 but they should really have won the Fourth Test at Headingley, and it could even have been 3-2 to England or a 2-2 series draw with the Edgbaston match drawn, had the luck been with them. And yet it is the series that time forgot.

Working through reports and personal reminiscences it is hard to understand why the series failed to catch on and is scarcely remembered today. No book about the Rest of the World series graces the bookshelves of a lover of cricket history and when mentioned to modern cricket fans the series is frequently mistaken, at least initially, for the World Series Cricket financed by Kerry Packer towards the end of the decade. The cricket played by so many outstanding players was enticing enough to have warranted a far greater attendance than those few thousand who showed up most days. The only explanation lies in the basic desire of international cricket spectators to watch one country being pitted against another. Yet apart from Australia and to a lesser extent South Africa (as was) and West Indies, England's matches against New Zealand, India and Pakistan, the other nations playing Test cricket in 1970, rarely attracted significant attendances until immigration from the subcontinent assumed significant proportions.

The story of the cancellation is not really a cricket story *per se*. If anything it is the story of generations in conflict. The MCC members, who in December 1968 had voted overwhelmingly in favour of their committee and their 'skilled' handling of the D'Oliveira affair, were the bedrock of support for another series against an all-white team from South Africa. However, they were joined enthusiastically by many cricket lovers who were not necessarily dyed-in-the-wool members of the right wing of the Conservative Party. South Africa had in 1970 what was widely considered the best team in their history and the best team in world cricket at the time. The desire to sit in the sun and watch them play a full season of cricket including county and festival matches as well as the Tests was very strong among such people. For those of them who had fought in the war, watching cricket was the fundamental birthright of every Englishman. It was partly what they had been fighting for and it accounted for the remarkable and sustained boom in attendances at all kinds of cricket matches in the years following the end of the war in 1945. Anyone who wanted to stop them watching cricket were fascist killjoys.

That was odd because the people who opposed them thought that *they* were the fascists. If the stereotypical supporter of the tour was a middle-aged or elderly, home-owning Caucasian, wore a jacket and tie as a matter of course, read *The Times* or the *Daily Telegraph* and lived in a middle-class suburban neighbourhood in the south of England, the stereotypical demonstrator against the tour was a young student with long hair, living in rented accommodation who was fiercely opposed to American military involvement in South East Asia and was part of the wider movement for civil rights in America, Ban the Bomb and the Anti-Apartheid Movement. The fault line ran down the spine of the country. It wasn't identical to but it certainly had similarities to the way in which Brexit divided the country after the 2016 referendum. Each side was convinced of its own virtue and of the fundamental evil of its opponent. On each side there was a spectrum from moderate to extreme, from David Sheppard's Fair Cricket campaign to Peter Hain's Stop the Seventy Tour movement on one side and from Wilf Wooller and the alt right of MCC to men like Doug Insole and Billy Griffith on the other who could see the evils of apartheid but believed that playing cricket with South Africa and keeping diplomatic channels open was more likely to instigate a reform of apartheid than sending the country into sporting isolation.

It was a time of open political conflict in the country, not just between politicians and voters of left and right but between young and old. In 1970, people aged between 18 and 21 (including this author) were given the right to vote in a general election for the first time. As part of that youthful, politically conscious generation I remember only too well how difficult it was to convince our parents and those who wished to be regarded as our elders and betters that not only did we not want what they wanted, we bitterly resented what they wanted for us and what they thought we should be wanting. The generation that went to university in the 1960s, annoyingly for those who probably didn't have the chance to go to university in the 1930s, wanted a different world from the one that had been fought for by those who had gone to war, they believed, on our behalf. Somehow all the tributaries of cultural dissonance flowed into the raging torrent of a river that was heading inexorably for some kind of gigantic political waterfall.

As the 1969 cricket season came to an end it would have come as an enormous surprise to cricket lovers who had watched Glamorgan win the County Championship, Yorkshire beat Derbyshire in the final of the Gillette Cup and Lancashire win the inaugural John Player Sunday League that before the following season began there would be, to paraphrase Orson Welles in *The Third Man*, warfare, terror, murder and bloodshed in the streets of St John's Wood but it produced Garry Sobers, Mike Procter and five Test matches of inestimable quality. Without the Stop the Seventy Tour, MCC believed the country would have enjoyed five months of a South African tour engendering brotherly love, democracy and peace which might have produced more than Harry Lime's cuckoo clock. The fact remains, however, that the world of English cricket fundamentally changed in 1970. This is the story of how that happened.

1968 TIMELINE

5 January Alexander Dubcek elected First Secretary of the Czech Communist Party.

The reforms known as the Prague Spring begin.

30 January Tet Offensive begins in Vietnam.

16 March Robert Kennedy announces his decision to run for President.

17 March Anti-Vietnam war riots in Grosvenor Square, London.

31 March Lyndon Johnson refuses to run again for the Presidency.

4 April Memphis, Tennessee. Martin Luther King assassinated. Violence erupts nationwide.

11 April German student leader Rudi Dutschke shot in the head by an anti-communist. There follow riots by West German youth aimed at the pro-war Springer press.

23 April New York City. Students barricade themselves into Columbia University buildings and lock the dean in his office. Police beat up and arrest hundreds of students.

25 April Spain. Students start protesting anti-Franco and pro-democracy for the first time since the Civil War. The University of Madrid is closed for 38 days.

2 May The University of Paris closes its Nanterre campus following weeks of protests.

3 May Students migrate to the Sorbonne. Latin Quarter riots as French police advance.

13 May French trades unions announce General Strike. Public transport stops. Petrol stations close.

21 May Ten million workers in France now on strike in solidarity with students.

30 May De Gaulle dissolves the Assembly and calls a general election.

5 June Robert Kennedy assassinated in Los Angeles.

23 June De Gaulle wins an overwhelming majority in the new Assembly.

8 August Miami Beach. Richard Nixon nominated as Republican Party's candidate for President.

20 August Russian tanks invade Czechoslovakia and occupy Prague.

23 August Protests begin on the streets of Chicago. 'The whole world is watching!'

24 August Mayor Daley's police react with unprovoked brutality transmitted live on TV.

27 August MCC selectors omit Basil D'Oliveira from the party to tour South Africa.

28 August Hubert Humphrey nominated Democratic Party candidate for President.

16 September Tom Cartwright withdraws from the MCC squad to tour South Africa.

17 September Basil D'Oliveira announced as replacement for Cartwright.

17 September John Vorster announces D'Oliveira will not be allowed to play.

24 September MCC announces cancellation of its tour to South Africa.

26 September The office of Lord Chamberlain is abolished.

27 September The musical *Hair* opens in the West End.

2 October Police open fire on student protestors in Mexico City. Hundreds reported dead.

12 October Olympic Games open in Mexico City.

16 October John Carlos and Tommie Smith give the Black Power salute after the 200m.

5 November Richard Nixon elected President of the United States.

5 December Motion of no confidence in MCC defeated by 4,357 votes to 1,570.

The scheduled 1970 tour of England by the South Africa cricket team is reconfirmed.

CHAPTER ONE

1968

IT is impossible to understand the passion that consumed
both sides in the first six months of 1970 until the events of
1968 have been appreciated. As the timeline demonstrates, in
September 1968 the South African government decided to cancel
the tour of their country due to be made that winter by the England
cricket team (still known outside the Test matches as MCC) in the
wake of the decision to include, belatedly, the South African exile,
Basil D'Oliveira. This was in line with government policy as stated
in the House of Assembly in Cape Town by the South African
Prime Minister B.J. Vorster on 11 April the previous year which
had reaffirmed that there would be no mixed sport played in the
country, no matter who the participants were. The Worcestershire
all-rounder was categorised in the country of his birth as a Cape
Coloured and as such was therefore ineligible, according to the laws
of apartheid, to play cricket with or against white men. Vorster was
simply stating the law as it applied to all South Africans and in
his view MCC, persuaded by the Anti-Apartheid Movement, was
breaking the law by including D'Oliveira in its touring party.

More importantly, the passion of 1970 cannot be understood
without setting it in its wider cultural and historical context. The
battle that raged at Lord's, the headquarters of MCC where the
selectors met to choose the England cricket team and to defend its
subsequent decision to extend its invitation to the South African
Cricket Association to tour in 1970, was in many ways a similar

battle to what had taken place elsewhere. The disturbances at the Sorbonne in Paris in May 1968, on the streets of Chicago during the Democratic National Convention in August, in Grosvenor Square, London in March, in Rome, in Spain and on the streets of Mexico City before the start of the 1968 Olympics all fed off each other. The three astronauts of Apollo 8 which had orbited the Moon over Christmas 1968 returned to Earth as heroes. NASA and the Nixon White House immediately sent the astronauts on a good will tour round the world during which they received uniformly enthusiastic welcomes everywhere – except on American university campuses where they were jeered, heckled and jostled because they were seen as symbols of an Establishment that was responsible for the continuing prosecution of an unpopular war.

In May 1970, the month when the Stop the Seventy Tour movement finally succeeded in its aims, four young students, who had been protesting about President Nixon's decision to escalate the war in South East Asia by sending armed troops into Cambodia, were shot dead by the National Guard on the campus of Kent State University in Ohio. The following month the *Washington Post* published what became known as the Pentagon Papers, documents from the Defense Department which showed that as early as 1965 Robert McNamara, the Secretary of Defense, was telling President Lyndon Johnson that the war in Vietnam could not be won. President Nixon tried to prevent publication but the Supreme Court ruled 6-3 in favour of the newspaper. The result was a national outcry and a feeling that the people had been lied to by their government. It wasn't, of course, the first time that had happened but it was the first time so many Americans had been made aware of the bare-faced mendacity of the men they had elected into power.

When Bob Hope made one of his many trips to Vietnam to entertain the troops, as he had been doing to American soldiers since 1942, he told the assembled crowd of GIs that he had a message for them from President Johnson who wanted them to know that their President was doing all he could to bring the boys home. The cheerful atmosphere that tended to accompany the indefatigable but now elderly entertainer changed abruptly to be replaced by booing. Hope looked shocked. This had never happened to him before. The soldiers knew they were being lied to, knew that Johnson had no intention of calling a halt to the war. Hope's idea of cheerful optimism belonged to World War II, possibly also to Korea but in Vietnam in 1968 the vast majority of the soldiers were there because they had to be there, not because they believed in a cause. There was considerable respect for those who had dared to burn their draft cards and fled to Canada. Nancy Sinatra went to Vietnam and found herself in instant sympathy with the troops who responded empathetically to her big hit 'These Boots Are Made for Walkin''. She returned home to a big row with her pro-war father.

It took till 1968, by which time 300 Americans were dying each week in Vietnam in pursuit of a war that could not be won, for the tide of support at home to turn. In 1966 there was still a widespread belief that the President told the truth to the American people, that American democracy was good, that Soviet and Chinese communism was evil and that the war could and would be won. That year the best selling record was the song 'The Ballad of the Green Berets' sung by Staff Sergeant Barry Sadler at a time when the charts were usually headed by Motown, the Beatles, the Rolling Stones and the Beach Boys. It propagated the myth of American exceptionalism that was to dominate John Wayne's flag-waving film *The Green Berets* released in 1968. It was the reason Richard Nixon won, however narrowly, the Presidential election which took place in 1968.

It was 1968 when the tide of support for the war finally turned. In February that year, with the Tet offensive still in operation, America's most trusted newsman, the anchor of the CBS nightly news, Walter Cronkite, went to Vietnam and reported back to a stunned nation that the war was unlikely ever to be won and it could be ended only by negotiation. Allegedly, President Johnson grimly predicted that if he had lost Cronkite he had lost America. A month later Johnson announced he would not run in that year's presidential election. In Chicago in August, Cronkite opened the CBS coverage of the convention that elected Hubert Humphrey as the Democratic candidate for president in the midst of the infamous street riots, provoked and prosecuted by Mayor Richard Daley and his brutal police force, with the withering observation, 'The Democratic Convention is about to begin in a police state – there doesn't seem any other way to say it.'

The street protests both in America and in other countries were part of an ongoing war between the haves and the have-nots, between authority and the counterculture but above all between the young and the old. In America, the anti-war protests gathered pace in the late 1960s and then spread rapidly throughout Western Europe. America, which had been a beacon of hope to oppressed people throughout its history, now appeared to be sending young men who didn't want to be there halfway across the world to kill people they didn't know for no reason they could understand.

America's failure to win the war in Vietnam in rapid time against what many Americans believed to be a raggle-taggle army of ill-prepared peasants came as a shock to everyone. President Johnson's response was to widen the draft and to send more and more young men to fight in the jungles of South East Asia. Although Johnson was horrified by the numbers requested by General Westmoreland and rarely sent him all the recruits he asked for, the Pentagon Papers revealed that it was administration practice to announce a lesser figure to the American public than the number of troops actually shipped overseas.

On the first day of February 1968 South Vietnam's chief of police fired a revolver into the head of a handcuffed Vietcong prisoner at point blank range on a street in Saigon, an act which was filmed by an NBC cameraman and photographed by an Associated Press photographer. The image of the executed youth who looked about 12 years old horrified the world, never mind Americans. Fifty years on the images of death and dying on the nightly television news have become depressingly familiar but in 1968 the impact was devastating. Dr Benjamin Spock, whose books on baby and child care had influenced the mothers of the children who were being sent to fight in Vietnam, made a passionate denunciation of the war and advised that half a million of 'his' young men refuse the draft. Many of those peaceable mothers now turned against a war they had previously acknowledged had to be supported as mothers had supported all previous wars in which the United States had been a combatant.

This might all seem a long way from Lord's, from a summer of Test cricket and even further from South Africa, a country ruled by apartheid. In fact it isn't. The narrative of the Stop the Seventy

Tour is intimately bound up with the contemporaneous worldwide struggles for civil rights and the anti-war protests in America which, when they joined up with the traditional idealism of youth, created the atmosphere in which the Stop the Seventy Tour campaign developed.

Martin Luther King had initially wanted to keep the issue of Civil Rights separate from the anti-war protests because he needed Johnson's Congressional support to pass legislation, in particular the Civil Rights Act of 1964 and the Voting Rights Act the following year. Eventually the pressure became too much and he spoke out against the war, bringing his supporters into line with the anti-war protesters. On 4 April 1968 King was shot dead outside a motel in Memphis, Tennessee. Despite appeals for calm from Bobby Kennedy, there were riots all over the country. The National Guard was sent in to restore order. In Washington DC alone 12 people were killed, over 1,000 were hurt and more than 6,000 arrested. King's Christian philosophy of non-violence was starting to feel outmoded to black Americans in 1968. The future to them now appeared to belong to Stokely Carmichael, Bobby Seale, Angela Davis and the Black Power movement. They saw the impact of the marches and the street protests on Lyndon Johnson's decision. The whole world now understood that direct action worked.

Just over two weeks after Martin Luther King was assassinated, Enoch Powell delivered his notorious 'Rivers of blood' speech at a hotel in Birmingham. The problems for black people in Britain were by no means as bad as they were for African Americans suffering under the Jim Crow laws or for the Africans in South Africa but they demonstrated that British society struggled to assimilate recently arrived, particularly non-white, immigrants into the mainstream of society. Lord's might not want to concern itself with the problems of apartheid, however much it claimed to look on racial discrimination with distaste, but it could not bury its head in the sand for much longer. The colour problem was everywhere apparent.

MCC remembered that even in the peaceful far-off days of 1960, the South African cricketers had arrived for their tour of England just five weeks after the massacre outside the police station in Sharpeville, Transvaal, when 69 protestors had been shot dead by white policemen and a further 180 had been injured. The massacre had so outraged the civilised world, that the South African touring party had been met at Heathrow airport by 200 demonstrators carrying placards. Others were waiting for them when they arrived at the Park Lane Hotel as the players disembarked from the coach. Small scale picketing had occurred spasmodically throughout the tour but as far as the British news media were concerned, such events were less interesting than the English umpires Frank Lee and Syd Buller's consistent no-balling for throwing of the young South African pace bowler Geoff Griffin.

The 1970 tour would bring MCC, the Cricket Council and the Test and County Cricket Board into direct conflict with those who regarded playing cricket against a white South Africa team as condoning apartheid. Racial tensions in some British cities were growing, fanned by Powell's deliberately provocative outburst. East End dockers in London marched, carrying banners proclaiming 'ENOCH WAS RIGHT'. In South Africa, black cricket lovers knew that their government would never permit D'Oliveira, their local hero, to return and play on the hallowed turf of Newlands. In America during the long hot summers of the 1960s the black ghettoes in Watts, Detroit, Chicago and Newark continued to burn. Their occupants similarly had no stake in white society.

A disproportionate number of the 58,000 Americans who were eventually killed in the war in South East Asia were young black men. In 1967, the world heavyweight boxing champion, Muhammed Ali, was fined $10,000 and risked imprisonment when he refused the draft. Ali wouldn't fight a white man's war when his own people had their own struggles for justice and freedom. He pointed out the absurdity of black men being sent to Vietnam to kill other people of colour when they were subject to so much discrimination and violence at home.

> My opponents are white people not Viet Cong or Chinese or Japanese. You are my opponent when I want freedom, you are my opponent when I want justice, you are my opponent when I want equality. You won't even stand up for my religious beliefs in America and you want me to go somewhere and fight when you won't stand up for me at home.

When Ali made his charge in 1967 he was not widely supported outside the black community and his refusal of the draft led to his being stripped of his world title to general approval. At the Mexico Olympics the following year two African-American sprinters, Tommie Smith and John Carlos, won gold and bronze medals respectively in the 200 metres final. When the American national anthem was played on the victory rostrum they each raised a fist encased in a black glove in recognition of their support for Black Power. The response at home from white America was one of overwhelming fury and far from being welcomed home as Olympic heroes, the two men were ostracised.

At the start of 1967, certainly amongst white Americans over the age of 30, there was still a strong belief in the concept of 'My country right or wrong'. The government had fought two world wars and the Korean War on the side of truth, justice and the American way. If the government said 'Go', young men went. It was their sacred duty to do so. Young people who protested the war by burning the American flag were a disgrace, they spat in the faces of the noble dead who had given their lives for the exact same cause in earlier wars. What made these young people think they knew better? It was young people who were the target of this ire because they were most at risk of dying for a cause in which they did not believe. The men who excoriated them were frequently men now middle-aged who had fought fascism and Nazism in Europe and the South Pacific, who had watched their friends die, who had emerged from the heat of battle ever more certain that democracy had to be fought for. If Hitler had been stopped in 1936 ....

It was a familiar refrain among the generation that had fought World War II. It led to Anthony Eden's decision to invade Suez in 1956 and it led successive American presidents from Truman to Nixon to believe that Communism must be resisted wherever in the world it threatened to spread like a contagion. In the 1960s, the battlegrounds were Berlin and Vietnam. The former was comprehensible, the latter was not. Americans found themselves in the uncomfortable position of supporting and dying for a corrupt 'democratic' regime in South Vietnam and fighting an enemy looking for national self-determination. Robert McNamara later observed ruefully, 'We thought we were fighting Hitler or Stalin; in fact we were fighting Tito. We thought we were fighting communism; in fact we were fighting nationalism.' It was a mess and young people simply did not recognise that the government had the right to call on them to die in a cause that was anathema to them.

The world was changing but the old men who ruled the world were not. In April 1968 the 'hippy' musical *Hair* opened on Broadway and mesmerised audiences watched young men and women taking off all their clothes on a public stage for the first time. In *The Producers*, a film made the previous year, Mel Brooks portrays the first audience to see 'Springtime for Hitler' as literally staring at the stage with their mouths wide open in shock. Something like that must have happened at the Biltmore Theater when Joseph Papp moved his off-Broadway production there in April 1968. The musical of course became instantly notorious for the nudity and the hash it unashamedly displayed but just as significant as the bare flesh and the spliffs was the 'desecration' of the American flag on stage which now sent Broadway audiences into paroxysms of rage. Their theatre had moved on from Rodgers and Hammerstein, even from Arthur Miller and Tennessee Williams, as it became the arena for protest politics. *Hair* was a musical that placed the 1960s counterculture on stage. It thrust bisexuality, interracial relationships and the rejection of monogamy in front of audiences who had previously been 'protected' from such taboo subjects.

In 1968 students all over the world saw direct action in the form of street protests as the most effective means open to them. It applied not just to the draft in America but to every aspect of life in which young people and their aspirations were being frustrated by an older generation who exhibited no interest in their grievances. It wasn't just a question of rich against poor. It was a generational existential anxiety which the older generation simply could not grasp. At the start of *The Graduate*, along with *Bonnie & Clyde* the hit film of 1967, Dustin Hoffman in his first starring role plays a recent college graduate who has worked hard in school all his life and has achieved all the academic honours his parents had wanted for him. Flying home into a wealthy middle-class suburb of Los Angeles, he tries to explain to his proud father the unease that is gnawing away at him. He is worried about his future. He wants it to be different from the life his father had led, different from what had been mapped out for him. His parents have arranged a celebratory party for him from which he does his best to escape until he is cornered by one of his parents' friends:

Mr McGuire: I want to say one word to you. Just one word.

Benjamin: Yes, sir.

Mr McGuire: Are you listening?

Benjamin: Yes, I am.

Mr McGuire: Plastics.

Benjamin: Exactly how do you mean?

Mr McGuire: There's a great future in plastics. Think about it. Will you think about it?

Embarrassed by the affair he is having with Mrs Robinson, the wife of his father's business partner, he drifts for days on an air mattress in the pool outside the family home until his father looms over him.

Mr Braddock: Ben, what are you doing?

Benjamin: Well, I would say that I'm just drifting. Here in the pool.

Mr Braddock: Why?

Benjamin: Well, it's very comfortable just to drift here.

Mr Braddock: Have you thought about graduate school?

Benjamin: No.

Mr Braddock: Would you mind telling me then what those four years of college were for? What was the point of all that hard work?

Benjamin: You got me.

It was a problem for the baby boomers, particularly in the United States and Western Europe. Their parents had known depression, war and austerity. Their solution was a passionate belief in material prosperity, early military action to defend any threat to democracy and a determination to ensure that their children benefited from all their sacrifices. The problem was that not all of those children wanted those benefits and those who did not utterly rejected the philosophy behind them. They wanted to make love not war. They wanted, in Timothy Leary's words, to 'turn on, tune in and drop out' of the society their parents had created in the post-war world. It was obvious the authorities were not going to give their passive approval to the counterculture which they regarded as a threat to everything they believed in. If young people wanted a more caring, a more just society with fewer material values, they were going to have to fight for it.

British culture changed visibly after 1963, the year that sexual intercourse began according to Philip Larkin and the year that the Beatles found themselves with four successive number one hits. It was the start of 'Swinging London', James Bond, Carnaby Street, Mary Quant, Terence Stamp, Julie Christie, BBC2, *The Avengers*, the white heat of Harold Wilson's technological revolution and of course the introduction of the Gillette Cup in cricket. The political turmoil which occurred in the aftermath of the MCC selectors' decision not to pick Basil D'Oliveira in August 1968 was part of this change in the culture.

One of the justifications for the maintenance of sporting links with South Africa was that it was 'only' the government in South Africa that was the problem, the implication being that all the white cricketers and all their supporters were opposed to the policy of apartheid. Yet immediately after John Vorster decided to cancel the 1968/69 tour the veteran South African sports journalist Louis Duffus wrote an article for the *Star and Argus* group of newspapers in which he made clear the essential logic of the government's action.

> D'Oliveira was for so long a dagger directed at the heart of South African cricket that surprise and shock at the cancellation seems synthetic.
>
> Most of all D'Oliveira must have known the conditions as they affected his whole life. The law of the land says you drive on the left. D'Oliveira was told to come out and drive on the right.
>
> Was it to be expected that the South African Government would change its whole policy for a cricketer?

Because of one cricketer the great players produced in this country and the game itself have been victimized.

Posterity will surely marvel how a player, helped to go overseas by the charitable gestures of White contemporaries, could be the cause of sending the cricket of his benefactors crashing into ruins.

Had he read the article, D'Oliveira would have been surprised to learn that his passage to England had been facilitated by the charitable gestures of white contemporaries. Duffus's sentiments were repeated in his book *Play Abandoned* published in early 1970 and reviewed with withering contempt in the March edition of *The Cricketer* by the poet and cricket writer Alan Ross.

All posterity is likely to marvel at, I'm afraid, is the gutlessness, self-interest and downright subserviency of 'sportsmen' who underwrite a vile policy without so much as a squeak of protest, though many in private claim to detest it. [Duffus's] book, quite apart from its inadequacy as literature and general slipshod quality, is yet another indictment of terrible South African inadequacy. When will a South African cricketer or sporting journalist stand up and be counted? For then, and only then, will there be signs that the idiocy will ever stop.

Duffus's book and article might have been a fair reflection of the white South African reaction but it is important that the cricket authorities in England are not portrayed simply as reactionary fools, insensitive to the demands for change in many aspects of society. In November 1962, only four years after the last investigative committee had come to the conclusion that the anachronistic status of the amateur cricketer should be preserved, a new committee looking into the same problem recommended that it be abolished. The recommendation was approved by the full MCC committee and from the start of the 1963 season there was no longer a formal divide between amateur and professional cricketers. During that same season the first one-day limited-overs knockout competition was introduced into county cricket. It proved to be an enormous commercial success. In 1969 the Test and

County Cricket Board introduced a 40-overs league whose matches would take place every Sunday even if it meant a team that had begun a three-day County Championship match on the Saturday had to travel a hundred miles to fulfil the Sunday engagement and be back in time to continue the Championship game on the Monday morning. The point is that MCC, which considered as a fundamental part of its job the guardianship of what is now called the spirit of cricket, found it perfectly compatible with this new commercialism. When confronted with the politics which were inevitable if England continued to play cricket matches against South Africa it should be clear that the cricket authorities were not ignorant of the world outside St John's Wood. The problem was the difference in political and social philosophies which were ranged on either side.

Britain had long been used to street protests, from the Jarrow marchers in the 1930s to the Eastertime CND marches from Aldermaston to Trafalgar Square. They were essentially peaceful, although the speeches in Trafalgar Square could get inflammatory and certain CND members had been arrested including the 91-year-old Bertrand Russell and the playwrights John Osborne and Robert Bolt. Osborne and Bolt spent the night in prison, appeared in front of the magistrate next day and were fined £1. It was serious and well-intentioned of course but it read largely like Bertie Wooster stealing a policeman's helmet on Boat Race night. What happened in Grosvenor Square on 17 March 1968 was entirely different.

A march from Trafalgar Square to Hyde Park was planned to demonstrate against the war in Vietnam. It was to stop at 10 Downing Street on the way to hand in a petition. It must have been somewhat galling to the Prime Minister, Harold Wilson, who, although unwilling unequivocally to express the opinion in public, was equally opposed to the war and was trying desperately to resist the efforts of Lyndon Johnson to drag Britain into it. It was a manoeuvre made particularly difficult by the weakness of sterling and Britain's dependence on American financial support. The marchers were variously estimated at between 10,000 and 30,000 and although most of them followed the prescribed route, a significant minority broke away just before the march reached Hyde Park and headed for Grosvenor Square, the site of the American

Embassy. A strong cordon of police, anticipating such an event, was waiting for them.

Police horses charged the crowd, the officers laying about them with their truncheons. Inevitably, innocent people were badly hurt and the press photographs and television newsreels made it look like another Peterloo. For students, young mothers with toddlers in push-chairs and middle-class pacifists who were caught up in the violence, that was exactly what it felt like. The public was deeply shocked by the images of faces streaming with blood caused by overt police brutality. British police had traditionally been the envy of the world precisely because it was widely believed that they did not behave like that. After 17 March 1968, to a generation of British youth, the police became 'pigs' just as they were referred to in America and the rest of Western Europe. To the law and order generation the police were defending the rule of law and the noisy, unruly mob got what it deserved. Battle lines were being drawn up.

Much of the political and social agitation was the result of actions taken by students. The mid-1960s was the time when the first baby boomers, those born immediately after 1945, reached university age. In most cases they were the first members of their family to achieve such an exalted state. Their parents had left school at 14 and gone into jobs, if they could find them, because money was so tight at home or they had joined the armed forces as the tide of war consumed them. When they were demobbed they went back to their jobs or, in the case of most women, they returned to domestic duties. Their children were not subject to the same economic and political forces so when they returned home during university vacations they took back with them social and political attitudes their parents struggled to understand. As tertiary education expanded in Britain and student numbers increased after the government accepted the recommendations of the Robbins Report in 1963, this gap widened significantly.

In other countries the problem was much the same although there were national variations. In France in the decade up to 1966 the student population trebled but French society was still in the grip of the Catholic Church and the position of women, who were legally prohibited from wearing trousers to work, was seriously circumscribed. President Charles de Gaulle, who was 78 years old in

1968, might have been the hero of liberation to the Free French but to the intellectuals and students of the 1960s he ran an old-fashioned paternalistic regime that symbolised everything that was backward and repressive about the country. It was somehow appropriate that the challenge to his authority which climaxed in May 1968 began at the start of the year on the rather more prosaic battleground of young men wanting to sleep with their girlfriends.

A German student called Daniel Cohn-Bendit was the youthful articulate leader of a student revolt which began on the Nanterre overspill campus of the University of Paris, whose authorities had refused their male and female students' request to share accommodation. The men now in authority hadn't been allowed to sleep with their girlfriends when they were 19 so they were unlikely to approve the idea of this generation, who hadn't been through the war, being permitted that sort of sensual pleasure on a campus designed to promote higher intellectual aspirations. Nanterre's buildings were new but its administration was traditional and autocratic and it pointedly refused to listen to its students' requests.

The Nanterre protests inevitably assumed some input from militant anti-Vietnam war demonstrators who had been influenced not only by a visit from Stokely Carmichael (when he had been immediately arrested by police) but also by events in New York where, on 23 April, students at Columbia University had begun a sit-in to protest at the university's blatant hypocrisy at announcing a tribute of respect for the dead in Vietnam whilst continuing to do weapons research for the Pentagon. In addition, it had compulsorily purchased neighbouring land in Harlem for further expansion and had evicted the black tenants and demolished their houses. The police, summoned by the university authorities, arrested 700 students and hauled them away to jail.

On 2 May the University of Paris closed its revolting Nanterre campus and Cohn-Bendit's supporters descended on the Sorbonne in Paris. The following day the police arrived and the clashes that were to be such a feature of the month began in earnest. Cohn-Bendit was ordered to appear before a disciplinary hearing at the Sorbonne. When hundreds of students came to give him their support, de Gaulle ordered riot police to arrest them and then closed the Sorbonne itself. The students marched through the Latin Quarter singing the 'Internationale', the anthem of world communism. They were opposed to capitalism but they were not traditional communists because they were only too aware of the reality of Soviet totalitarianism. Their revolutionary imagination was seized by Mao and Che Guevara, not by Lenin or Trotsky. When they learned in early May that Czechs had poured on to the streets of Prague to celebrate Dubcek's reforms, French students cheered. In response the police confronted them with the threat of force.

Adopting tactics from previous French revolutions, the students began to rip up the cobblestones in the streets outside the Sorbonne and used them as weapons. Cars were overturned and shops ransacked. Barricades which would have been recognised by the Parisians of 1848 were erected, sealing off the area. By now there were 40,000 students on the streets and every street leading to the Sorbonne was blocked by waves of riot police. In the early hours of the following morning the police were ordered to attack. The Prime Minister, Georges Pompidou, tried to calm things by reopening the Sorbonne. The students swarmed in and claimed a permanent occupation.

Les Evenements as they became known were French in particular circumstances but they were an international defining moment of the year. The students were supported by respectable intellectuals like Jean-Paul Sartre and Simone de Beauvoir. France's best known stage actor Jean-Louis Barrault, who had transformed L'Odeon into a great theatre, came out on the students' side and invited them to occupy L'Odeon, which they did. They then trashed it, much to Barrault's mortification. Sartre also helpfully advised the students to smash their universities and join forces with the workers. It was this alliance with the workers that turned a student revolt into a nationwide industrial paralysis.

On 13 May the French trade unions announced a general strike. Despite long working hours, French workers found that their wages were the second lowest in Western Europe. Unemployment was growing. By 16 May, 50 factories were occupied and by 21 May ten million workers were on strike. The Cannes Film Festival came to a halt. The director Jean-Luc Godard harangued the festival crowds, complaining that he wanted to talk about solidarity with the workers and the students but the festival-goers, perhaps predictably, only wanted to talk about tracking shots and close-ups. 'Dix ans, ca suffice', cried the anti-Gaullists as they marched, referring to the time since 1958 when de Gaulle had become President. Theatres closed, public transport stopped, petrol stations ran out of petrol. The country ground to a halt.

On 22 May the French government deported the Jewish Daniel Cohn-Bendit back to Germany which inevitably evoked memories of events 25 years previously. On the 24th, students set fire to Le Bourse. Now de Gaulle had had enough. He called a referendum promising that if he lost it he would resign. Students celebrated, chanting 'Adieu, de Gaulle' and waving white handkerchiefs like football supporters eagerly anticipating the sacking of an unpopular manager, but a week later the President abandoned his plans for a referendum. The violence that erupted in response that night, however, killed off widespread general sympathy for the students, although the strike continued for another fortnight. De Gaulle might have been brought down by the trade unions but ultimately they shied away from striking the fatal blow and, after de Gaulle consulted secretly with the army, he broadcast his refusal to resign or change the Prime Minister. Instead he dissolved the old Assembly and announced plans for a general election.

De Gaulle feared that the anarchy in the streets was the prelude to a takeover of totalitarian communism which he alone could prevent. The students believed this was effectively a *coup d'etat* with de Gaulle seizing more power. The Gaullists, fed up with revolting students and striking workers, marched into the Place de la Concorde singing 'La Marseillaise' to demonstrate that the student protesters did not represent their idea of France. Their chants included a call to send Daniel Cohn-Bendit to Dachau. The revolution of 1968 was running out of steam. Petrol stations began to reopen, trains started to run, workers drifted back to the factories and the girls at the Folie Bergere, who had also expressed their solidarity with other workers and the students, started to take off their clothes again. Three people had been killed during the May riots. On the Bank Holiday weekend at the end of May, 70 people were killed on the roads. By the end of June, de Gaulle emerged with the greatest electoral victory in French parliamentary history. He ordered the cobblestones of the Left Bank, which had proved such handy missiles, to be paved over with asphalt. The revolution was over.

The workers had gained a 10% pay increase, a rise in the minimum wage and shorter working hours. The students got a grudging acceptance from university authorities that some reforms were necessary. In Cambridge, the author of this book struck his long-planned blow for revolution when he sat on a student committee calling for a reform of the ludicrously outmoded syllabus in the History Faculty and failed miserably to achieve almost anything of significance. However, despite his victory, de Gaulle's public support started to weaken and in 1969 he lost a referendum in which he asked the French people to support his intended reform of the parliamentary system. Immediately after the result he retired to his rural retreat in Colombey les Deux Eglises. Like Lyndon Johnson, he eventually accepted that he could not win the battle against the tide of history.

The utopian dreams of May 1968 were not realised but then utopian dreams very rarely are. However, despite the Russian tanks rolling into Prague in August 1968, presaging the destruction of Dubcek's Prague Spring, this re-imposition of Soviet repression on the suffering people of Czechoslovakia lit a torch that was to be held proudly aloft for 20 years by successive generations of students and young people. Amidst the inevitable reverses as the Old Guard tried to suppress the agitation for changes of which they disapproved, there emerged some of the great liberal triumphs, widely recognised as part of the social transformation of the 1960s. Out of the Stonewall riots surfaced the movement for gay liberation. The second wave of feminism grew out of the realisation that even in a revolutionary movement promoting egalitarianism the fact remained that it was the men who talked about politics and went on television, the women who did the typing, made the tea, washed up and went to bed with the leaders of the revolution. By the end of the 1960s they had, understandably, had enough.

In England, Parliament had already passed legislation permitting gay sexual relations between consenting adults over the age of 21 and an Abortion Act that ended some of the dire consequences facing women whose lives were threatened with physical or mental devastation when they discovered they were pregnant. In 1968 the office of Lord Chamberlain was abolished and theatres were thereby permitted to stage any political or sexual work of a radical nature that did not transgress the law. The following year the Divorce Reform Act was passed, permitting couples to divorce after a separation of two years. The old certainties were disintegrating.

In the light of these and similar events it was perhaps unsurprising that the mandarins of English cricket found that the tidal waves of social revolution were now crashing against the Grace Gates. It was no longer possible for Gubby Allen, Billy Griffith and the other men whose influence dominated the MCC and hence English cricket to dismiss the demand to stop the 1970 tour with lordly disdain. Their desire to continue playing cricket against their old white friends from South Africa was to be confronted by an entirely new and seriously armed opposition.

CHAPTER TWO
FEBRUARY–AUGUST 1969

MCC set out its stall with regard to the tour of England in 1970 by South Africa shortly after it had won the vote of no confidence in its committee in December 1968. The following month the newly formed Cricket Council of 28 members of the elite of English cricket voted unanimously that the tour should go ahead. It was a position they were to stick to stubbornly and in the face of all reason, until overwhelmed by an order from the British government.

The difference between the newly formed Cricket Council and MCC was hard to understand, particularly as the two bodies appeared to be populated by exactly the same men. Peter Baxter, the veteran producer of *Test Match Special*, says it as well as anyone.

> The MCC was being turned into a private members' club so it couldn't be the recipient of any Sports Council grant and the Cricket Council was then formed to fulfil that purpose. Under the Cricket Council was the TCCB which regulated first class cricket and the NCA which performed the same function for the amateur side of the game. The Cricket Council was the overall governing body and covered all aspects of the game. The MCC was involved in all those discussions because of Lord's and because of Gubby Allen. The MCC has always had a seat on the board of the TCCB and then the ECB and probably the Cricket Council as well.

The principle of the Council as relayed by its secretary, S.C. (Billy) Griffith, was that, 'It is our wish to play and foster cricket as widely as possible in England and all over the world ... the Council would welcome any cricketer selected to tour this country by South Africa.' It was noted that simultaneously a statement from the all-white South African Cricket Association (hereinafter SACA) announced that it was in talks with the (non-white) South African Cricket Board of Control to pursue matters of mutual interest. For the Council this was proof that South Africa was moving surely towards desegregation of sport and entirely justified the Council's determination to maintain its much-cherished links with South Africa by confirming the tour. The Council clearly didn't bother to look out of the window in the Long Room to watch the pigs flying over St John's Wood.

In its defence it was also announced from South Africa that the Australian cricket team would play four Test matches in that country early in 1970. Writing in *The Guardian* on 23 January 1969, John Arlott generously gave the Cricket Council the benefit of his considerable doubt.

> ... the fact that it is the establishment sometimes obscures this fact but for the moment at least it must be accepted on trust as a body of good intent. If its first achievement should be the first visit to this country of a mixed team of South African cricketers it will have made an amazingly creditable beginning.

South Africa, along with Australia and to a lesser extent the West Indies, was one of the countries most England cricketers looked forward to touring. The hotels were decent, the hospitality boundless. Keith Fletcher summed up South Africa then and now pithily.

> In South Africa if you could ignore what was going on with apartheid and if you were Anglo-Saxon it was a brilliant tour. Life has changed and you couldn't get away with that now.

The subcontinent aroused no such emotions. As Ian Botham was later to remark, Pakistan was the place you would like to send your mother-in-law to, thereby offending both Pakistanis and mothers-in-law. Few England cricket tours there seemed to conclude without some sort of diplomatic incident having taken place.

In the 1950s and 1960s, many senior England players did not feel the need to tour India and Pakistan at all. If fit, May and Cowdrey, Trueman and Statham would always reclaim their places in the England side for the first Test the following summer. As late as 1972, the captain Ray Illingworth, John Snow, Geoff Boycott and John Edrich all indicated their unavailability for the tour of the subcontinent. Peter Baxter believes that Colin Cowdrey led the tour of Pakistan in 1969 only because the party had originally been chosen, of course, to tour South Africa. 'Cowdrey would never have signed up for a tour of Pakistan,' Baxter avers.

It wasn't just the oppressive humidity, the poverty, the inedible food (and its unwelcome consequences), the inadequate hotels and the unwelcome evidence of the natural world in what passed for a bedroom or a bathroom, there was also the question of dubious umpiring. All in all it was a trip young players went on in order to establish their place in the side for the following summer and future trips to Australia and South Africa.

In September 1968, the TCCB decided to replace the cancelled South Africa tour with one that would play one first-class fixture and three Test matches in India over a month followed by a similar programme in Pakistan.

On 24 November, the Indian section of the tour was cancelled when the Indian Finance Ministry could not find the sterling to guarantee MCC £6,000 for each Test and £2,000 for the other match. A three-day match in Ceylon, as Sri Lanka was then known, was then added to the tour of Pakistan, a decision that was not greeted with acclaim by the players. The early up-country matches were a nightmare even to county cricketers who were used to driving after a Tuesday or Friday afternoon finish from Middlesbrough to Taunton to start play at 11.30 the following morning, along roads that as yet boasted only the beginnings of a motorway system. For an early match on the 1969 tour of Pakistan, John Snow recalled that the players were assembled at 5.30am for the coach journey to the ground. One quick look inside told them that their de luxe transportation vehicle had been used as a cattle truck the day before and was now presented to the England players with all the traditional interior furnishings of straw and cow dung.

On this tour, it wasn't just the transport arrangements, the hotels, the umpires, the humidity, the lack of washing facilities or the food that so bothered the intrepid explorers. They found that MCC had thoughtfully sent them to Pakistan in the middle of another political storm, only this one included the threat of potential violence that had been simmering on the streets for some months as East Pakistan agitated for independent status and separation from West Pakistan. It was to be another two years of trouble before East Pakistan became the new state of Bangladesh but the political turmoil in which Pakistan appeared to be almost permanently mired led during the MCC tour to the fall of the President Ayub Khan and the imposition of martial law by his replacement General Yahya Khan. When the England party arrived there at the start of February the players were not reassured by the British High Commission's bare-faced lie that they would be perfectly safe because order had been restored in the capital. In fact, on the drive from Dhaka airport, they had already discovered that the police and army authorities had withdrawn and the city was effectively in the hands of rioting students.

These were not students in the sense that the England players understood the word. What they found in Dhaka was not peaceful protesters carrying placards demanding the American troops leave Vietnam or a bunch of inebriated young people vomiting in the streets or throwing eggs at Harold Wilson, all of which British students in the late 1960s indulged in but were nowhere in evidence in Dhaka in 1969. The England party thought that perhaps their best plan was to fly out of Dhaka the following morning. The students told them if they tried to do that their coach would not reach the airport. The British High Commission official who hosted a cocktail party for the cricketers after reassuring them that they were all perfectly safe spent most of the party in discussion with other Commission staff about evacuation plans.

The first Test match in Lahore had passed off quietly enough, possibly owing to the presence of army marksmen with rifles trained on potential troublemakers in the cheap seats. The players were not unaware that if the marksmen did start shooting they were directly in the line of fire. However, they steeled themselves to the task in hand and on a typical low, slow subcontinental pitch England gained a first innings lead of 97 thanks to a century from Cowdrey, which turned out to be the last of his 22 Test hundreds. After a hard fought 83 by Keith Fletcher in the second innings, the tourists set Pakistan a daunting 323 to win. Majid Khan and Hanif Mohammad played out time with ease, the captains shaking hands with Pakistan on 203/5. Tom Graveney and Roger Prideaux between them bowled eight overs in that innings, conceding eleven runs.

The match in Dhaka was a different story altogether, the England team reluctantly carrying on with the tour against a background of incessant gunfire which seemed to them to be taking place directly outside their hotel. The students were reported to be patrolling the streets with guns seeking out those whom they believed to be corrupt. Those whom they designated to fall into this category were bound and gagged and then tossed into the river to drown. For the terrified England players it must have been hard to think about ways of bowling out the opposition when they were in fear for their lives.

The Bangabandhu National Stadium in Dhaka was a half-finished concrete bowl rising out of a piece of waste ground. The windowless dressing room comprised four bare concrete walls under the main stand lit by a single 40 watt bulb. There was nowhere from which to watch the cricket. The players remained in their dungeon until a player who was out returned to inform the next man in that he was expected at the wicket shortly. The sanitation was predictably primitive and the food to English tastes inedible. Until it ran out, the England party survived on oranges, bananas and whatever tinned food still remained from the stocks they had brought with them.

The journey of a few yards from the bowels of the stadium to where their coach was parked was a trial in itself. The crowd pressed in on the players who carried their cricket bags high over their heads, thereby allowing wandering hands to search for small change that could be skilfully extracted from the pockets of players who were more interested in preserving their matchday equipment. Colin Milburn joined the party in the middle of the Dhaka Test match, having flown from Perth where he had been playing for Western Australia. The journey, involving multiple changes of plane, took nearly 72 hours and he arrived in the middle of a religious festival in which cows were slaughtered in the streets. It all fazed even that most sunny of North East temperaments, and he must have wondered if his journey had been entirely necessary.

The students were in evidence in the ground when the England players arrived to start the match, having relieved the stewards of their duties, but surprisingly a proper cricket match broke out. The Pakistan captain Saeed Ahmed won the toss and elected to bat but laudable bowling by Snow, Brown and Cottam who took nine of the wickets between them kept the total down to 246. D'Oliveira scored 114 in the England first innings of 274 but Pakistan revealed no sign of urgency in their second innings of 195/6, scored at less than two runs an over, to set England 168 to win in 20 overs. John Edrich and Roger Prideaux showed exactly what they thought of this outlandish target by scoring exactly 33 runs without loss off the 20 overs. It must have made everyone wonder whether this entire tour was ever really necessary.

The intention of the MCC was to bring cricket to Pakistan in the hope of fostering a spirit of amity and goodwill. The third Test at Karachi showed what a vain hope this had always been. Local supporters, who objected to the elevation to the captaincy of Saeed Ahmed over the claims of the local favourite Hanif Mohammad, made their displeasure apparent from the start and play was frequently interrupted and delayed. Over the course of the first two days an outstanding innings of 139 by Colin Milburn and a typically serene century by Tom Graveney had put England in a very strong position. On the third day Alan Knott, with assistance from Keith Fletcher, John Snow and David Brown, was heading for his maiden century in Test match cricket as the England total climbed towards 500.

The atmosphere in which the match was played, however, was turning distinctly hostile. The population of Karachi was upset to learn of the death of one of the anti-government leaders who had been fasting in protest at what was regarded as government oppression. The England team was warned that it had to join all other traffic in Karachi on the third morning of the Test by flying a black flag from its coach. The manager Les Ames refused to comply, maintaining stoically that his players were in Pakistan on an apolitical cricket tour and would not be party to any kind of domestic political protest. The truck carrying the armed guards who were supposed to accompany and protect the England players disappeared at the first road junction. It made for an anxious journey to the ground, particularly when angry demonstrators were seen marching towards the stadium. Keith Fletcher remembers the chaos well but says he never felt personally threatened.

> We knew they were coming because you could hear them coming. We didn't feel particularly unsafe because they weren't coming directly for us. They marched up to the cricket ground from the Karachi town centre. There was a big gate at one end of the ground and I don't know if someone opened it for them or they forced it open but they all came in through that gate.

They stormed their way into the National Stadium and tore up the seats which they proceeded to use as weapons.

Alan Knott, at the business end, was concentrating on the approach of that century. He was 96 not out when he failed to read a googly from Mushtaq Mohammad but breathed a sigh of relief when the ball bounced over the top of the middle stump, wrong-footing the wicket keeper, Wasim Bari. He re-marked his crease and prepared to face the next ball, determined to squeeze out those final four runs. Meanwhile, at the non-striker's end, David Brown had been watching the behaviour of the rioters with increasing alarm, as had the Pakistani fielders. As Knott settled over his bat again, the incursions on to the field began in earnest. The Pakistani fielders and the umpires turned and with one accord fled towards the pavilion. David Brown raced down the pitch and grabbed Alan Knott, who was showing no inclination to leave the crease. He wasn't going to abandon his post at this stage. He was on 96 for heaven's sake. Surely the rioters understood the importance of a maiden Test century. David Brown did not believe that was what the rioters were primarily thinking and an extremely reluctant England wicketkeeper was forced to race off after his partner who remembers the occasion well.

> He was 96 not out and I had to tell him there was no point staying out there because nobody was going to bowl at him. The Pakistanis knew exactly what was going to happen and they were gone.

By the time they had reached the relative safety of the dressing room the rioters were busily venting their fury by digging up the pitch.

Alan Knott soon realised to his frustration that even if the police managed to calm the rioters the pitch would take days and maybe weeks to repair. He was right. The England innings closed at 502/7 with Alan Knott stranded on 96 not out, the match was abandoned and declared drawn and the series finished 0-0. Unfortunately, getting off the field was one thing, getting out of the ground and then out of Karachi was another. Loudspeaker appeals to the crowd for calm included a promise that play would resume as soon as order had been restored, however unlikely the players and officials thought that to be. Meanwhile, the England team were quickly packing their bags prior to a quick escape when they discovered that they had been locked into their dressing room for their own safety. They remained there for over an hour but once the Pakistani Board of Control had abandoned the tour, Les Ames managed to get everyone booked on an evening flight to Cairo. They must have felt like the American Embassy hostages felt when they finally left Iranian airspace in January 1981.

Ironically the party was delayed in Cairo because the engines would not re-start, delayed again in Rome and finally in Paris because London airport was fogbound. The official Pakistan tour brochure had made great play of the pleasure the country was taking in acting as stand-in host for MCC after the cancellation of their South Africa tour. 'Thanks, Basil' read the tongue-in-cheek headline. The England players were not slow to echo the sentiments addressed to their now notorious all-rounder, although this time they were accompanied by a distinct note of irony. The embattled nature of the England cricket team was to become more pronounced before the start of the South Africa tour in 1970. The violence of the Pakistan tour would start to cloud the judgement of MCC, the Cricket Council and the Test and County Cricket Board. Political demonstrations and student activists were anathema to them and they would not be permitted to gain any traction during a domestic English season.

Colin Cowdrey was not part of the frantic exodus on the third day of the Karachi Test. He had received news of the death of his father-in-law and had flown home the previous day. He saw no reason why he should not resume the captaincy for England's next scheduled

Test matches against West Indies and New Zealand in the summer of 1969. Unfortunately, within three weeks of the start of the season he snapped an Achilles tendon which put him out of action until the last match of the County Championship in September. In his place the England selectors chose Ray Illingworth who had just begun his tenure as captain of Leicestershire after a fractious departure from Yorkshire, who would not give him the security of the three-year contract he had requested. His rivals, Graveney and Close, had both had their brushes with authority and were overlooked. Illingworth, who had never really set the world on fire as a Test player and had been in and out of the Test team for over ten years, would be unlikely to bar Cowdrey's smooth path to regaining the captaincy in time for the South Africa home series and the Ashes trip the following year. In fact, Cowdrey would never captain England again as Illingworth demonstrated facets of captaincy that the Kent batsman had never approached.

Cowdrey was a fine batsman and an immaculate slip fielder but he rarely convinced as a captain. Few England players who had been professionals until the start of the 1963 domestic season thought much of Cowdrey's captaincy ability. On the other hand he was a genial man whose affability clearly convinced the England selectors to appoint him with possibly a measure of relief after Brian Close had forfeited the position because of his time-wasting at the end of a County Championship match at Edgbaston in August 1967. In a fractious climate in the West Indies with various islands gaining long-sought independence from Great Britain during the first months of 1968, it was felt that the suave, diplomatic Cowdrey was a much safer choice than Close, whose Yorkshire bluntness was not an asset in that situation. Illingworth was awarded the captaincy for the 1969 season on what appeared to be a temporary basis, whilst Cowdrey made a slow recovery.

After the chaos and the trauma of the flight from Karachi, the England cricket team was relieved to find themselves back in the sedate atmosphere of Old Trafford for the start of the series against West Indies in June 1969. The efficacy of the new captain's diplomatic skills was not called upon as a century from Boycott and fine seam bowling from Snow and Brown gave Illingworth a comfortable victory by ten wickets in his first Test match as captain.

West Indies were a pale shadow of the irresistible force that had won the series in England in 1963 and 1966. Eleven of the touring party of 16 were newcomers to English conditions. Hall and Griffith no longer opened the bowling and Conrad Hunte, Seymour Nurse and Rohan Kanhai were all missing from the batting order. Clive Lloyd was just starting his Test career and looked more than promising but Basil Butcher was past his best as was Lance Gibbs and even the incomparable Garry Sobers had, by his own extremely high standards, a tour of modest proportions. David Brown remembers the cunning plan to get him out in the first innings which worked nearly perfectly because he dismissed Sobers when the batsman had only made ten.

> We aimed to get him caught at slip so we practised bowling wide of the off stump. We had a cordon of slips. We only had one man on the off side other than the slips and third man and that was John Edrich at extra cover. I bowled to Garry as wide as you like and he just smacked it straight into Edrich's hands. It wasn't supposed to work like that. The plan was to get him caught at slip, not caught at cover.

The second Test at Lord's was drawn, England finishing 37 runs short of victory with three wickets left and Illingworth in partnership with Barry Knight when time ran out. The final Test at Headingley was won by England's resolution at a moment when lesser sides and lesser captains might have panicked. In the last innings West Indies had reached 219/3 in pursuit of 303 to square the series when Butcher fell to the traditional combination of caught Knott bowled Underwood. When Barry Knight bowled Sobers fourth ball for a duck and Clive Lloyd went caught behind off Illingworth, the West Indies were facing defeat. In the end they lost by 30 runs and England thus won two consecutive series against the West Indies, a feat they were not to repeat again in the 20th century when a series draw was the height of their achievement. Michael Parkinson writing in the *Sunday Times* had not been impressed by what he had seen.

> Watching what I take to be the best bowlers in England and the West Indies performing in the current Test series is a

depressing and boring task. After a time, stupefaction sets in and the mind plays tricks. Shepherd merges into Knight who is Shillingford who is Brown who in turn becomes Holder and so on. They are as characterless and indistinguishable as a row of jelly babies. My Kingdom for one over of wristy leg spin.

If he read the column, it seems unlikely that his old mate, the new captain of England, would have been impressed.

Once West Indies had been dispatched, Illingworth's England were ready to do the same to New Zealand. At Lord's, New Zealand competed well enough during the first innings, conceding a small lead to the hosts but a gritty hundred from John Edrich meant that when England were bowled out early on the fourth morning, New Zealand needed 362 runs for their first ever victory over England. Although Glenn Turner carried his bat for a hard fought 43, Derek Underwood soon put an end to those dreams taking 7-32 as England glided serenely to a comfortable win by 230 runs. Rain, which wiped out nearly the whole of the last day's play at Trent Bridge, saved the New Zealanders in the second Test match when they were still nearly a hundred runs behind England's first innings total of 451/8 declared.

In the final Test of the 1969 summer at The Oval, Derek Underwood was again the destroyer taking 12 wickets as England cruised to victory by eight wickets. For Ray Illingworth, it brought to an end a summer of Test cricket that could hardly have gone better. For English cricket as a whole it seemed to steady the ship after 18 months of turbulence. Even at the time, however, it was realised that the summer of 1970 would present significant challenges. Indeed, had the Cricket Council bothered to look beyond NW8 it would have spotted a number of incidents that must have worried them for what they portended for the following year.

As early as the 16 May 1969 edition of *The Cricketer*, its editor, E.W. Swanton, was writing of his anxiety when contemplating the following year's tour. He called for a multi-racial South African touring party to play outside South Africa which, he believed, white South African players would accept. If no non-whites were good enough to be selected for the team currently, a second party could be sent which would be made up of promising youngsters from multi-racial backgrounds who would play alongside the official tourists. If SACA were to show itself open to integrated cricket in this way, Swanton was sure that MCC would campaign for South Africa's readmission to the ICC.

> To me, the prospect of a South African side coming next year to England and encountering the sort of atmosphere they would be likely to find if they had been due this summer is depressing to a degree. Rather than this, surely it would be preferable to sever – who can say for how long? – links that have endured for the best part of a century. They can be preserved but the initiative as I see it must come from South Africa.

In the *Daily Telegraph* in April 1969, Swanton found it sad that SACA had shown itself ignorant of the depth of feeling in Britain against apartheid in sport.

Around the time England were playing the West Indies at Lord's in late June, an all-white team of South African cricketers sponsored by Wilfred Isaacs, a wealthy Johannesburg businessman, had arrived to play a number of matches in England, at Swanton's suggestion. Swanton had also suggested Isaacs included two black players in the party but Isaacs suspected a trap and discussed the matter with Frank Waring, the Minister of Sport. Waring told Isaacs to inform Swanton that the squad had already been chosen on merit and it was too late to make such artificial changes.

Isaacs had brought over a squad to play in 1966 which had included the young Mike Procter, Lee Irvine and Barry Richards as well as seasoned internationals Roy McLean, Neil Adcock, Jackie McGlew and Hugh Tayfield. Three years later they returned to play four first-class games against Essex, Oxford University, Surrey and Ireland, although subsequently these matches had their first-class status removed. This time the party included the Test wicketkeeper John Waite, Graeme Pollock and the young Vincent van der Bijl who was later to form such a fearsome opening bowling partnership for Middlesex with Wayne Daniel. Young Liberals led by Peter Hain, who will make increasingly frequent appearances in this book, decided to test the policy of direct action which meant interrupting sporting events to draw attention to the question of apartheid in South Africa. The authorities were prepared and when the small number of protestors arrived in Basildon to interrupt the first match between the Isaacs XI and Essex they found a daunting array of police officers, squad cars, motorbikes and a mobile radio headquarters. Nevertheless, being inconspicuously dressed, they managed to get into the ground unobserved.

Keith Fletcher was playing for Essex that day and remembers the match clearly.

> It was rumoured that they were going to cause disruption to the game. We never thought much about it to be honest but then they came on to the field while we were playing and sat down in the middle of the wicket. At first we thought it was all a big joke; it was so unfamiliar to us then and then we realised it was a demonstration against apartheid.

The police seemed unsure whether or not to disturb the hallowed sanctity of the cricket field but Brian 'Tonker' Taylor, the extrovert Essex captain and wicketkeeper, had no such reservations. He shouted from behind the stumps to Keith Boyce, the young Bajan fast bowler whom Fletcher and Trevor Bailey had spotted on a recent International Cavaliers tour of Barbados and Jamaica and immediately signed for Essex. Taylor's instructions were quite clear. Boyce was to run up and bowl as if Hain and his colleagues were not there.

> Boycey couldn't bowl. If he had, he would have killed someone. Tonker said, 'Come on Boycey. Carry on bowling.' Well, that's exactly what Tonker would say.

Taylor's view was that if the idiots sitting in the middle of the wicket were hit by the ball it was entirely their own fault since they shouldn't be there in the first place. Boyce, not wishing to offend his new captain but clearly reluctant to hurt a spectator who was protesting at the injustices being done to other people of colour, remained at the start of his run. The incensed Taylor decided to take unilateral action and started kicking the protestors in the back as they sat in the middle of the pitch. Finally the police arrived and carried the protestors bodily from the field of play.

The fact that the Essex players did not have a lot of time for the protestors who were disrupting the play simply confirmed the young South Africans in their traditional prejudices. Barry Richards, who had been visiting Britain to play cricket since 1963 when he was 17, wrote later of his youthful attitude.

> I defended South Africa down to the ground, with all the fervour one would expect from someone who had enjoyed the benefits of a system and who had never known any other lifestyle. If I was cross-questioned on the absence of a 'one man, one vote' system, I would glibly reply that it was impossible because black people were educationally inferior, after all, some could not read or write. At the time I would never question why they were illiterate, or whose fault it was. It would take me other visits before I could appreciate the injustices.

The next match of the Isaacs tour took place at Oxford, a town with a much more highly organised body of university students and trade unionists from the car factory at Cowley who were determined to show their opposition to apartheid. Three days before the game began, somebody dug up the wicket and when the game did eventually start thanks to a sterling repair job by the groundsman at The Parks, at the sound of a whistle, 70 well-rehearsed protestors stopped the match, causing such mayhem that play was abandoned for the day. Throughout July nearly every match played by this all-white side was interrupted at some point or other. If this amount of disruption could be caused by a relatively few people, the chances of major disruptions when the official South African tourists arrived in 1970 increased significantly.

In the Winter Annual 1969/70 edition of *The Cricketer* magazine, Michael Melford, the cricket correspondent of the *Sunday Telegraph*, wrote a review of the Isaacs tour.

> It seems that the young South Africans had been told to respect the views of any demonstrators who might interrupt their matches. But what did they find?
>
> Louts who spat in their faces using foul language, others armed with barbed wire under their jackets, hooligans who

by digging up the pitch, digging heels into it, or throwing stones on to it were prepared to ruin many other uninvolved people's pleasure. The players began to recognise the faces – some were apparently being paid for demonstrating – but one ringleader dropped out when he was arrested for stealing between demonstrations.

The Communist Party was much in evidence and was shepherded off one pitch singing The Internationale.

Many of the stereotypes commonly used to describe anti-war and anti-tour protesters are in evidence in Melford's attack. The heroes are respectful. The villains are violent, abusive, crude and borderline criminal. The whole mixture is neatly topped off with a sprinkling of communism. It is of course entirely possible that the ranks of the protesters were swelled by those who had gone along to join in the mayhem but the wholesale dismissal of them as all behaving as described was unfair and untrue.

While the Isaacs cricketers were making their way uncertainly round England, South Africa's Davis Cup team arrived to play Great Britain in Bristol. Letters were sent by the Young Liberals warning of disruptions to play during the three days of the tie lasting from 17 to 19 July.

Again, despite the best efforts of the local constabulary, Hain, another man and two women, all Young Liberals, got on to the court during the first match when the British No 1 Mark Cox was 5-2 up in the first set against Robert Maud. They unfurled their banners proclaiming 'No Davis Cup play against Racialists' and 'Take Apartheid out of Sport'. One of the women tried to interest the players and the embarrassed officials in reading one of her leaflets but without success. The referee, Mr Maurice Cornford, angrily tore up the leaflet he was handed. There was a smattering of applause from the stands but it was drowned out by the jeers of those who had come to watch the tennis. A polite request asking the Young Liberals to leave now that they had registered their protest only persuaded Hain and the other three to lie down on the court. Mr Cornford then summoned eight shirt-sleeved policemen to remove the four protestors from the court and take them off to Redlands Police Station in Bristol.

David Gray, the tennis correspondent of *The Guardian* observed mildly,

> There was no violence. It was a kind of ritual of protest, so smoothly performed that it might almost have been rehearsed, and the television cameras caught the whole scene. The Liberals were not detained and a police spokesman said afterwards that any further action would be by summons. What did annoy the police and which may result in serious repercussions was the planting of a dummy bomb under one of the stands. This was found to be a harmless mass of wires but inquiries are still being made about the hoax. Both the Communists and the Young Liberals promised there would be further demonstrations... When it was all over the LTA breathed a sigh of relief and the match continued.

Great Britain eventually triumphed in the tie by three matches to two. It was a win-win situation for the LTA, the crowd and the demonstrators. A few months later South Africa was barred from the Davis Cup.

It had been coming for some time. The Rhodesia Davis Cup team of 1968 had been due to play a tie against Sweden but such was the force of the anti-apartheid demonstrations that the match was abandoned in Sweden and all the players and officials had to fly to France to find a relatively tranquil setting for the match to proceed. The accompanying South African journalist, Louis Duffus, wrote in response:

> I have never admired South Africans and Rhodesians more than when watching their dignified reaction before the idiotic political provocation of immature, ill-informed and often scruffy adolescents.

Clearly, the age and the manner in which political protestors dressed was incontrovertible evidence of the mistaken nature of their views.

These two protests were conducted with a certain amount of polite apology on all sides. At this stage Hain and his fellow activists were really quite uncertain about their tactics, had never been in trouble with the police and did not particularly wish to become martyrs for the cause. Their entire purpose was to demonstrate, to what they felt would be a sympathetic British public, the abhorrent practices of apartheid which could only be destroyed from the outside by the sporting isolation of South Africa. As they constantly repeated, there could be no normal sport in an abnormal society. Taking encouragement from the success of his tactics in July, Peter Hain wrote a warning letter that was published in *The Guardian* on 22 August 1969.

> At its coming council meeting the MCC will have the opportunity of calling off next year's tour by a white South African cricket team to Britain.
>
> The consequences of another refusal by the MCC to cancel the tour should not be underestimated. The token disruption during the recent tour of the Wilf Isaacs XI to Britain and the Davis Cup match at Bristol demonstrated the seriousness of threats to massively disrupt the 1970 tour: next summer could see a season consisting of an endless series of protests and disruptions.
>
> The MCC ought to have the courage to call a halt to collaboration with racialism in sport. White South Africa should be made to realise that there will be no future compromise with apartheid, either inside or outside sport. There is a need for a clear moral lead from British sportsmen on this issue and MCC have the chance to provide this at its council.

In September 1969, details of the South African tour were published. There was to be a full season of matches running from 2 May to 8 September, including five Tests and matches against all 17 counties. No acknowledgement was made of the possibility of serious disruption although Denis Howell, the Minister for Sport in the Labour government, said, when interviewed on television, that in his opinion the South African team should stay away from Britain. The policy of the Cricket Council and MCC was just as determined as the policy of apartheid that was enforced by the South African government. They believed in the maintenance of sporting links with South Africa and the majority of the men on these committees managed to reconcile such a policy with a frequently expressed polite distaste for apartheid.

The principal objective of the newly formed Stop the Seventy Tour was to force MCC into withdrawing their invitation to the South African Cricket Association but, as fate would have it, the Rugby Football Union had arranged a tour of the British Isles by the Springboks in the winter of 1969/70. Cricket and tennis in South Africa were largely the sports played by the descendants of British settlers. Rugby was much more the sport of the Afrikaaners, the political originators of the policy of apartheid. The names of the cricketers were largely of Anglo-Saxon origin – Jack Cheetham, Roy McLean, Jackie McGlew, Trevor Goddard; the names of the rugby players included Piet Botha, Sakie de Klerk, Hannes Viljoen and Johan Oosthuizen. These Springboks were to play 26 matches in three months including a Test match against each of the four home nations. This time there would be no polite requests to leave the field of play so that the match could continue. From the moment the squad arrived in London in October 1969 they would face the full wrath of the whole British Anti-Apartheid Movement. MCC looked on with some trepidation. Whatever happened during the rugby tour would very likely be replicated during the cricket tour the following summer. As it transpired their very worst fears were soon realised.

CHAPTER THREE
AUTUMN AND WINTER 1969/70

THE focus of the Stop the Seventy Tour, as its name implies, was the cancellation of the cricket tour in the summer of 1970. The demonstrations against the Wilfred Isaacs tour and the Davis Cup tie in Bristol were regarded as rehearsals for the main event and initially so were protests planned for the rugby tour. However, the violence and the hostile atmosphere that surrounded the rugby tour from its start were of a different order from Peter Hain and three friends sitting down in the middle of the pitch in Basildon and causing uncertainty in the mind of Keith Boyce or tennis officials in Bristol politely requesting them to leave so the match could be continued.

The first match against Oxford University on 5 November was initially abandoned when it was discovered that weed killer had been sprayed on the Oxford rugby ground and the words 'Oxford Rejects Apartheid' had appeared in letters 5ft high. The match was rescheduled to be played at Twickenham where a line of 200 policemen stood shoulder-to-shoulder behind a 4ft high fence. Several hundred anti-apartheid demonstrators from all over southern England had turned up but few managed to scale the fence and those few who did were quickly ejected from the ground as the match proceeded, accompanied by jeers and counter cheers. 'Don't Scrum with a Racist Bum' was the inelegant slogan of the day.

Hain was one of those ejected but professed himself very pleased with the impact the protest had made. The match had been played with three of the four sides of the ground unoccupied which allowed the police to concentrate their forces but inevitably it gave the game an unnatural air. The university side was selected to be the Springboks' first opponents because they would presumably give the tourists a decent game but nobody expected any result other than a convincing win for the Springboks. Although Oxford University were captained by the All Black scrum-half Chris Laidlaw, their victory by 6 points to 3 was an astonishing result to the rest of the rugby world and it suggested to the delighted demonstrators that their actions were already getting under the skin of the players, even at this early stage.

On the morning of the game the London Welsh and Wales flanker John Taylor, who had toured South Africa the previous year with the British Lions, gave an interview to *The Guardian* in which he announced that after much careful thought he would not play against the tourists in the two games in which he expected to be selected – for London Counties at Twickenham and for Wales in the international in January – because of what he had seen on that tour. Taylor, known familiarly as 'Basil Brush' because of his wild hair, gave a highly articulate point of view to the journalist Christopher Ford which encapsulated much of the STST campaign's thinking.

I disagree with apartheid as I believe quite a lot of rugby players do. I don't like politics in sport but the South Africans are the ones who have brought politics in .... By playing I would merely be helping to perpetuate an objectionable regime.

I've been to South Africa and I know people are going to say I accepted their hospitality under false pretences. But I didn't go there thinking about politics. I'm just as keen as the next player to get on with the game and indeed our brief was not to talk politics at all. Inevitably though the subject came up and I couldn't see anything in apartheid except the fact that it was condemning most of the population to second class citizenship.

Having seen it in action I can't go on burying my head in the sand ... as far as I am concerned bridge-building has achieved nothing in twenty years and the time has come to try something else.

It was exactly what the STST campaigners had been saying but now it was being said by a respected rugby international and the impact was to worry the rugby authorities still further and elicit new support from a wider cross-section of British people for whom, just over year since the D'Oliveira controversy had erupted, the issue of South Africa was becoming increasingly important.

For the next game the following Saturday at Welford Road against Midland Counties East, all police leave in Leicester was cancelled. Tickets were restricted but after 3,000 protestors had marched to the ground despite attempts to divert them by the local constabulary, a hundred of them produced legitimate tickets and got into the ground. They made little impact on the game itself which the tourists won narrowly by 11 points to 9, but the following week saw another defeat as the tour moved into Wales and South Africa was humbled by Newport. Again, the result indicated that the players simply could not perform to their usual standard under such difficult circumstances. Now a section of public opinion started to swing behind the Springboks and in his report on the Newport game, U.A. Titley, the rugby correspondent of *The Times*, was already expressing that paper's political standpoint.

> It was difficult not to have sympathy for the visitors who are battling at the start of their tour not only a crop of normal misfortunes but also against things that are beyond their control. Although two stoppages by spectators were affairs of only seconds it was hard not to suspect that although the flesh was willing, the spirit in the sense of natural anxiety, was weak.

Three days later in Swansea, violence between demonstrators and the police broke out and reports indicated that it was reminiscent of troubled times in the 1930s. It might have been the intention of the police simply to maintain law and order but the violence with which they did so convinced demonstrators that the police were acting in collusion with the rugby supporters. A hundred demonstrators got on to the pitch just after half-time and caused play to be suspended for more than five minutes. As soon as they sat down the police dragged them away, being noticeably as aggressive with the women as they were with the men which, in those unenlightened times, appalled many neutrals. One police sergeant and 21 demonstrators had to be treated in hospital. The police made great play of injured policemen, attacked for simply doing their duty. The STST statement released the day after the match painted a very different picture.

> The private army of rugby thugs was responsible for some of the most systematic and brutal mob violence ever seen on peaceful demonstrators in Britain. The introduction of the vigilantes into the protest arena must now call into question the whole future of the tour. Unless something is done now, someone may get killed.

The National Union of Students and the student unions at Leicester, Reading, Southampton and Swansea universities reiterated the plea for the tour to be called off. Danie Craven, the president of the South African Rugby Board, responded in Durban that the tour would continue no matter what protests were held. Peter Hain, for all his stated belief that protests should be non-violent, warned that matters would only get worse until the tour was abandoned. In the play that was possible South Africa beat Swansea by 12 points to 0. It seemed almost incidental.

Perhaps sensing the political climate might be more receptive than it had been previously, the South African golfer Gary Player chose that day to plead with the authorities in his country to permit Papwa Sewgolum, of Indian origin but living in Durban, to play in the South African Open golf tournament. The appeal was rejected in a blunt official statement. 'Participation by a non-white in the tournament is against Government policy.' Player's action was dismissed in some militant quarters as what would in future years become known as 'virtue signalling'. In this case it was believed that Player was making the plea because if all South African golfers were to be banned from international tournaments this would destroy the better part of what was left of his career. It was remembered that when Sewgolum had won a tournament a few years earlier and had to submit to the farce of being presented with the trophy outside in the rain because the clubhouse was restricted to whites only, Player had made no public comment. The following spring, after Arthur Ashe had been refused a visa by South Africa, the black tennis player said he thought that Gary Player's life was in danger from black extremists whose campaigns were getting increasingly violent. All he had to do, added Ashe, was to make a public statement of his disapproval of apartheid which he had currently not done.

On 10 November 1969 a passionate debate took place in the Cambridge Union and in front of television cameras from London Weekend Television on the motion 'This House believes that political commitment should not intrude upon sporting contacts'. It was proposed by Cambridge graduates Ted Dexter and Wilf Wooller, the larger-than-life former captain of Glamorgan, and opposed by Denis Howell, the retired Football League referee and now Labour MP for Small Heath Birmingham and Minister for Sport. Wooller had already crossed swords with Peter Hain and left the student in no doubt as to his intentions.

> I debated with him down the radio with me in London and him in Cardiff. The first thing he said to me was, 'I want to see you behind bars and I am going to make sure that happens.' Billy Griffith was an administrator softly spoken but deeply, deeply hostile although hostile not in an aggressive way. My attitude to him was, 'You're the enemy but you're not a bastard.' Whereas Wooller I thought was a bastard.

Griffith, as its secretary, tended to be the unwilling recipient of the stream of letters Peter Hain deposited in person with MCC.

> Billy Griffith was conservative with a big C and a small c. He was polite whenever I handed him a letter which wasn't often, maybe a couple of times at most, a clipped politeness which was very much not the case with Wooller who was always extremely aggressive towards me.

Wooller, supported by Dexter, advanced in the Cambridge debate the now traditional argument that it was unfair to punish cricketers and cricket lovers when it was clear that British businessmen had no trouble trading with South Africa. Indeed, many British actors were free to appear in touring adaptations of Agatha Christie novels and other plays designed to appeal to the expatriate community. Those who chose to go tended to be excoriated by the left-wing members of Equity, the actors' union, but the British government made no attempt to stop them and the actors themselves presumably managed to find an accommodation with the principle of the segregated audiences before whom they had to play. The argument that cultural bridges were better for everyone than isolation was the same as the one that was used in 1980 when Mrs Thatcher tried to persuade the British Olympic Association to join the American boycott of that year's Olympic Games in Moscow. Politics and sport it was believed, principally by sports administrators, should be kept separate.

In the Cambridge Union debate the speech of the night was made by Denis Howell's seconder, John Arlott. Hands plunged deep into the pockets of his jacket and speaking without notes, he captivated the Union for 15 minutes. He argued persuasively that:

> It is political commitment and political belief that can make a man think that his opponent's views are so obnoxious that he will abstain from playing any game with him as a protest against what the other man believes... I cannot believe that any gentleman on the other side of the house would happily have played a round of golf with Hitler or Goering, nor I trust do any of them want to make up a football match with the people who directed or carried out the suppression of the Hungarian revolution or who battered down the rise of thought in Dubcek's Czechoslovakia.

His speech culminated with an impassioned, 'Mr President, sir, anyone who cares to support this motion will not exclude politics from sport but will in fact be attempting to exclude sport from life.' It was enough to defeat the motion by 344 votes to 160 and indeed after a late-night drinking session it was enough to convince even Wooller and Dexter that there was some merit in his argument.

Arlott had travelled to South Africa for the 1948/49 MCC tour there. It was the first days of government by D.F. Malan's National Party but already the change in the quality of life experienced by non-whites was apparent and Arlott was appalled. On his return,

Arlott was invited to sit on the panel of the radio programme *Any Questions* as he was a fairly regular guest. When the subject of South Africa arose he made his feelings abundantly clear, calling the Malan government 'Nazi' in character. It was a justifiable accusation for as he pointed out, most of the members of the Malan cabinet had supported Nazi Germany during the time of the Second World War. However, in 1950 when the programme was broadcast, South Africa was still a member of the Commonwealth and calling it Nazi provoked an immediate reaction. BBC news relays were banned by the South African Broadcasting Corporation. Arlott was disciplined by the BBC for breaking the rule of political impartiality that BBC employees had to observe. He was not invited back on to the panel of *Any Questions* for another three years, which greatly distressed and worried him. Arlott was at the time a producer in the BBC's Poetry Department, although he was far better known as a cricket commentator. It is hard to understand why he should have been invited on to *Any Questions* in the first place if he was not going to be allowed to express an opinion. Nevertheless, the fact that he was not asked to appear again on the programme for three years was a decision that cut Arlott to the quick. His mind, however, was made up. He never visited South Africa again and he remained vocal in his detestation of apartheid.

Arlott's oratory at the Cambridge Union was disseminated by the television recording and captured the feelings of many British people who, prior to Basil D'Oliveira's initial exclusion from the MCC touring party in 1968, had given very little thought to the iniquities of apartheid in South Africa. This shift in public opinion turned the STST campaigners and their increasingly successful attempts to disrupt the rugby tour from objects of scorn and derision to objects of admiration. Even if they remained objects of scorn and derision to those who did not agree with the message they were sending, they were nevertheless having the impact they wanted. On 19 December, Stoke-on-Trent Council cancelled a badminton match between England and South Africa due to be played in March 1970. It was feared that there would be damage to the council-owned venue, King's Hall. South Africa's sporting isolation was increasing.

STST stepped up the pressure. On 27 November a deputation arrived at Lord's hoping to speak to Billy Griffith whose health was to deteriorate significantly during the course of this crisis. Robin Marlar, the former captain of Cambridge University and Sussex, was deeply opposed to the STST and he sympathised greatly with Griffith's plight.

> Billy Griffith was another magnificent fellow, very brave and a splendid chap. Billy liked his pipe and would have done anything for a quiet life.

Unsurprisingly, Mr Griffith was seeking his quiet life elsewhere and was not in a position to greet them. A letter was solemnly handed over by Louis Eaks of the Young Liberals whose contents were thereafter released to the press.

> The current campaign against the Springbok tour confirms my earlier prediction that any campaign of militant action to disrupt matches next summer will turn Lord's into the Ulster of the cricket world.

At the same time the press reported an attack by a hundred demonstrators on the South African Ambassador's car in Newcastle upon Tyne.

Whether or not it was the pressure exerted by these demonstrations and those against the rugby tour it would be difficult to prove but in the middle of December, SACA announced that its cricket squad to tour England in the summer would be chosen strictly on merit and on a non-racial basis. John Arlott certainly thought the two could be linked.

> It must now seem that the demonstrators, by their actions against the Springbok rugby team have in a few months achieved more than the cricket officials have done by 15 years of polite acquiescence. The South African Government has cause to understand that a thousand active demonstrators probably bespeak a hundred times as many silent objectors.

Whilst generally welcoming the principle only the MCC and its supporters thought the announcement would bring the STST movement to a close. It didn't take a genius to work out that so deprived had been non-white South African cricket it was impossible to imagine anyone from the townships displacing on merit Graeme Pollock, Mike Procter or Barry Richards or indeed any player from the 1970 side that would face the Australians the following spring. The announcement was made by Jack Cheetham, now president of SACA but formerly the well-respected captain of the South Africa team that had toured England in 1955, losing a hard-fought series only in the last session of the last day of the Oval Test match. Cheetham, wrote Arlott,

> is an honest man. As a cricketer and a captain he was one of endeavour and integrity. Anyone who knows him will feel that his statement was one of sincere belief and intent. It is unlikely that personal mistrust of Cheetham lies behind the decision of three of the four non-white cricket unions to reject the offer of £30,000 towards their fund. Nonetheless, such self-denial is unusual and weighty evidence of mistrust. This is a late but determined effort, engendered by alarm at the demonstrations against the rugby team to save the cricket tour from ruin by public opinion.

Peter Hain and his supporters were not quite so charitably disposed.

> Cheetham's announcement we all realised at the time was just pure PR. What it reflected was the MCC and SACA saying to themselves 'Crikey, these guys are having a real impact on the rugby tour, we have to do something, anything' but the fact was they couldn't do anything significant even if they genuinely wanted to and some of them certainly did.

If Cheetham and SACA truly believed that this announcement constituted some kind of breakthrough, he was immediately disabused of the notion when John Vorster refused to deviate from his previously stated position.

> If the demand is made that our Springbok teams will not be welcome overseas if they do not include all race groups, we

will not be prepared to comply with that provision, and the relationships will necessarily have to be broken.

Nevertheless, the Test and County Cricket Board, which comprised representatives from the Minor Counties as well as the 17 first-class counties, maintained the robust defence of its principles and of the tour which it confirmed on 11 December would definitely go ahead.

> In reaffirming their decision they repeat their aversion to racial discrimination of any kind. They also respect the rights of those who wish to demonstrate peacefully. Equally they are unanimous in their resolve to uphold the rights of individuals in this country to take part in lawful pursuits, particularly where those pursuits have the support of the majority. A sub-committee has been appointed to deal with all matters relevant to the tour and to report to the TCCB.

The sub-committee was not due to report for two months and, as far as the Cricket Council was concerned, matters would remain as they were until the middle of February. They refused categorically to accept that there was a connection between a tour of England by an all-white South African cricket team and any implied tacit approval of the policy of apartheid. Sport had to be kept separate from politics at all costs and in any case a sporting ban was a very weak weapon with which to persuade the South African government to alter one of its central policies.

The Cricket Council's stance enraged Michael Parkinson who now began a prolonged campaign of ridicule in his column in the *Sunday Times*.

> The Cricket Council shows itself to be imbued with incompetence, insensitivity and plain bloody daftness. It can now be called without any doubt the Test and County Clodpoles Board.
>
> The TCCB's decision which virtually ensured Vorster's XI would tour England next year is one which will please barbed wire manufacturers and those awful people who

believe in giving encouragement to that loathsome mob in South Africa.

I had hoped the rugby tour reaction would have found at least one sensitive conscience at Lord's. So far the image presented by the people who run cricket is that of Wilfred McWooller, whose contribution to the debate thus far has been characteristically militant and unsympathetic to people who oppose apartheid. I for one do not care to have someone like him as the figurehead of our national game.

The rugby tour continued on its way, the games sometimes being interrupted and sometimes remaining free if the demonstrators, who were present at every match, failed to evade the presence of the police whose determination not to be bested could occasionally turn ugly. Outside the White City stadium in Manchester, before the match against North West Counties, 2,300 policemen were needed to contain the 7,000 demonstrators. When the Springboks played London Counties at Twickenham, Hain climbed over the fence straight into the arms of policemen who delighted in dragging him away through a puddle of water as rugby supporters tried to kick him and hurled abuse at him. After having his name taken in an atmosphere of open hostility he was ejected from the ground although he managed to get back in again through another turnstile but he couldn't get back on to the pitch and had to watch South Africa win the match 22-6. The interruptions were not deemed worthy of press reporting.

The match against Ulster at the end of November was called off for fear of encouraging trouble at a time when 'The Troubles' had just started. The first Test match was against Scotland at Murrayfield the following week and ended in yet another upset, Scotland winning 6-3. It was played out with two of the four sides of the ground kept deliberately vacant and the spectators compared to normal Test matches were half the number who usually attended.

Beer bottles, cans, stones, coins and fireworks were hurled at 300 police as they advanced across the terraces. There were 26 arrests, all but five of them after the match. Sixty-five people were ejected from ground. A policeman was kicked in the stomach. The Chief Constable of Edinburgh said he was satisfied with the way his men had handled the situation. Students later claimed that they had been dragged out from the barrier, their arms pinioned and their faces forced into the ground. They were, they said, hit by truncheons concealed inside policemen's sleeves and gloves. The following day the *Sunday Times* published a photograph taken by its staff photographer Frank Herrmann which showed a female demonstrator being grabbed roughly by her hair and dragged away. Shortly after taking it, Herrmann was approached by a police superintendent who said, 'You can't do that', and stopped him from taking more. Although he was allowed to keep the film in his camera, he was barred from the touchline.

The cricket authorities noted what was happening to the South African rugby players and reacted with alarm. On 8 December, Mike Turner, the man who ran Leicestershire cricket, wrote to Lord's that he had just had a letter from the Chief Constable of Leicester and Rutland Constabulary warning of costs of £140.2s 5d per hour, exclusive of meals and travelling, as the price for his men guarding the Leicestershire match against the tourists. He concluded:

> I think that unless the advice given by the Bishop of Woolwich [David Sheppard] is accepted by the anti-apartheid demonstrators, the country has to face a situation which, if it slides much further, will lead to complete anarchy.

The Lancashire secretary J.B. Wood popped across the road to see Lancashire County Constabulary which was then located in Stretford Town Hall. He wrote to Lord's:

> The [police] had a terrible experience with the Springboks at the White City the other week with over 2,000 police involved in the whole operation.

On 18 December, the sports promoter Derrick Robins met the Assistant Chief Constable of Sussex and the Chief Superintendent of the Eastbourne Division to discuss security arrangements for the first match of the tour due to be played against his team at The Saffrons starting on 28 April. Amongst the proposals considered was the idea that admission would be by signed invitation only, making it a private match between the Derrick Robins XI and South Africa. The police officers thought a minimum of 200 constables would have to be on duty, incurring a cost estimated at between £6,000 and £15,000 for the match but a later letter from the Chief Constable suggested £10,000 a day might be a more realistic figure. However, cricket just didn't have that sort of money available.

A Cricket Council Emergency Executive Committee was held at Lord's on Monday 29 December, in which the members sounded hopeful that their press magnate friend, Sir Max Aitken, could be persuaded to run a helpful campaign in the *Daily Express*, appealing for funds to pay for this new expense. Any money left over would go to furthering non-white cricket in South Africa. An alternative, much shorter schedule of five Test matches and six three-day games was discussed and sent to SACA. South Africa was assured that it would not have to contribute to police costs but the share of the gate revenue would have to be revised to ensure that MCC did not end up in the bankruptcy court. Jack Cheetham wrote back from his home in Johannesburg with counter proposals including a tour starting on 20 June with five Tests and seven three-day games finishing at The Oval on 2 September. The matter would be fully discussed when the appropriate sub-committee reported to the Cricket Council in mid-February.

The rugby tour continued to be an unmitigated disaster for the visitors. They were made to feel unwanted wherever they went and their sporting prowess was only intermittently in evidence. When the law pounced, as it did after a match against The North in Aberdeen and 98 students were arrested and fined an eye-watering £1,500, a bright student wrote to his hero, John Lennon, wondering if he would be prepared to put on a concert in order to raise the money. Lennon replied that he was too busy to do that but enclosed a cheque for £1,500. Instead of being taught a lesson, as had been hoped by the Aberdeen magistrates and their supporters, the demonstrators were instead congratulated by one of the idols of Generation X.

Any pretence the authorities might have harboured that the matches could proceed with just a few demonstrators being hauled away to the applause of the crowd was abandoned when the stadium at Cardiff Arms Park was surrounded by barbed wire. Conversely, the anti-apartheid campaigners stepped up their actions too. For the Test match against England which was due to take place at Twickenham on the Saturday before Christmas, a group was delegated to sit down in front of the tourists' coach and others planned to handcuff themselves to the goalposts. Two STST supporters, Mike Findley and Peter Twyman, spent hours rehearsing for this particular moment by running up to a pole that had been planted in the back garden of Peter Hain's parents' flat in Putney and handcuffing themselves to it at speed. Others booked into the South Africans' hotel on Park Lane and tried to superglue the locks on the doors of the players' bedrooms. On the night before the game, one dedicated young woman was prepared to go so far as to seduce one of the South African players when asked to do so by Peter Hain.

> The girl just got groped for her troubles. She was serious but in a happy-go-lucky sort of way. She worked hard in the movement but she wasn't particularly intense. She never quoted the latest ideological arguments, she was just a practical, down to earth young woman, a really nice person who had boyfriends attracted to her like moths to a flame. When we asked her to do it she just said okay. It was our idea not hers for her to seduce one of the players but of course we needed an attractive co-operative woman to do it. If one of us had gone into the hotel we would have attracted suspicion which she didn't.

In the end the plan didn't work because when she approached the player in question he turned out to be alcoholically incoherent and physically incapable.

In the morning, outside the hotel, the next part of the plan clicked into operation. A well dressed man, looking quite anonymous in a business suit, climbed on to the coach and told the driver he was wanted inside the hotel. Hain explains:

> The man who got on the coach was called Michael Deeney; he was a City banker, a financier who wore a suit at work. I was too well known to go into the hotel but even the average STST supporter, scruffy and long haired, could never have done it because they would have attracted instant suspicion.

That's why the driver never gave a second thought to this chap coming and telling him he was wanted in the hotel.

The coach driver obediently got off the bus and Deeney took his place. Half the team had still to board when the 'driver' started the engine and started to pull out into Park Lane. The police outriders were caught by surprise. Deeney turned left into Piccadilly by which time the players realised they were being hijacked. As the coach accelerated past Green Park underground station one of them managed to get his hands round Deeney's neck. The bus thereupon bounced off half a dozen cars and crashed into a red Post Office van. The police soon arrived but it was total chaos as Deeney immediately handcuffed himself to the steering wheel.

On the forecourt outside Twickenham railway station, a deputation from the Commons and Lords stood waiting to engage with the rugby supporters pouring off the trains. The Church of England was led by David Sheppard, the Bishop of Woolwich, Mervyn Stockwood, the Bishop of Southwark and Trevor Huddleston, the Bishop of Stepney, the Lords Soper and Brockway and MPs including Ian Mikardo, Anne Kerr and Andrew Faulds. One man approached David Sheppard and demanded to know why he was in Twickenham and neglecting his parish. 'It's my day off', replied the former captain of Sussex shortly. The demonstrators continued to chant as they marched side by side towards the ground. One student yelled, 'What did you do during the war? Support Hitler? You're supporting Nazis now.' He was confronted by a rugby fan built like a second row forward. 'I was fighting for you,' he replied in a tone that clearly suggested he now wondered why he had bothered. It could be argued that both sides had a point.

Outside the gates of Twickenham stadium, Jack Bailey and Raman Subba Row, former county cricketers for Essex and Northants respectively but now working for the Cricket Council and MCC, handed out pamphlets enlisting the support of what they supposed would be a sympathetic crowd for saving the 1970 tour. Unfortunately for them, they met with limited success because most people mistook them for the other side and either ignored the pamphlets being offered or threw them away without reading them.

Just after the match started Michael Findley succeeded in his ambition of cuffing himself to a Twickenham goalpost but Peter Twyman was tackled by a policeman ten yards short of the try line. The cheers from the demonstrators which had accompanied the appearance on the pitch of the two intrepid invaders were replaced by cheers from the other side when Twyman was brought down by a tackle that was fully appreciated by the Twickenham crowd. The match, however, was delayed whilst bolt cutters were found and used to release Michael Findley from his fervent embrace of the goalpost.

One side saw the protests as evidence that Britain still believed in justice and morality. The other side saw the police precautions and the arrests as a bulwark against anarchy. Jack Bailey wrote later:

> The police ringed the touch-line and faced the crowd, not the play. They were magnificent. I was particularly impressed by the demeanour of one black policeman, who was plainly disgusted by the antics of the demonstrators in front of him and the obscenities being hurled his way. Nonetheless, he remained stoically calm throughout, still facing the crowd as the final whistle blew.

The match was played in the now familiar atmosphere of hostility and simmering tension. It ended in yet another defeat for the tourists, this time by 11 points to 8, their first defeat by England since 1906. Bailey and Subba Row had taken to the match as their guests Jack Cheetham and Arthur Coy from the South African Cricket Association. Neither man felt that what he had seen there warranted calling off the tour but the MCC men knew in their hearts that cricket simply could not be played under the circumstances they had witnessed at Twickenham and that their cricket tour would have to be truncated. Only Test match grounds could possibly be defended to the extent that would be necessary for a cricket match to be played uninterrupted.

Nevertheless, as the South Africans were showing no signs of caving in under pressure, it was important to MCC that they continued their support for their old friends. They must have appreciated the letters in the MCC archives that reveal that they were also being supported by 'ordinary' people who felt the same way they did, even if they expressed themselves more forcibly. On 6 December a letter was written by Alexander Buchan in Bury to the Secretary of MCC.

> What makes me so very cross is that those who protest have never visited South Africa and know very little about that which they are protesting. Many agree that apartheid is not the be-all and end-all of South Africa but it is the best method of dealing with the problem that has been tried so far and I am sure that time will tell that the present South African government are treading on the right lines. Whilst segregation is not the best method of dealing with the matter I have it on the highest authority that the South African native is better off to-day than ever before.

That would probably have come as a surprise to a family living in Soweto but the letters in a similar vein continued to arrive in the Lord's postbag. An anonymous letter to Billy Griffith, written on 11 December, made clear its author's disenchantment with the Labour government.

> We are absolutely against our democratic right to watch whatever sport we like being taken away by thugs supported by the Labour Government. A minority of people in this country might be against apartheid but the majority are against the invasion of the coloured people to this island taking our houses, jobs, National Assistance, also the abhorred Race Relations Law. ... This country is not democratic any more but a Police state. We can muster up several thousands and the coloured teams [West Indies, India and Pakistan] will be as welcome as the anti-Apartheid people have made the Springboks. We are sick to death of the encouragement the Labour Government have given all the Tariq Alis, Coloured anarchists and disruptive students... One would have thought the election results would have taught the Liberals and Labourites just how the country feels about the coloureds, but it seems they will never learn.

There is no suggestion that, despite the letter being archived, the MCC committee echoed these racist thoughts. Indeed, they gave the same treatment to a flimsy telex which is equally unpleasant to read.

THIS IS THE FINAL WARNING TO THOSE ORGAN-ISING THE TOUR OF WHITE SOUTH AFRICAN CRICKETERS. SINCE ALL APPEALS TO REASON HAVE OBVIOUSLY FAILED AS THEY WERE BOUND TO AND THE ONLY THINGS THE PIGS EVER LISTEN TO IS VIOLENCE WE NOW DECLARE THAT IF THE TOUR GOES ON THE LIVES OF EVERY ONE OF THOSE CRICKETERS AS WELL AS OF THOSE PEOPLE RESPONSIBLE FOR INVITING THEM AND THEIR FAMILIES WILL BE AT STAKE. WE HAVE THE GUNS AND THE EXPLOSIVES AND METHODS WHICH WE WILL NOT AS YET DISCLOSE. WE SHALL NOT BE SO FOOLISH AS TO STATE NOW WHICH MEMBER OF THE ROYAL FAMILY OR WHICH MCC PERSONAGE WILL BE THE FIRST TO BE KIDNAPPED.

IF YOU DO NOT THINK THIS WARNING IS SERIOUS CONSULT THE SOUTH AFRICAN SPECIAL BRANCH AND MENTION TO THEM THE NAMES OF PRATT TSFENDAS AND HARRIS. THEY WILL KNOW WE MEAN BUSINESS

It was signed

THE THIRD WORLD LIBERATION ARMY (AFRICAN DIVISION)

Peter Hain gave an interview to the *Financial Times* on 13 December which reflected his concern that MCC would have to be dragged 'kicking and screaming into the 20th century' because otherwise it would proceed with its fingers in its ears. The interview incensed Arthur Alvey of 42 Kensington Square who wrote to Maurice Allom, the chairman of MCC the following day in a fine fury.

I could scarcely believe my eyes when I read this. Are you going to take this from a 19 year old boy who, I understand, was not even born in this country and only came to Britain four years ago. How dare this young fellow speak in that way of the MCC?

I should like to know whether you intend to reply to this young fellow. If you do then I suggest your Committee ought to stop apologising and appearing diffident about the whole affair. Dammit, you are grown-up men like me and you should make it crystal clear that you are not going to allow a 19 year old boy and his followers to disrupt the tour. For heaven's sake what have we come to if a fellow like this can be allowed to hold our cricket to hostage. He is showing the same intolerance that he complains about in South Africa.

The letters were not all from racist bigots by any means. Many of them were simply protesting that their right to watch cricket in peace was being threatened by lawlessness and violence. On 9 December Billy Rees-Davies QC, the Liberal MP for Pembrokeshire, wrote:

I feel most strongly that under no circumstances should the MCC be virtually blackmailed into giving up the proposed South Africa tour. Many of my colleagues in the House feel the same way that I do, as indeed do my constituents amongst whom are many lovers of cricket.

On the field, the South African rugby players were demoralised by the hostility with which they seemed to be greeted everywhere they played and depressed at their own poor form. Linking the two together, the players voted to abandon the tour and return home. The South African government, aware that such a move would be tantamount to a defeat not just for the rugby team but also for the government and its fundamental policy of apartheid, made it quite clear that the players were expected to grit their teeth and complete the tour as scheduled.

It staggered to a conclusion at the end of January after draws in the Test matches against Ireland and Wales. In Dublin, 10,000 people marched on Lansdowne Road, led by Bernadette Devlin, the Independent Republican MP who, a few months previously, had famously been elected to the Westminster parliament at the by-election for Mid Ulster, at the age of 21 the youngest member ever. The match was played behind another barbed wire fence and the post-match reception was disturbed by the throwing of eggs and stones. When they arrived at Galashiels to play South of Scotland, they were met by a peaceful protest headed by the local MP, David Steel. The last Test match was a 6-6 draw at Cardiff Arms Park where Wales's popular and innovative coach Carwyn James gave his pre-match talk to the players but then walked out of the ground to register his own protest. Almost certainly more upsetting to the South African players was the try that Gareth Edwards scored in the last minute to secure the draw.

On the day of their departure, the protesters chased the team's coach all the way to Heathrow airport, calling incessant messages about the disgrace of whites-only sport from a loudspeaker tied to the roof of an old Bentley. It was intended that the weary players returned to their own country bearing the message that all-white South African teams were not welcome in Britain. At the airport, a further 50 anti-apartheid demonstrators were waiting for them in the pouring rain. Police had to shepherd the players through a side entrance to avoid a direct confrontation. The demonstrators then rushed upstairs into the terminal and made for the window overlooking the duty free shop where the players were buying last-minute gifts. They banged on the window yelling their message that the South African rugby players should go home and tell their cricketers that they were not wanted in Britain either.

They certainly returned home chastened by their inability to win a single Test match against any of the home nations and it would have been impossible to have separated the latter result from the impact caused by their public excoriation. However, contrary to their expectations, the welcome that greeted them on their return to South African soil was fulsome. Their home fans realised perfectly well that the players had been under enormous strain and though results had not been triumphant their dogged determination (as the government had predicted) to complete the tour under such provocation and at the hands of inhospitable hosts evoked nothing in South Africa apart from admiration.

The demonstrators were largely seen as either long-haired communists or decadent drug addicts and sexual deviants whose political views were both predictable and reprehensible. Forty-seven

Conservative MPs tabled a motion in the House of Commons congratulating the South African players for the sporting spirit they had displayed under such duress. However, as far as the believers in liberal gradualism were concerned, it had been demonstrated that their traditional idea that South African players could come to Britain and see how wonderful the community relations were in a multi-ethnic society where there was no legal discrimination against people of colour was quite misguided. At the end of the tour few people had changed their minds and attitudes had hardened on both sides.

Already SACA would have been made aware that it was the intention of protesters in the summer of 1970 to continue the policy of direct action. That meant not just placards outside the ground. It meant sitting down on the pitch and reflecting sunlight from hand mirrors into the eyes of the batsman at the crease. Police wouldn't need to be on full alert just for the 80 minutes of a rugby match but for the full seven hours (including lunch and tea intervals) of the five days of Test cricket.

The police authorities had been made aware by the rugby tour of the excessive demands that would be placed on them. On the day of the last match of the rugby tour the Police Federation announced that it was going to demand a 10% pay rise for all officers. They warned that 5% would not be good enough even though the government was at the time engaged in a desperate struggle to impose a prices and incomes policy that would control all wages in the public sector.

> Inspector Reg Gale, chairman of the Federation said, 'Our opinion on the South Africa [cricket] tour has nothing to do with the rights and wrongs of it. But anything that throws an extra load on the police we can well do without.' He said the Police Council accepted the staff view that the manpower shortage was seriously deteriorating to the point that a grave situation would exist soon if nothing was done.
>
> 'Already a great number of policemen have had to be diverted from other work – largely at public expense but not exclusively so – to cover the Springbok tour and I understand the cricket tour will be much more difficult to deal with.'

These were exactly the words the STST people wanted to hear and the Labour government did not. A pay rise of 10% for 98,000 police officers up to the rank of chief inspector would be a blow to the government's Prices and Incomes policy, not just because of what it would cost the Exchequer to settle the police claim, but because it would undoubtedly encourage similar demands for pay rises from many other professions within the public sector. On the other hand, the prospect of riots on the streets, which an understaffed police force could not contain in the months leading up to a general election, was probably even worse.

It surprised even Hain and the STST that public support for the anti-apartheid demonstrations had grown so fast. There was of course genuine indignation and revulsion at the South African government's policy of apartheid but the explanation as to the rapid growth of direct action during the rugby tour must have owed something to the ubiquity of student protests against authority in the developed world and the unpopularity of the Vietnam war in particular. 1966 might have seen the triumph of the 'Ballad of the Green Berets' and even in 1968 the flag-waving John Wayne film *The Green Berets* did surprisingly well at the box office but the cultural tide was turning significantly against the war.

In November 1969 the world was shocked by the revelation of the massacre at the South Vietnamese hamlet of My Lai. The appalling events had actually taken place in March 1968 but for more than 18 months the knowledge of what happened when, in an attempt to destroy a battalion of Viet Cong, American troops actually murdered 500 unarmed Vietnamese women, children and old men was successfully covered up. Twenty women and girls had been raped, some of them as young as ten years old. The American Army initially described what happened at My Lai as a great military victory in which 128 enemy combatants were killed. The journalist Seymour Hersh broke the true story in November 1969.

From that moment, people who might have been sympathetic to America as the Land of the Free and the Home of the Brave, who had applauded its efforts in World War II, praised the foundation of the United Nations and lauded the Marshall Plan as a generous way to rebuild Western Europe and bolster it against the advance of the new Soviet empire, turned decisively against the war and the

Americans who prosecuted it. To a generation of young people there was little difference between Sharpeville and Selma. The tour of England by the South Africa cricket team in the summer of 1970 was going to be the latest battle in the war of the generations and the MCC grandees, Gubby Allen, Billy Griffith, Arthur Gilligan and others, were firmly lined up on the wrong side of history.

The same barbed wire which had so disfigured the rugby Tests at Cardiff Arms Park and Lansdowne Road was now being delivered to Test cricket grounds in England. It was still only January but the cricket war had started. Michael Parkinson kept up his relentless campaign with a coruscating attack on the sycophantic BBC. On 18 January he wrote dismissively of the interview on *Sportsnight with Coleman* that the eponymous host conducted with Ted Heath, lately the winner of the Sydney to Hobart yacht race, and suggested a discussion on the South Africa tour to be conducted in the *Sportsnight with Coalhouse* studio as he called it. The panel should comprise the politicians Heath and Enoch Powell and the cricketers Ted Dexter and Colin Ingleby-Mackenzie. The 'impartial' chairman could be Wilf Wooller. Parky went on to reveal the Cricket Council's 'secret' plan for the 1970 Tests which would now be held successively on the Isle of Mull, at the Eddystone Lighthouse, in the vaults of the Bank of England and in a jumbo jet. The fifth Test could be played out in the *Sportsnight with Coalhouse* studio with the attendance limited to 14. Application for tickets to the latter event should be addressed to The Secret Committee, c/o the Maximum Security Wing of Parkhurst Prison on the Isle of Wight. The South Africa cricket tour as a subject had passed from satire to ridicule.

CHAPTER FOUR
JANUARY/FEBRUARY 1970

T HE *Cricketer* magazine began the new decade with a page
of contributors setting out their hopes for the 1970s. David
Sheppard opened the batting by writing of the importance
of cricket standing up to racialism in cricket and that the coming
protests against South Africa would take place without violence. The
distinguished umpire, Syd Buller, who sadly had only six months
to live, hoped that the new lbw rule would stop batsmen padding
the ball away. In those two short pieces it is possible to see both the
deeply entrenched desire for cricket lovers to talk about cricket and
the recognition that in the year of grace 1970 this was simply not
going to be possible.

The day after Parkinson attacked the BBC and the Cricket
Council with humour, the whole issue of the tour was once more
brought to the attention of the world beyond cricket when, in a
coordinated attack organised by the Young Liberals, ten county
grounds were infiltrated on the night of Monday 19 January.
Slogans were daubed on the walls and some pitches dug up. At
Bristol, weed killer was poured on the pitch and slogans painted
on the glass-fronted Jessop scoreboard. At Hove, the paint also
went on to the covers and the heavy roller. In Southampton, at the
headquarters of Hampshire CCC, the scoreboard was defaced and
slogans were daubed on walls both inside and outside the ground.
In Cardiff, the outspoken Wilf Wooller's notoriously short temper
was not improved when he found that in addition to digging up the

Glamorgan pitch and pouring tin tacks into the hole the 'hooligans' had given his car an entirely unwelcome and inexpertly delivered coat of paint.

There was also damage at Lord's where a small fire had been started but no significant damage sustained, at The Oval, Headingley, Old Trafford, Leicester and Taunton. A.K. James, the Secretary of Somerset, officially informed Lord's that he too had discovered similar slogans on the walls of the County Ground and on the wicket covers at Taunton. The damage, he reported solemnly in the manner of the forensic scientist giving Inspector Montelbano the approximate time of the murder, had been perpetrated between 10pm and 11pm. It had not been possible to ascertain if weed killer had been sprayed on the pitch. At New Road in Worcester, however, traditionally the venue for the first county match of any major tour, weed killer had been sprayed on the square covering an area of 33 square yards. The following day, two students and a housewife who had been caught in the act were each fined £4 at Marylebone Court after pleading guilty to putting up anti-apartheid posters at Lord's.

The reaction to these attacks was almost unanimously negative. The Anti-Apartheid Movement disclaimed all responsibility and its president, David Steel, who had been sympathetic to the aims of the protesters at the rugby matches, also sought to distance the Liberal Party as a whole declaring, 'The outbreak of vandalism at cricket grounds will do nothing to end racialism in sport. It is counter-productive on [sic] public opinion.' John Pardoe, the Liberal MP for North Cornwall, warned similarly: 'Wanton destruction even in support of a good cause is only a step from anarchy. If anti-apartheid demonstrators can destroy property in support of their cause why should not Enoch Powell and his friends destroy property in support of their cause?' Even the liberal *Guardian* commented adversely in its leader for 21 January.

> It is the existence of such men of conscience [as David Sheppard] that makes yesterday's attacks on cricket grounds self-defeating as well as wrong. They are wrong because the right to protest does not encompass the right to shove one's views down the throats of others and to interfere with their

freedom. They are self-defeating because they will make it more difficult for people like David Sheppard to increase the numbers of cricketers opposing apartheid.

The obvious culprits had to be the Stop the Seventy Tour movement. Hain had always believed in the efficacy of direct action and intended it to be non-violent. He phrased his response very carefully, truthfully denying any direct involvement in the coordinated attacks, but it seems reasonable to deduce that he had prior knowledge of them and in any case he had been quite open about advocating disruptive protests. Such actions made him vulnerable to prosecution because the conspiracy laws as constituted in 1970 were designed to curb such behaviour. However, it was impossible for STST to change its tactics because it was the public declaration of direct action that was causing the debate about the tour to be discussed so openly. Peter Jackson, the Labour MP for High Peak and a leader of a 100-strong group of MPs opposed to the tour, said bluntly, 'This sort of activity is inevitable if the tour goes ahead.' Hain confirmed as much to the press. 'From now on we are going ahead full steam.'

Zealous police officers did not necessarily appreciate the intention of Hain's clearly expressed desire that any direct action should involve no violence on the part of the demonstrators and they tended to react with a predictably heavy hand. The violence that then occurred as demonstrators defended themselves and/or fought back was blamed largely on the protesters. Right-wing publications always concluded their reports of such incidents with the numbers of policemen who had been hurt and the numbers of arrests they had made. The implication was clear that the fault was all on the side of the protesters and it inevitably influenced readers who were only tangentially interested in South African politics and sport.

Most of the letters in the press found the nocturnal attacks of 19 January to be regrettable. Sir Peter Wintringham Stable (aged 81), the former High Court judge, wrote to the *Daily Telegraph* that preparations to hold up cricket matches by trespassing on the grounds and digging holes in pitches constituted a criminal conspiracy. On the other hand, the attacks had coincided with the night the BBC transmitted a programme on the state of race relations in South Africa. The Reverend John White, vicar of Broadstone in

Dorset, had seen the programme and had determined that South Africa should be totally excluded from all sport only to wake up the following morning to news of the previous night's raids. His letter was written more in sorrow than anger but it concluded:

> I cannot think of anything more stupid being contrived, for I for one will have nothing whatsoever to do with those who support violence which I must assume appears to be the policy of the Stop the 70 Tour committee.

At the end of December 1969 the Professional Cricketers' Association had sent out a ballot paper to its members, openly soliciting their views on the tour. In view of the situation that had arisen with regard to the tour, 'your executive feel that your feelings should be ascertained – in your interest and in the interests of cricket itself'. On 8 January, the secretary of the PCA, Jack Bannister, was quick to make the announcement that with over half the votes returned within a week of the forms being sent out, the result was that 82% of county cricketers had indicated that they wished the tour to go ahead. Bannister told the *Daily Express* that, 'most of the remainder were concerned with the practicality of the tour. The moral issue hardly affected the voting.' When asked about the identity of some of the voters Bannister remarked that it had been a secret ballot and that the cricketers had been guaranteed their anonymity. Nevertheless, Crawford White writing in the *Express* was quick to release the information that the former Test captain Colin Cowdrey and the symbolic figure of Basil D'Oliveira had both voted for the tour to go ahead. The *Sunday Times* revealed that Maurice Hallam, the Leicestershire opener, had voted against the tour on the grounds that it would damage English cricket financially, Roger Prideaux had voted in favour and John Edrich was still undecided.

PCA president John Arlott lobbied the cricketers with the passion and sincerity with which he had addressed the Cambridge Union. It must have pained even if it didn't surprise him to learn that D'Oliveira, whom he had helped to find his first job in England as a professional for Middleton in the Central Lancashire League in 1960, had voted with the majority in favour of maintaining sporting links with his home country that was showing no signs of abandoning the hateful policy of apartheid. Bannister was right in predicting that the interim vote would accurately reflect the final vote. Ultimately, approximately 350 cricketers voted for the tour to go ahead and fewer than 20 voted against. One of the dissenters was certainly Mike Brearley and another he believes was the Surrey batsman Mike Edwards. He also feels that one of them must surely have been Tom Cartwright with whom Brearley had toured South Africa in 1964/65 when they had struck up an immediate rapport.

Jim Cumbes, fast-medium bowler for Lancashire, Surrey and Worcestershire, remembers the atmosphere surrounding the vote.

> Looking back I think we as county cricketers underestimated or didn't understand what apartheid was all about and how badly people had suffered. In that meeting of the PCA I remember John Arlott addressing us and saying, 'If you had been out to South Africa, as I have, and seen how apartheid operates your views would be a lot different.' I think our view was a bit cosmetic. We thought, 'Is it going to do much good, our not playing them? They are good cricketers and we want to bring good cricketers over.' Cricketers were pretty right-wing it was true and they didn't think calling off the tour was going to do much and frankly they didn't know much about it. They didn't like the barbed wire and digging up the pitches. There was an article, maybe in *The Telegraph* that said for goodness sake, take the barbed wire down and just get on with the game of cricket. The line everyone came out with was 'Don't mix politics with sport.'

The humorous and commonly accepted view of the PCA was that it was one of the few workers' organisations that was more right-wing than its employers.

Even Arlott would not have been surprised by the result of the PCA vote because in truth he was torn himself. His own stand on South Africa was straightforward but he had accepted the position of the PCA because of his lifelong admiration for the journeymen of the game. This issue as to whether or not they should play cricket in South Africa and against South Africa struck at the heart of what it meant to be a professional cricketer. Coaching in South

Africa during the winter months when they were not paid by their counties was a vital source of income for English players. If there was a political ideology to be explored it was the players' belief that politics and sport did not mix as Keith Fletcher explains.

> We were great believers that politics shouldn't come into sport. That was the crux of it as far as we were concerned. Sport is sport and we felt we should be able to play against anybody. I felt that then and I still feel that way. John Arlott was very passionate but it was soon obvious that as far as the tour was concerned we couldn't play the games under those conditions. You only need two people to keep coming on the field from different parts of the ground and it was going to become a complete farce.

The attacks of 19 January would have stiffened the resolve of the cricketers as they had stiffened the resolve of the authorities. They confirmed the opinions of MCC and the Cricket Council that the summer tour had to go ahead if only to show that decent people could not be defeated by bullies. To that end the Cricket Council ascertained, through every available channel, that the playing of cricket in England was a legal pursuit. Preventing it therefore was not. The tour, according to the opinion polls, was still supported by the vast majority of ordinary people in Britain. As far as they were concerned, cancelling the tour would be bowing to the pressure of hooligans and fascists, the sort of people Britain had fought the Second World War against. For these people the tour had become the symbol of hope and the defence of liberty – the exact opposite of what the STST was advocating. If the tour was going to be called off it would have to be the government that would do it. The rule of a minority, many of whom, it was believed by *Daily Telegraph* readers, did not wash as often as they should, no matter how well intentioned they claimed to be, was not part of the British way of life. Marylebone Cricket Club would not yield to any illegal force exerted on it.

On the other hand, they could not proceed without the implementation of unwelcome, innovative and expensive security measures. They discussed in detail their initial plans to protect the pitches.

Concertina barbed wire, 8' ditch dug round the playing area, 6' chainlink fence with 8' angle-iron stakes every 8 yards – two small gates for players and groundsmen. Mobile special constables, 15' wide and 8' high units consisting of metal frame or chain link screen topped by barbed wire. 7' high treble system of electric fencing of fairly high voltage in form of a continuous barrier backed by rolled barbed wire barrier.

When the scale of the costs became apparent, counties soon realised that they would not be able to absorb these new expenses without a significant contribution from spectators. Yorkshire CCC was the first county to announce its plans. For the match between Yorkshire and the touring South Africans it was planned that spectators would be asked to pay a further three shillings whether they were members or day visitors. For the Test match between England and South Africa at Headingley the charge would rise to five shillings. Juniors would have to contribute an extra half a crown to the club coffers in order to pay the police to guard against disruptions. Since the price of admission for a day's play in a Test match at the time was about ten shillings, less of course for a county match, this new poll tax was the equivalent of a 50% rise in the cost of watching cricket.

For the counties, the situation was even more serious since they had no option but to take these expensive precautions. Since the halcyon days of the immediate post-war years, county cricket had faced the reality of consistently declining numbers of spectators so that at best most counties were just about keeping their heads above water. It was feared that the costs of security for the visit of the South Africans might send some of them into bankruptcy. An annual membership of Somerset CCC in 1969 cost precisely one pound to admit spectators to every day of the 12 home county cricket matches except Gillette Cup ties. Given that the county won only one game all season and finished bottom of the table this was perhaps a fair price. At the top end, membership of Surrey CCC who finished third still cost only seven guineas and that included entry to all five days of the Oval Test match. There was a great reliance on subscriptions and matchday income and very little sponsorship of county cricket. Bearing in mind these facts it is easier to see that the cost of security could easily reach a level at which the more vulnerable county clubs would be staring into the financial abyss. The Test and County Cricket Board had stated that it was prepared to dig into its own pockets to ensure that the tour went ahead but those pockets were not bottomless.

It got even more difficult for the cricket authorities when they were opposed not by scruffy long-haired layabout students but by the Bishop of Woolwich and his supporters. David Sheppard agreed with Peter Hain that the 1970 South African cricket tour should be cancelled. They differed, however, in their methods, although they never fell out. Sheppard was an object of admiration even to many of those people who thought the tour should go ahead. He had been an outstanding player. Cyril Coote, the groundsman for many years at Fenner's, who had seen all the great Cambridge University players of the post-war era, always believed that Sheppard was the best of the lot, a better batsman even than Peter May who was widely regarded as the best batsman in world cricket in the late 1950s, after Sheppard had temporarily left the game to work in the Anglican Church. In 1953 Sheppard had captained Sussex to second place in the Championship, at that point the highest position in its history. When he briefly popped back on to the Test scene in 1956 he immediately made a century in what subsequently became known as 'Laker's Match'. On the 1962/63 tour of Australia he made a match-winning century at Melbourne having played very little first-class cricket for seven years. MCC was forced to take him seriously.

Geoffrey Howard, the Surrey CCC secretary who had managed the victorious England tour of Australia in 1954/55, had previously been a believer in the maintenance of sporting links with South Africa on the well worn grounds that British liberal gradualism would eventually show South Africans the error of their apartheid ways. Sheppard arranged for a group of black teenagers to see Howard and tell him that they loved cricket but if an all-white South Africa side played at The Oval as scheduled they would not enter the ground. They would be on the outside protesting. Howard had not been influenced by the direct action of the Stop the Seventy Tour but these conversations convinced him that the tour should be cancelled.

Also involved was the Anti-Apartheid Movement, all of them working in Britain to make British people aware of the appalling nature of apartheid and to campaign for the cancellation of the cricket tour. The difference in tactics, however, led to some awkward moments as Peter Hain remembers.

> We had an ambivalent relationship with the Anti-Apartheid Movement. They tried to stop me setting up STST because they didn't control it. As far as they were concerned we were out of their control. We were the militant direct action powerhouse of the whole thing, we had the teeth that got the tour stopped but then you had the AAM which advocated traditional peaceful forms of protest, marches, placards, letters, meetings and so forth. The spectrum was important. People could identify with the Anti-Apartheid Movement or they could identify with the Committee for Fairness in Sport in a way that felt part of the wider opposition to the tour even if they disagreed with our 'illegal tactics'.

In the files of the MCC archive is a letter from N.E. Mustoe of the Britain and South Africa Forum, which subtitled itself An Objective Expression of British Goodwill. It was attached to a copy of the list of 50 people who attended the Annual General Meeting of the Anti-Apartheid Movement which had been held at the National Liberal Club on 26 October 1969. Mustoe helpfully marks with a cross 'those who are known to be Communists'. Although Peter Hain and his parents are all on the list, their names are not adorned with the mark of Marx. Amongst people who thought like N.E. Mustoe, there was a ready willingness to identify those opposed to South Africa and apartheid as communists since white South Africans saw themselves as a bulwark against the wind of change that was also blowing communism through the African continent. A letter to *The Times* in London published on 2 December from a man in Johannesburg described people like the Hains:

> Most of the leaders of this movement have fled from South Africa because of their well known communistic activities amongst the Africans and their attempts to overthrow this Government, in other words the stable White Government of South Africa and Rhodesia .... The members of the anti-

apartheid group would only fire a gun in the dark at some
unarmed woman or child ... not one of them nor their parents
have ever lifted a finger in defence of democracy.

The government knew exactly how explosive the whole issue of
South Africa was because in 1968 and 1969 they were themselves
embroiled in a controversy about whether Britain would sell arms
to the country. The Labour government had always refused to
countenance the sale of arms to South Africa but in the wake of
the financial crisis around the time of devaluation in October 1967,
South Africa had applied to purchase naval weapons. The cabinet
was persuaded by Denis Healey, the Defence Secretary, to reconsider
an amendment of the embargo on the grounds that such weapons
could not be used to enforce apartheid and the ban on selling spare
parts for South Africa's Centurion tanks would remain in place.
There was also a strong economic argument in terms of the jobs such
an order would create but both the Cabinet and the Parliamentary
Labour Party dissolved into uproar at the idea. After much heated
debate, the ban on arms for South Africa was retained. The embargo
on sales of weapons to South Africa was one of those ideological
divides that had always separated Labour from the Conservatives.
Edward Heath had made it quite clear that if his party won the
next general election he would overturn the embargo. Denis Healey
candidly admitted later that as soon as he saw for himself the reality
of life in apartheid South Africa he realised he had made an error
of gross insensitivity.

It was now clear that the cricket tour like the ban on arms sales
would split the country along party political lines. The Labour
Party made clear its fundamental opposition to the tour but the
Conservative Party bought into the idea that to cancel it would be
to give in to those social and political forces of rebellion of which it
fundamentally disapproved. If the tour went ahead and there were
riots on the streets, the Tories believed that it could only be beneficial
for a party, one of whose principal tenets was a strong belief in 'law
and order'. To that end, Sir Peter Rawlinson, the Shadow Attorney
General, called for injunctions to be taken out against the Young
Liberals, Peter Hain and Louis Eaks. He believed that both men
had made inflammatory statements which were designed to lead

to criminal behaviour. The reluctance of the Home Secretary to act under such blatant provocation indicated that Callaghan was giving these louts a licence to riot and that Labour was 'soft' on law and order – exactly what the Conservatives wanted the electorate to think. Rawlinson told an audience in Slough that Callaghan's 'strictly neutral' attitude towards the tour was exacerbating the problem. He went on to point out that:

> The Government by its weakness is acknowledging the licence to riot. What if the Czechs turn Wimbledon into a battlefield when a Russian is playing, or the Jews oppressed in the Soviet Union, disrupt the Russian ballet dancers or Arabs riot when Israelis perform?

A Commons motion, sponsored by seven Tory MPs, accused Callaghan of 'encouraging wreckers, rioters and hooligans'.

Tory Party chairman, Anthony Barber, who was to be the Chancellor of the Exchequer in the next Conservative government, returned from a two-week visit to South Africa and made a public statement before leaving on a flight from Jan Smuts airport. He said there was much goodwill towards South Africa in Great Britain and that her much publicised racial problems were unique and more easily criticised than solved. He felt the world should therefore show more realism and understanding towards them. The leader of his party was quite clear that should the Conservatives win the next election he would resume arms sales to South Africa and reopen negotiations with Ian Smith in Rhodesia. It is a measure of how attitudes have changed in the past 50 years that these policies were considered perfectly acceptable by much of the electorate. At the same time, a number of Labour MPs had announced their intention of joining the protestors who planned to sit down on the pitch if the tour went ahead. Frank Cousins, formerly General Secretary of the powerful Transport & General Workers' Union, a member of Harold Wilson's Cabinet from 1964 to 1966 and now chairman of the government-sponsored Community Relations Commission, told the Home Secretary that if he permitted the tour to proceed, it would do untold harm to race relations in the country.

The Conservatives slowly edged their way towards a tougher stance on the law and order issue. Writing in *The Guardian* on 3 February, Michael Lake noted that:

> Conservative leaders have not yet formed definite views on how to strengthen law and order should they become the government in spite of their growing preoccupation with disorderly behaviour and violence. Conservatives have generally been roused to tighten the law following a year of student disorders, occupations and squatting, and anti-apartheid demonstrations. In fact many student demonstrations have been against Mr Enoch Powell whose views on race relations Mr Heath has several times repudiated. And it is puzzling that Mr Heath should concentrate on more law and order while at the same time publicly welcoming the South Africa cricket tour which even the Police Federation has condemned because of the extra burden it would place on hard pressed staff.

The mood of the country was moving slowly but consistently towards cancellation, fuelled at the end of January 1970 by two more acts by the South African government which demonstrated its implacable determination to maintain white supremacy. Arthur Ashe, who had won the US Open Tennis Championships at Forest Hills in 1968 and had just achieved his second Grand Slam by winning the Australian Open, was told by the South African government that he would not be granted a visa to enter their country. Ashe had given a guarantee that were he to be granted a visa he would refrain from commenting publicly on any matters other than questions posed to him about tennis. Ashe was one of the more moderate of public African American figures. The prospect, however, of a black man winning a tournament in South Africa, the home of apartheid, and thereby damaging the myth of white superiority, was too dangerous for the South African government to take. A Japanese jockey, Sueo Masuzawa, who wanted to ride in races on courses in Pietermaritzburg and Johannesburg was also refused a visa, although visas filed at the same time by jockeys from the United States, England, Scotland, Ireland, Australia and Italy were approved by the Ministry of the Interior.

When the Cricket Council met Jim Callaghan on 29 January to discuss the problems of the tour in the wake of the attacks of 19 January, the subject of Arthur Ashe never came up. The Home Secretary and the Minister for Sport, Denis Howell, stared coldly at Maurice Allom, Billy Griffith and Jack Bailey, the deputation from the Council and inevitably the meeting broke up with nothing resolved, each side eyeing the other with profound suspicion.

Instead the popular press was thrilled to release the information that cricket authorities had thoroughly examined the possible responses to direct action by anti-apartheid forces and had come up with the following responses. Under the page 1 banner headline of BARBED WIRE PLAN FOR TESTS the *Daily Express* listed the cunning plans devised by the Cricket Council:

> BARBED WIRE entanglements 5 feet high encircling the entire playing area

> VIGILANTE squads of supporters to guard grounds and prevent damage or disruption of play

> GHOST GAMES with the place not known until the last moment to avoid demonstrator damage

> GUARD DOG patrols on grounds before and possibly during play.

The decision to ban Ashe from entering the country made the expulsion of South Africa from the International Lawn Tennis Federation and a complete boycott of tennis in South Africa by all the major players in the world almost inevitable. The following day the International Cavaliers, a team that would have included the most famous cricketer in the world, Garry Sobers, and that had always included cricketers from all the Test-playing countries and had been welcomed all over the world, was told by white cricket officials that the presence of non-whites in their party was the reason that they would not be permitted to tour South Africa. When Yorkshire members arrived at Bramall Lane for the AGM of Yorkshire CCC they found 'No Racist Sport', 'Shame, Yorks', 'YCCC, don't provoke violence' and 'Dolly, Ashe, who next?' daubed on the walls. They were met by a deputation from STST who handed out leaflets asking them not to attend the Yorkshire v South Africa game scheduled to be played at Bramall Lane that summer.

On 4 February a memo was written by Jack Bailey for the meeting of the Cricket Council due to take place in five days' time in which he tried to lay out the grounds why it was perfectly reasonable for the Council to proceed with the tour.

a) They are traditional opponents.

b) We are satisfied that SACA are making every possible effort to further the cause of multi-racial cricket.

c) No minority group should be able to dictate to the majority in this country. No amount of blackmail or pressure should influence this decision.

d) The Tour is practicable and profitable within the terms of the revised itinerary.

e) The ultimate good of all cricketers in South Africa is best served by the Tour taking place.

f) In the interest of world cricket in the long term, expediency, however desirable it might seem in the short term, should not be a consideration.

g) Public opinion is on our side and therefore the majority of people would be disappointed if the Tour did not take place. Furthermore, it would be difficult for them to reconcile our constantly stated intent with any change of heart.

Much to the fury of Wilf Wooller, Dr Glyn Simon, the Archbishop of Wales, called upon the members of Glamorgan CCC to follow his example and resign from the club if Glamorgan were to play against the visiting South Africans. Writing in the diocesan magazine, the Archbishop laid out his case calmly.

I shall give up my membership and I hope many others will do so as well in view of the great principles involved. Better still would it be for the players themselves to follow the example of Mr John Taylor the London Welsh international forward in refusing to take part in matches against South Africans. To those who say that all they want is to enjoy watching a game without bringing politics into it at all, I say it is right to oppose such views which are based on ignorance of what apartheid really means for the grave and grievous suffering of the bulk of the South African nation.

The infuriated Wooller spluttered that the Archbishop was using his ecclesiastical office to stir up trouble among Glamorgan's members and that he was 'in the sporting sense a completely useless member'. They sent back his annual membership dues of £3. The Archbishop returned one pound of it as a contribution to the players' testimonial fund. The Right Reverend George Sinker, the Provost of Birmingham, resigned his membership of Warwickshire CCC in protest against the match with South Africa to be played at Edgbaston. The Bishops of Durham and Exeter let it be known that they were joining the Bishops of Woolwich, Stepney and Southwark in training for the forthcoming fight against the cricket establishment. Gubby Allen, in his tied cottage in St John's Wood, must have been glancing anxiously out of the window expecting the imminent arrival of a gang of angry mitred bishops brandishing crooks outside the Grace Gates. The much more moderate Rev. Roy Henderson, formerly of Malvern School and Brasenose College Oxford, wrote to his Oxonian contemporary Donald Carr on 10 February:

> The more one hears of the difficulties for non-white cricketers in South Africa and the effect on South African opinion if they are completely isolated in the realm of sport, the more one realises that we have an opportunity to do something to bring to an end the present injustices.

Third World countries were beginning to flex their political muscles on the international stage and there was no easier arena than apartheid. Uganda cancelled a scheduled match against a touring MCC party, reducing the tour to matches only against Kenya. Two days later Kenya's Minister for Co-operative and Social Services cancelled the Kenyan leg as well, noting that as long as MCC wished to play South Africa it was up to the member states of the Organisation of African Unity to demonstrate that they would no longer allow themselves to be humiliated by South Africa and Rhodesia. Accordingly, no

Kenyan athlete would be permitted to race against anyone who had competed against South African athletes in the past three years. The Commonwealth Games were due to take place in July in Edinburgh and early rumblings were heard by the British government that if the South Africa cricket tour were allowed to proceed, a number of Commonwealth countries from Africa, Asia and the West Indies would send no athletes. The government was more concerned than the Cricket Council at the prospect of such a move but even the authorities at Lord's could see that they were perhaps setting out on a road that would eventually lead to a complete separation of white and black Test-playing nations with India, Pakistan and West Indies refusing to play against England and possibly Australia and New Zealand unless their official cricket bodies came out and condemned the South Africa tour.

SANROC, the South Africa Non-Racial Olympic Committee, had written to many county cricketers asking them not to play when their counties took the field against the tourists. Mike Brearley's feelings were clear on this and Peter Lever had already had words with his chairman, Cedric Rhoades, informing him of his reluctance to play in the match between Lancashire and South Africa. He remembered:

> Earlier that year in January I'd asked the chairman not to play against South Africa and he said he'd suspend my contract for four days so I would have that time off. It disappointed me that there were so few players who would do anything about it. There were one or two who came out afterwards when it was all over and said they would never have played but they didn't say it at the time. The Lancashire players didn't say anything and they didn't do anything either. If Clive [Lloyd] and Farokh [Engineer] had gone to ask the chairman as I did they would probably have got the same reply. Maybe they were waiting to see how the thing developed, I don't know. I've never discussed it with either of them to this day.

Shortly afterwards, Lancashire members raised the question at the club's AGM as to whether they should in fact be playing South Africa at all but a motion proposing the county withdrew from the fixture was defeated, much to Cedric Rhoades's satisfaction. He announced the decision whilst reiterating his belief that playing cricket against an all-white South Africa team would 'build bridges'. The bridges did not appear to be facilitating any sort of traffic into the townships. Labour Party leaders in the North West though pledged their 'full and active support' of anti-apartheid demonstrations that had been planned if the Lancashire v South Africa match were to go ahead. The following week some Yorkshire members who were taking five minutes off from their highly enjoyable game of internecine warfare, also proposed that their county's match against South Africa should be called off if the tour went ahead. The Yorkshire committee, preparing to demolish Brian Close at the end of the season, did the same to the motion.

Attitudes were hardening and by the time the Cricket Council met to hear the report of the sub-committee it had charged with the task of examining every aspect of the tour it had become clear who was on which side. The Council had the support of the committees of all 17 counties, representatives of the Minor Counties, the Professional Cricketers' Association, the Rugby Football Union, the League of Empire Loyalists, the shadow Cabinet and most of the Conservative Party. Ranged against them were numerous student bodies and all the groups of the far left, most Labour MPs, the Liberal Party and the trade unions. It wasn't entirely Old versus Young but the spokesmen for the supporters of the tour certainly appeared to be all white, middle class and by their own admission middle-aged. The student bodies opposing them clearly believed that 'middle-aged' was a euphemism for 'old and out of touch'.

Public debate took the discussion beyond the mere confines of that summer's tour. The secretary of the cricket authority on the West Indian island of Antigua made it clear that he believed that the West Indies should sever all ties with England if the South Africa tour were permitted to proceed. If the issue were raised at the ICC, which it would have to be, there was a strong conviction that not only West Indies but Pakistan, India, Ceylon, East Africa, Malaysia and Fiji would follow in support. England would then be left to play cricket only against Australia, New Zealand and the all-white South Africa. What then of the much vaunted bridge building? Looking further ahead, it was also noted that in the wake of the current immigration, it would take only another ten to fifteen years before children born of West Indian, Pakistani and Indian parents would become eligible to play for England. Then it would hardly be possible for England to omit diplomatically their players who would be unacceptable to the South African government if it maintained its policy of apartheid. D'Oliveira's poor form in the West Indies and his form with the bat in county cricket during the summer prior to the Oval Test match in 1968 had allowed MCC to make a cricketing case for his exclusion but it would not be practical to do so when England's best team contained four or five black cricketers.

The Cricket Council, which had issued the invitation to the South African Cricket Association, was clearly in no mood to take this scenario seriously. Instead, it suggested to the counties that they start to invest in barbed wire, searchlights and guard dogs. At Old Trafford and Headingley, they moved more slowly than at Trent Bridge where Nottinghamshire CCC quickly informed Lord's that it would cost £250 to install the floodlights which would add a further £6 a week to the electricity bill. At Edgbaston, Warwickshire estimated it would cost £300 to install the lights and £120 a week to pay for security patrols to make sure the events of 19 January were not repeated. At Lord's, MCC had already spent £200 on Danert wire which was a superior form of barbed wire and could only be obtained from one factory in Great Missenden, as well as £200 on other miscellaneous related costs.

When the much anticipated Cricket Council meeting took place in the Long Room on a cold, dark February evening it was possible to look through the windows and see not the run stealers flicker to and fro but barbed wire starkly silhouetted against the hallowed, snow-covered turf. The addition of watchtowers and guard dogs all added to the unwelcome impression that the long shadows on county grounds were now those of concentration camps. In a sense the grounds had taken on some of the aspects of their wartime experience. Lord's had been commandeered as an air crew receiving centre, The Oval had been a prisoner of war camp and Headingley had been closed and taken over by the Royal Army Medical Corps, which had fitted it out as a mass mortuary. Ironically, in defence of liberty and freedom, the cricket authorities seemed prepared to turn the grounds back into the sort of fortified camps which everyone thought had been consigned to history when Victory in Europe was proclaimed 25 years before.

After the meeting on 12 February, it was announced that the counties and MCC had agreed unanimously that the tour by South Africa would go ahead but the number of fixtures would be more than halved, from 28 to 12, comprising five Test matches, five county matches and two representative games. Instead of arriving at the end of April to open their tour at the start of the domestic season, the South Africans would now arrive on the first day of June and instead of playing every county as tourists had traditionally done if the summer was not shared with another country, they would play essentially only at the major city grounds where it was easier to maintain some kind of security. The 12 matches would be played at only eight grounds, the six Test match grounds plus Bramall Lane and Swansea, instead of the original 22 and artificial pitches would be installed to prevent the possibility of the threatened vandalism. Matches would start on conventional grass pitches but could then be moved to the artificial one that would be installed somewhere on the square if there was damage to the natural one. MCC was certainly relieved when the BBC announced that current standing financial contracts would not be affected by the change.

Preaching from his *Daily Telegraph* pulpit, E.W. Swanton regretted that there was no olive branch extended to 'those countries to whom apartheid has a special anathema', merely the 'chilling' announcement that artificial pitches would replace damaged ones. He also regretted a similar silence from the SACA but he looked forward to five weeks at the start of the shortened tour and three at the end when County Championship matches would take the full spotlight in peace and relative tranquillity. He felt that, at the time of writing in the middle of February, only somewhere between 20% and 33% of the British population were in favour of cancellation. He saw no harm in the sort of peaceful demonstrations he knew had taken place in Dublin and Cardiff when the South African rugby team had played its recent Test matches and he concluded in typically Swantonian magisterial fashion that 'the Cricket Council cannot surely deal again with the SACA in its present form'.

The England captain, Raymond Illingworth, was cross that Leicestershire's match against the South Africans had been cancelled as it had been a match he had greatly anticipated. He knew who to blame for it though.

> I don't think we have been hard enough with these demonstrators. Those who stopped matches on the recent rugby tour should have been jailed and any students taking part in the demonstrations should have their grants taken away.

It was as well for this author that Illy was only captain of the England cricket team and not the Secretary of State for Education to whose good offices the author was beholden for his postgraduate research grant in 1970.

Students were not terribly popular in February 1970. The day after the Cricket Council statement, Cambridge University undergraduates, who had gathered to demonstrate against a Greek gourmet banquet because of their distaste for the Greek junta, fought with guests at the recently built Garden House Hotel, at the time the most exclusive hotel in Cambridge. Demonstrators broke into the ballroom where 120 guests were eating and drinking at the £3 a head banquet and dancing to the music of Theodorakis, no doubt pretending to be Anthony Quinn and Alan Bates dancing in *Zorba the Greek* which was much in vogue at the time. The 500 protestors did damage to the hotel estimated at £1,000 before hurling red paint at the police. The *Telegraph* reported in hushed tones that Charles Goodhart, the unreconstructed rightwing Fellow of Gonville and Caius College and a university pro-proctor, had been taken to Addenbrooke's hospital with a severe gash on his forehead caused by a half brick hurled at him. There would be consequences for the arrested students that would not be apparent for a few months. Meanwhile, on that same night in Canterbury, Edward Heath faced a barrage of toilet rolls and fireworks as he struggled to make himself heard in a speech at the University of Kent.

John Woodcock, the cricket correspondent of *The Times* who was in South Africa covering the tour by Australia, reported that the Cricket Council's decision to proceed with a shortened tour had been greeted warmly. Graeme Pollock expressed a certain disquiet that the new tour meant that there were only three matches before the Test series was scheduled to begin, but he was very pleased to be playing in England and all the players were looking forward to it. MCC had issued the invitation, stood by it and had now confirmed the tour would go ahead. It would be reasonable from the point of view of a South African player to think that the decision had finally been made and that the tour, in whatever shape it finally assumed, would proceed as planned and they were very pleased.

STST did not see the announcement as a triumph but as a declaration of war. Peter Hain responded quickly and with a determination that could not be misconstrued.

> The MCC has been under pressure by everyone from bishops to trade unions. They seem to have destroyed every principle for which cricket stands. They don't debate the issue; they just take up entrenched stands. I don't think they have a leg to stand on and they leave us no option but a sustained and militant campaign. By shortening the tour they have made it easier for us to concentrate our forces.

He told the press that STST tactics had other methods of disrupting play without resorting to digging up the pitches which could be construed as violence. They included letting rabbits loose on the pitch; demonstrators handcuffing themselves to the umpire; extra fielders moving on to the pitch; a bogus 12th man going out with the drinks tray; setting off fireworks, using flashing mirrors, calling 'no ball', invading the pitch and sustaining generally noisy scenes. He could almost have been predicting the average mayhem at an alcohol-fuelled T20 on a Friday night but in 1970 this was a serious warning. Shortly after the announcement, anti-apartheid slogans were discovered daubed on the walls of the Edgbaston cricket ground where the South Africans were due to play twice on the shortened tour. It must have disheartened the cleaners who had only just succeeded in removing the slogans that had been painted on the walls during the incursion the month before.

Michael Parkinson continued to lampoon the efforts made by MCC to protect cricket grounds.

A spokesman for Rentadog said they had sold their last Alsatian at the weekend and the British Knobkerrie Manufacturers' Association said he'd never known a year like it. At Lord's, Colonel Ponsonby Gherkin, commanding officer of the 1st Battalion Argyle and Bolton Wanderers, which is on loan to MCC for the defence of Lord's, said that his men were dug in and ready for anything.

A letter to the *Sunday Times* on 22 February from Donald Rich of Andover indicated that he intended to watch the South Africa games because he refused to be intimidated by threats of violent action. He added a warning to the humorous columnist.

> Michael Parkinson can be one of the most entertaining writers on sport but he loses all sense of proportion when he writes about MCC.

A surprising addition to the debate was provided by George Best, currently the finest footballer in Britain and possibly the world but a man better known for his celebration of wine, women and goalscoring than politics.

Best, despite a reputation which his alcoholism did its best to diminish, was no fool and perfectly capable of expressing a political opinion if anybody ever asked him about anything other than the aforementioned wine, women and football. 'Writing' in that organ of responsible political journalism *The Sun* only a few months after its launch as a right-wing tabloid now under the ownership of Rupert Murdoch, Best made plain his feelings without prevarication.

> I think that it is an absolute disgrace that we are allowing the South African cricketers to tour this summer ... We have been playing them for years but they have done nothing about their scandalous apartheid policies. Put them in isolation till they see sense.

Previously Best had defended the sit-down demonstrators during the Springboks' rugby tour and had indicated that he would have joined them had he not been otherwise detained making a large number of First Division defenders look foolish.

David Sheppard issued his own reaction to the decision of the Cricket Council to carry on with the truncated tour.

> I appreciate that the MCC council did not want to seem to give in to the threat of violence but more than that is at stake. Today's decision means that the tour will take place under siege conditions. The first thing to suffer might well be good race relations in this country.

The Anti-Apartheid Movement was even blunter in its condemnation. 'Cricket will suffer, race relations will be damaged and the Vorster regime will be delighted by today's announcement.' John Arlott, as ever, wrote with passion but detachment:

> The Cricket Council has tried to put itself, no doubt to the exclusion of all else, into the position of thinking solely for cricket. It is not possible to think solely for cricket. Cricket is part of a greater world which the English cricket establishment in all its innocence or its political stubbornness has refused to recognise. Now the point has been reached where we face a summer where cricket is subordinated to acrimony when performance at Test level will be distorted by political issues. No one has won.

In vain did the Cricket Council point out that talks had already started in South Africa between SACA and the non-white cricket bodies in the hope of improving relations. Unfortunately, they had as much a chance of success as those between Conservatives and Labour over Brexit. The two sides were simply so far apart and unwilling to make any concessions on which each side believed to be their fundamental points of principle that failure was inevitable. Yet out of these talks came SACA's declaration to the English cricket authorities that future South African touring sides would be chosen on a non-racial basis and that merit would be the sole criterion for selection. It was a laughably hollow promise but MCC and the Cricket Council trumpeted it abroad as if it were the Declaration of

Independence. SACA of course, whatever their real feelings, could only go as far as their government permitted them to stray.

The threat of inevitable violence as articulated by John Arlott meant that James Callaghan was under considerable pressure to cancel the tour but he was reluctant to do so at this stage. Cabinet papers, released in the year 2000 when Peter Hain was a serving Labour minister, indicated that in the discussion with ministers as to whether or not Hain should be prosecuted, the Home Secretary was in favour. He had been on his feet in the House of Commons earlier that day answering questions from irate Labour MPs who wanted to know why he had not already insisted that MCC cancel the tour and irate Conservative MPs like John Boyd-Carpenter, who had served as a minister throughout the Conservative governments of Churchill, Eden, Macmillan and Home, who demanded that the police should waive any charges that might be incurred whilst ensuring that the cricket matches could be played by South Africa.

Sir Patrick Wall, MP for Haltemprice in East Yorkshire, was an outspoken supporter of Ian Smith in Rhodesia and of white minority rule in South Africa which he saw as a last bulwark against the insidious spread of communism throughout the African continent. He demanded to know if the Home Secretary understood that it was 'his duty to protect the rights of the majority and if the majority want to watch matches they should not have to pay extra to protect their own rights'. He sat down to cheers from Opposition benches. Callaghan struggled back up to his feet and tried to placate the House by informing MPs of his ongoing talks with police to ensure that whatever demonstrations took place, law and order would be maintained. He was cheered by his own side and received cat calls from the benches opposite. Normal parliamentary standards of behaviour circa 1970 were operating. It should be noted that neither side accused the other of being traitors or enemies of the people. Callaghan found it difficult to move politically, which was why putting Peter Hain in prison might have seemed to be the least worst option.

Ten days after the Cricket Council's announcement that the truncated tour was going ahead, Harold Wilson made his own opposition to the tour abundantly clear in a radio interview. He said that he thought the D'Oliveira affair had put South Africa firmly beyond the pale but he added that those who wanted to demonstrate peaceably and watch peaceably should be permitted to do so. He himself would not be watching even though he was a cricket supporter. The following day a petition protesting the government's hostile attitude to South Africa was handed in at 10 Downing Street by the Anti-Demonstration Association which helpfully offered to protect the county grounds with the use of lions and cheetahs. Kenneth Day, chairman of Graveney Sports Club in Ewell, Surrey, wanted all such clubs as his to send volunteers to help the police stand guard at The Oval during the nights leading up to the Test match there in August. On 6 March Yorkshire CCC installed rolls of barbed wire to protect the Headingley pitch.

Two Labour MPs on the left wing of the party, Joan Lestor and Ian Mikardo, set down motions calling on the National Executive to demand the tour be cancelled. Subsequently, all the members of Labour's powerful National Executive Committee unanimously approved Mikardo's motion congratulating the chiefs of the Armed Services for their decision to cancel the scheduled match between the Combined Services and South Africa. Callaghan was one of the members who voted in favour of the motion. Many of his colleagues told him they were prepared to join the sit-down protests and indeed planned to demonstrate in a non-violent way outside Lord's and The Oval when matches were played there but still the government shrank from ordering MCC to withdraw its invitation. It was still a private members' club and just as it couldn't order it to admit women into the pavilion it was felt that it was undemocratic for a Labour government to order the cancellation of a cricket tour.

Instead, Callaghan used the weapon that he thought would be the most effective by demanding that the cricket authorities be presented with the entire bill for the policing that would be required for the duration of the cricket tour. Figures quoted to Lord's by the Home Office ranged from £7,000 for a three-day county match to £18,000 for a five-day Test. The total merely for the two scheduled visits to Birmingham for the Warwickshire match and the Edgbaston Test was estimated at £25,000, a figure with which cricket would be unable to deal, easily wiping out the projected £7,000 that the TCCB had expected to distribute to each of the 17 counties if the tour were to proceed on its original schedule and without extra policing. The cost of protecting every match on the 28-match tour was unimaginable on that basis.

Having learned from the experience of the rugby tour Callaghan said that the cricket authorities would not be allowed to get off so lightly. It was estimated that policing for the rugby tour cost £50,000 of which the rugby unions contributed barely £5,000. For the match which took place in Manchester where the South Africans played North West Counties the 2,300 policemen assigned to provide security cost £8,985 without including any costs which could be attributed to the 29 policemen who were injured in the course of their duty and who could not then be redeployed the following week. Given that policing for the much longer cricket tour with more grounds and more matchdays to be protected, the costs would almost certainly soar beyond the quarter of a million pounds estimated at the end of January. The Cricket Council knew that law and order was likely to be a major issue in the forthcoming general election and as the Labour government could not afford to look weak under renewed attacks from the Conservative opposition, they had assumed that the government would be forced to deal severely with any demonstrations at cricket grounds. What they had not anticipated was that the government would raise the stakes by presenting them with the bill. It was getting to be a question of who would blink first.

To an extent Callaghan was bluffing. Whilst he was right to insist that the county clubs must take responsibility for what happened inside their grounds the Home Office was entirely responsible for what happened on the public highway. Callaghan, however, didn't want the county cricket committees to think they could hire the bare minimum of security staff for deployment inside their grounds in the sure and certain belief that the government would have to send significant reinforcements of the regular police if matters got out of hand. At Leicestershire's Grace Road ground, which had suffered in the attacks of 19 January, a satisfactory compromise was discovered. Although the ground was now protected day and night it was costing Leicestershire CCC nothing because the local police had recently lost their training ground and had moved into Grace Road at the suggestion of Mike Turner, the county cricket club's secretary.

On Saturday 7 March at Hampstead Town Hall, Peter Hain addressed 300 anti-apartheid delegates and promised to extend demonstrations to include tennis, badminton, athletics and hockey as well as cricket. Mike Brearley was also there.

> Peter Hain's organisation contacted me and invited me to come along to some day-long event where there were a series of talks in front of a public audience and I went in some nervousness because I thought I would be too conservative for that audience. I didn't want to sit on rugby grounds or put tacks on cricket squares. Temperamentally I was very cautious about that sort of thing. I was much closer to David Sheppard. They asked me I think because I'd been involved with and had seconded David at the No Confidence vote in the MCC Committee in 1968 so I became slightly well known. I was only 26 and I was rather nervous about conflict of that kind and feelings ran very deep in the cricket world. One of the things I learned from speaking at the Peter Hain event was Peter saying to me, 'We need all range of opinion. It's a conglomerate, it's like a political party.'

The men's singles finals of the Rothmans tournament staged at the Royal Albert Hall that night between Ken Rosewall and Marty Riessen was interrupted for five minutes by a sit-down protest against Rothmans' support for South African sport and those tennis players who were intending to play in South Africa. In response, Norman St John Stevas, addressing the annual conference of Scottish Young Conservatives in Edinburgh, said the tour must go on. 'Much more is now involved than cricket. The whole of our way of life is dependent on the observance of law. If the tour is called off, the government will have given way to blackmail.' Ted Heath said he would go and watch the South Africans play their cricket matches, a noble gesture as, despite being raised in the county of Woolley, Evans, Wright and Cowdrey, he clearly preferred the company of musicians and yachtsmen. Taken in concert with the intention to lift the embargo on arms sales and his stated intention to reopen talks with Ian Smith, this made clear the policy of the Conservative Party in respect of Southern Africa.

At their own annual conference in Cambridge a few days later, the Young Liberals stared back at their elders and betters. The Liberal Party had threatened to take away the grant of £1,500 they traditionally gave to their youngsters unless they dissociated themselves from the direct action taken on the night of 19 January for which Louis Eaks, their chairman, had taken responsibility. By a narrow but decisive majority, the Young Liberals reaffirmed their support for their chairman and, by implication, the attacks on the county grounds.

The National Union of Students held its annual Easter conference at Bradford University. Its president, the future Labour Cabinet minister Jack Straw, tried to explain the origins of the student unrest, elements of which were increasingly visible. Events like the 1970 tour he said were opening students' eyes to the injustices of the world and the students were determined to challenge society to live by their ideals. All British students were called upon to join the demonstrations planned for the South Africa matches. It should be noted, however, that the NUS was noticeably silent about anti-Semitism in Russia and the behaviour of the authorities in Eastern Europe towards dissidents. The following day a letter appeared in *The Times* from a student at Trinity Hall Cambridge explaining that as a member of the National Executive of the United Nations Student Association, he was responsible for helping to arrange a re-enactment of the Sharpeville massacre. He was doing so because nothing in South Africa had changed since that tragic event and, because of its colonial history, Britain bore a heavy responsibility for the tragedy of apartheid.

On a more prosaic level, many students refused to open bank accounts at Barclays, as it was the high street bank whose South African investments were most widely reported. The bank controlled a 54% holding in Barclays DCO which operated overseas and 53% of the branches of Barclays DCO were in Southern Africa, the vast majority in South Africa itself. There were demonstrations against Barclays by students in Cambridge, Oxford, York, Swansea and Southampton. At Essex University, perhaps the most militant of all universities in the late 1960s and 1970s, the campaign degenerated into a direct confrontation because a Barclays branch was sited on the university campus in Colchester. The student newspaper announced that it had gained hundreds of signatures in its attempt to force the university to divest itself of its investments, claiming Barclays now controlled a third of South Africa's banking assets. A bewildered spokesman for Barclays claimed he did not know 'why these people are making a beeline for Barclays. Trade between Great Britain and South Africa is legitimate'. Such attitudes did little to improve the temper of the students. An estimated one hundred of them invaded the campus branch of Barclays Bank, two of whom, symbolising the bank and the university, were carried high on the shoulders of the crowd and then dumped unceremoniously on the counter. A 'bomb' of red paint was thrown at the building and a mimed allegory of the Sharpeville massacre was then enacted on the floor of the bank that was ecstatically applauded by the students. No doubt it received an excellent review in the student newspaper. The students then solemnly closed their accounts though why they had opened them there in the first place given the widespread publicity that had been given to Barclays' South African investments for the past few years remains something of a mystery.

Students at every college of higher education in the country exerted pressure on their governing bodies to ignore the financial gains that could be gathered by investing in South Africa. Their parents did not approve of their slogans or their dress or their public behaviour, or of their music or of the length of their hair but for young people in Britain in 1970 that was their way of defining themselves as different from their parents' generation. For them, campaigning against South Africa's policy of apartheid was a litmus test of whether you believed in the struggle for political and social justice. Few students in 1970 believed in nuance. If you were not a believer in the struggle for Civil Rights or if you did not join the anti-Vietnam war protests you were in favour of setting dogs on non-violent black people or napalming little children in South East Asia. If you supported the tour, you were a supporter of white South Africa, a condoner of apartheid and a racialist.

It was now possible to sense a significant shift of mood in the country. South Africa had become a pariah state. On 29 March, the South African Cycling Federation was banned from competing at an international tournament to be held in Leicester in August. The Federation's president blamed Harold Wilson. The Co-operative

Party held its annual conference at Blackpool but even though its call for a government ban on the tour was defeated, delegates voted for an amendment which urged a boycott of all the matches if MCC did not call off the tour.

On 5 April, 20 West Indian organisations representing 150,000 West Indians in Great Britain decided to take action against South Africa and team up with STST. Two days later it became even more obvious that trade union opposition to the tour was increasing. A letter in that month's issue of the Post Office Engineering Union's journal suggested that its members 'black' all work on communications equipment used to promote or comment on the tour.

> Sport and politics cannot be separated in South Africa. Surely, when world stars of the calibre of Ashe, Sobers, D'Oliveira and [rugby league winger] Billy Boston have been banned, there can be no relaxation of the vicious apartheid laws.

Meanwhile, in South Africa, Australia's cricketers, who had retained the Ashes in England in 1968, were appreciating how superior was the current South Africa side.

CHAPTER FIVE

SOUTH AFRICA: JANUARY–MARCH 1970

I N the middle of March 1970 the South African cricket selectors sat down to choose the 14 players for the proposed tour of England that summer. They knew perfectly well that the players they would settle on would be widely recognised as the strongest squad of cricketers ever to leave the shores of South Africa and it was the main reason why the tour was so eagerly anticipated in England. The forthcoming Test series promised to be a feast of exciting cricket with the excitement emanating largely from South Africa.

In 1960 South Africa had been defeated 3-0 in a disappointing English summer dominated by a 'throwing' controversy. Their young fast bowler Geoff Griffin was no-balled at Lord's by England's most respected umpire, Syd Buller, and by the end of the tour he was opening the batting and not bowling. Neil Adcock and Hugh Tayfield were coming to the end of their careers and although Eddie Barlow and Ali Bacher made the 1960 tour their impact was limited. 1960 was the first tour to attract the attention of the Anti-Apartheid Movement.

The printed posters headlined:

APARTHEID ISN'T CRICKET
The selection of this all-white cricket team introduces apartheid policies into Commonwealth sport.

If South Africa were hosts to the MCC they would not accept Raman Subba Row, Vice Captain of England, as a member of our team.

England and Sussex batsman Rev David Sheppard has stated he will not play against or watch these all-white tourists.

We protest against this all-white team as a symbol of apartheid in practice.

NO POLITICS IN SPORT

On 14 April 1960, Keith Lye, the deputy director of the Anti-Apartheid Movement, wrote to J.P. 'Pom Pom' Fellows-Smith who had been an Oxford contemporary of Colin Cowdrey and M.J.K. Smith and was now an all-rounder in Jackie McGlew's tour party after the tourists had been heckled on arrival at Heathrow.

You have been greeted by demonstrations and pickets on your arrival in London, organised by our committee and you will probably be met by similar protests later in your tour. We would like you to understand clearly they are not directed at you personally, but they are planned to show British public indignation at the South African Government of apartheid.

We would be grateful if you would make known your views on apartheid in sport. Would you be prepared to acknowledge that your side cannot claim to be a representative South African team? What is your own attitude to race discrimination in sport? Are you planning any action that will help to abolish colour bar in international teams?

There is no evidence that any reply was sent and in truth, apart from the throwing controversy, the tour passed off peacefully. In 1960, so close to Sharpeville, British people knew what apartheid was, in principle would have disapproved of it but clearly did not wish to curtail the cricket in order to make that disapproval public. It took the events of 1968 to instigate a change in that attitude.

When England toured South Africa in 1964/65 they managed to hang on with some difficulty to the lead they had gained when they won the first Test match at Durban by an innings. Thereafter, the South African batting, now starring Colin Bland and the 21-year-old

Graeme Pollock, thrived against a pace attack that never rose above fast-medium. When they followed England home in the summer of 1965, they gained revenge by winning the three-match series 1-0. The sole victory came courtesy of a now legendary innings of 125 at Trent Bridge by Pollock. The 1968 tour was of course cancelled in the wake of Basil D'Oliveira's selection, at which point all thoughts turned to the tour that was due to take place in 1970.

What particularly whetted the appetite, even in the days when cricket scores were not available at the click of a mouse or a scroll of the thumb, was the four-match series played in South Africa in the first months of 1970 by the touring Australians against a side drawn largely from the touring squad that was announced at the end of South Africa's crushing four-nil victory. During their 22 years of isolation that followed the cancellation of the England tour, South Africans, and indeed cricket lovers who could temporarily lay aside their dislike of apartheid, recalled the details of that series lovingly. South Africa's batting was so strong that Mike Procter, who in the following season would score six consecutive hundreds, was batting as low as number eight or nine.

Australia did not have a bad team. In a sense they were recovering from the retirements of Benaud, Davidson and Simpson and the arrival of Lillee and Thomson as Test players was still a few years away but the batting was strong – Bill Lawry, Keith Stackpole, Ian Redpath, Ian Chappell, Doug Walters and Paul Sheahan – and while the bowling was not outstanding, it contained the mystery spinner Johnny Gleeson whom few batsmen could read from the hand. It probably didn't help that they arrived in South Africa immediately following a gruelling five-match series in India which, although it was won 3-1, had clearly exerted a physical toll on the players. Ian Chappell in particular had a miserable tour, scoring just 92 runs in the four Test matches for an average of 11.5. The South Africans, with months to prepare without competitive action, were irresistible and the Australians suffered heavy defeats at the hands of what became known as South Africa's greatest Test team. It was one of those Test series when, at least from the end of the second day of the second Test, the result of each match was predictable a long time in advance. The South Africans were triumphant but the Australians were a sad and beaten side long before the series finished.

The first match took place in Cape Town at the end of January. Despite a century from Eddie Barlow, Australia managed to restrict the hosts to 382 but they were themselves dismissed for 164 with only Walters making more than 20. Johnny Gleeson set his usual problems and no batsman looked entirely comfortable when facing him. Ali Bacher later confessed that he was determined to play him as a regular off-spinner (Boycott's infamous method), but every time he played forward to the ball he thought would turn in, it went the other way past the outside edge. When he thought he spotted a leg break it turned out to be an off-spinner. Despite all this confusion, South Africa still managed to set Australia 451 to win in their second innings. The Australians started brightly, reaching 130/1 before Lawry was trapped lbw by Procter when he was on 83. Thereafter the innings fell away badly and ended at lunch on the fifth day with South Africa winning by a convincing 170 runs. It made no difference that Gleeson was proving so difficult to read.

When the second Test was played at Durban, South Africa had effectively won the match by the close of play on the second day. Barry Richards, in only his second Test, having made modest scores in Cape Town, tore into the Australian bowling. When the other opener, Trevor Goddard, was out for 17 caught by Lawry off Gleeson made in an hour and 20 minutes, the total was already 88. By the time Richards himself was bowled by Freeman an hour after lunch the total was 229. However, Richards's innings was not the standout performance. Graeme Pollock batted for nearly seven hours to make 274, the highest score ever made by a South African in a Test match at that time. The innings closed on 622/9, made at the astonishing rate for those times of 3.7 runs per over. It allowed the Australians just about an hour's batting at the end of two days of returning the ball from the boundary and, as is frequently the case in such circumstances, they lost wickets immediately, finishing the day on 48/4 and virtually conceding the match and the series.

Henry Blofeld watched the partnership between Richards and Pollock, mesmerised by its awesome beauty, writing that during it, the art of batsmanship reached heights it rarely attained. It was the cricketing equivalent of Roger Federer and Rafael Nadal exchanging breathtaking shots as each brought out the very best in the other.

The hour after lunch produced the most incredible cricket of all. In this time Richards and Pollock put on 100 with a series of strokes that were as brilliant as they were made to seem simple. These two who are certainly among the half dozen best batsmen in the world, seemed to challenge each other stroke for stroke, and it will be a long time before such batting is seen in partnership again. In the past two seasons, Richards has shown while batting for Hampshire that he is one of the most outstanding players in the world but until this series he has not had the chance to prove himself at Test level. Now, in only his second Test in front of his home crowd he played the innings of his life.

On the second day, the Australian innings ended at 157 made at the fast rate of well over three runs an over and following on, with Stackpole, Walters and Redpath all passing 70, they managed a respectable total of 336 but still lost by an innings and 129 runs. Blofeld, predictably, was in raptures, saluting the strong possibility of a clean sweep.

In these two matches they have shown themselves to be a superbly organised cricket machine consisting of 11 players each of whom brings his own individual character to the game, which ensures that they are never dull to watch.

They are a wonderfully keen side and a joy to watch in the field, where almost everything is caught and the ball is chased to the boundary by fielders who seemingly give no thought to the consequences if they crash into the railings.

On the same February day as the South African cricket team was effortlessly demonstrating its superiority on the field, another British student union was in uproar over links to the country's despised apartheid government. The row broke over the refusal of Liverpool University's chancellor, Lord Salisbury, to distance himself from his previously announced support for the regime in Pretoria. Salisbury, of course, was a name redolent of Britain's colonial connections with Southern Africa. Salisbury, who was also not coincidentally president of the Anglo-Rhodesian Society, and his wife travelled from London to be the guest of honour at the annual Liverpool Students' Dinner and Ball but faced with crowds of antagonistic students, picketing the hall where the dinner was to take place, they decided to remain in their hotel. The president of the Guild of Undergraduates went to the hotel to present Lady Salisbury with the bouquet of flowers which had already been purchased for the occasion. There was a proposal that the university should sell its £28,000 worth of assets which had been invested in South African stocks and the proceeds donated to the South African freedom fighters. It was narrowly defeated whereupon the more militant students called a vote of no confidence in the committee which was passed by 28 votes to 24, at which point the entire committee resigned en masse and walked out, leaving the place in uproar. It was entirely typical of so much student politics of that time. Although this particular incident was not directly related to the cricket tour it revealed the depth of feeling caused by Britain's relationship with South Africa.

Also in February 1970 the Cricket Council released a short pamphlet titled *Why the '70 Tour? The Cricket Council Answer*. It is a memorandum that is difficult to read because the agonies of the people who have written it are apparent in almost every line. Although any argument in favour of the tour would have been dismissed out of hand by its opponents, seen across the divide from a distance of 50 years, it now arouses an odd sense of pity. The pamphlet is divided into six sections: Introduction, Recent Events, Cricket in South Africa, Why continue to play cricket against South Africa?, The Practical Side of the 1970 Tour and the Conclusion.

It begins by pointing out that 'the Council is totally opposed to any policy of the South African government that leads to apartheid in sport'. Already it has put its foot in its mouth. Nobody doubted that many of the people supporting the tour (though by no means all) were opposed to the principles behind apartheid. The Council would have been better advised to separate itself from apartheid in its entirety, not merely in those areas concerned with sport. It goes on to add that it does not need to emphasise the contribution made by the English cricket authorities to:

> the development of the game throughout the world with no thought of distinction between class, creed, or colour. For

many years, teams from this country have visited West Indies, India, Pakistan and Ceylon and, more recently, the developing countries in Africa such as Kenya, Uganda and Tanzania, without financial benefit to the cricketing authorities in this country, and the help given in this way will be readily acknowledged by those responsible for the game in the countries concerned.

So although it doesn't need to blow its own horn, it does so very loudly if a little self-consciously. It rehashes the D'Oliveira affair only in order to remind everyone that in the Special meeting called by Sheppard and Brearley, over 80% of the MCC electorate voted to maintain sporting ties with South Africa. The sub-committee set up in December 1969 had recommended the tour went ahead and the reasons behind the decision had been released to the press in February.

In the third section, the Council welcomed recent efforts by SACA to ensure that future touring teams were selected irrespective of race, creed or colour, whilst at the same time admitting that it would take time before non-white cricket produced players of sufficient calibre to merit selection on ability alone. The problem of the fractious relations between what they called the Coloured Boards needed to be resolved before they could sensibly negotiate with SACA. This was not an unreasonable proposition but the enormous emotional responsibility the Council felt towards their old friends in SACA was consistently highlighted.

> It cannot be over-emphasised that South African Cricket Association representatives have stressed again and again that they do not endorse any policy of apartheid in sport. As a team and as individuals they wish to be free to go anywhere and play anywhere against anybody. They mix freely on the field overseas but the laws of their land do not allow them to do so at home.

The Council goes on to acknowledge that some form of trouble would inevitably accompany the tour but to surrender to it in advance would be easy but spineless. Cutting ties with South Africa, the

Council believed, would not advance the cause of multi-racial cricket in that country to which they were devoted. The effect of isolation would simply be to increase the already apparent tendency of white South Africans towards introspection. This point of view was held by Laurence Gander, the former editor of the *Rand Daily Mail*, who had been honoured everywhere for the courage of his stance against prejudice in South Africa and who was an outspoken critic of the policies of the Nationalist Party. Gander pleaded for the retention of sporting links with South Africa, maintaining that 'South Africa can only benefit by continuing contacts with the outside world, whether in the cultural, academic, sporting or scientific field'.

Much was made of Basil D'Oliveira who, to many on the STST side and in the Anti-Apartheid Movement, was seen less of a graceful dignified cricketer than as an Uncle Tom, selling out in order to fit in with his new white friends. It was a harsh judgement but from an article written for the *Sunday Telegraph* at the end of 1969 it was possible to deduce that he would be voting with the majority in the Professional Cricketers' Association for the 1970 tour to proceed as planned. Whether or not he wrote it, he certainly allowed his name to appear at the head of the article in which he reminisced about the pleasure he obtained from playing with and against players from the South Africa Test team in the World Double-Wicket Competition in Australia.

> I believe that those few weeks we spent together were more valuable towards the ultimate breaking down of barriers than all the rushing on to pitches and violent scuffling which are the ways others prefer to protest. My short answer to those who feel compelled to break up events is to register a powerful protest. Remember that the thing we non-whites most of all want is freedom. If we are going to deny that choice to some who might not agree with us – are they likely to help us to achieve that right for ourselves?

That was exactly what the Cricket Council believed so it was no wonder it was lengthily quoted in the pamphlet. It also praised the South African Cricket Association for doing so much to help build up the standard of coloured cricket in the country to the extent that it expected coloured players would soon be able to take their proper place in the Test side. SACA needed encouragement not isolation to ensure further progress.

The essence of the Cricket Council's argument was contained in the section headed The Practical Side of the 1970 Tour.

> A traditional lawful pursuit supported by the majority of people in this country is none the less threatened by a small minority with illegal acts aimed at disruption. Increasing pressure has been brought and will be brought to bear on cricketers and administrators to give way. It is considered important, though, to consider the interests of cricket in the long term. Expediency in the short term will not be a consideration when assessing the situation. Yielding to pressure from a militant minority would subscribe to a victory for mob rule in our public life. This could lead to serious repercussions for the future of the game not only in this country but the world over.

Michael Parkinson in the *Sunday Times* didn't buy any of it.

> It is a rag-bag of cliché, red herring, zig-zagging, bobbing and weaving and as an argument in favour of the tour has all the watertight qualities of a string bag. The fact is that the damage to cricket will not be done by the so-called 'militant minority' (David Sheppard, where are your bovver boots?) but by those people responsible for inviting the white South Africans to play here. It is no good the MCC squealing 'foul' after it had delivered the first low blow.

The battle between the Cricket Council and John Arlott continued, with each side anxious to claim the moral high ground. Having digested the contents of the *Why the '70 Tour?* pamphlet, Arlott responded in some detail in a lengthy article in *The Guardian* on 20 February.

> The Cricket Council, which includes to all intents and purposes MCC, has taken the unusual step of presenting its case on moral grounds.

He then goes on to quote in full Billy Griffith's statement which included the passage:

In 1969, all the first class clubs including the Minor Counties who comprise the newly constituted TCCB recommended unanimously that the invitation to the South African Cricket Association to send a team to Britain should stand. Equally, they are unanimous in their resolve to uphold the rights of individuals in this country to take part in lawful pursuits, particularly when those pursuits have the support of the majority.

Arlott, though courteous as ever, was not impressed by the argument.

The questionable point is 'the support of the majority'. An 80% backing at the meeting of MCC or county committees does not automatically mean a national majority; nor even a large majority among those who pay money to watch cricket. To spell it out to one section that only reads *The Guardian* by accident or for the racing tips, Britain has at the moment a democratically elected Socialist government. It is significant that one county representative at the Cricket Council meeting abstained from voting in support of the motion to continue the tour.

Arlott dismissed the Cricket Council's stated distaste for apartheid because they only disapproved of it because of its adverse effect on cricket. They made no mention of that policy's deleterious impact on the rest of South African society, thereby revealing the blinkered approach which Griffith had desperately sought to deny.

Arlott was particularly irritated with Griffith's constant reference to the support the Cricket Council was receiving from 'a majority of the country'. It was true of course that a vast majority of the mail that poured into Lord's would have been supportive of the efforts to keep the tour going. The tour's opponents had long since given up the idea that the tour could be stopped by writing in sufficient numbers to the home of cricket and hoping the administrators would come to their senses. Arlott responded:

As the forces of opposition grow, it becomes increasingly wrong to label them 'a small minority'. Labour and Liberal MPs offer considerable opposition; and some Conservatives support them.

He went on to quote other examples of opposition from trade unions and other fraternal organisations. He concluded with a bleak prediction for the likely outcome if neither side made any kind of compromise.

Objective observation of these events, pronouncements and attitudes can only lead to the conclusion that 'progress' is towards physical confrontation. If this point is reached, those who seek to protect cricket may share its destruction equally with their opponents.

The to and fro of such verbal sparring kept the controversy alive and each side contributed to the debate on an almost daily basis. Yorkshire CCC, scorning the financial blackmail that it felt the government was threatening them with, announced that its members would be admitted free to the Headingley Test match and the proposed Northern Counties match against the tourists to be played on that ground. It also announced that barbed wire was now erected around the pitch in preparation for a match that was to be played three months later. It later transpired that it had been lent free of charge by the army but when the Ministry of Defence heard about it they insisted that the barbed wire was returned to the army as defending a cricket pitch against anti-apartheid protestors was not considered to be a national emergency. What F.S. Trueman's reaction was to this desecration of the ground on which he had taken so many wickets was not recorded but he would certainly have been forgiven for not knowing what was going off out there. This action was countered by the Transport and General Workers' Union, who threatened to (appropriately) 'black' the tour which, with fraternal support from other unions, would make life very difficult indeed both for the cricketers and the spectators.

One has to be careful in evaluating the support of trade unions. While the alliance between 'the workers' and the students had been one of the triumphs of 'Les Evenements' in France in 1968, the perfectly well-meant expressions of support by some trade unionists for a moral stand against the evils of apartheid has to be placed in the context of the reality of trade union life in contemporary industrial Britain. The attitude of many white British workers to the entry of black workers newly arrived from Commonwealth countries was anything but welcoming. It wasn't coincidence that Enoch Powell was probably the most popular MP in the country. It can be concluded that for many British trade unionists, it was all very well to register a protest against the iniquities of apartheid, but if black South African workers escaped from their country and came to work in a car factory in Coventry, the support for them would be minimal. Their attitude was very likely to be 'Go back to where you came from' which, given the unions' stated opposition to apartheid, made no sense at all. Such was the reality of the contradiction. More practically, the Birmingham Labour Party requested its members to boycott the profitable Warwickshire CCC football pool whose success had provided urgently needed funds for other counties besides Warwickshire.

South Africa responded predictably. SACA showed not the slightest interest in any kind of concession. It could have selected for the tour a promising young non-white player who might not play in the Tests but who would gain invaluable experience by being part of the tour and playing a few county matches. This option was never seriously considered. Instead, a hundred South Africans formed a group they called Guard the 70 Tour. These men declared they were prepared to travel to England and as Nicky du Preez, one of their key organisers, elegantly put it, 'If it comes to a punch up with the sort of long-haired hippies who tried to disrupt the Springboks' rugby tour, we will take care of that.' A prominent member of the Cricket Council's deliberations announced his support for this group and its stated intentions. Violence on the streets it appeared was now inevitable.

As the date on which the South African cricketers were due to arrive in Britain approached, all they could do was to play cricket when allowed to do so and maintain a dignified silence on what was happening in Britain. The Test series against the Australians was starting to follow a very familiar pattern as South Africa continued to torment the weary and outplayed opposition. In Johannesburg, the third Test followed the narrative outline of the first two as the hosts were strengthened by the return of their talented wicketkeeper batsman Denis Lindsay, which meant that Mike Procter would now drop from batting at sixth wicket down to bat at number nine. Although restricted to 279 in their first innings, the South Africans soon put their opponents under pressure. Peter Pollock took 5-39 and Procter 3-48 as the Australians conceded a first innings lead of 77. Opening the South African second innings in place of Trevor Goddard, who dropped down to number nine in his last game before his prematurely enforced retirement, Eddie Barlow scored 110 and, supported by Graeme Pollock who made a rapid 87 and Lee Irvine a solid 73, South Africa posted a total of 408, scored at the impressive rate of 3.35 runs an over. This set Australia a nominal target of 486 runs to win but Ian Redpath and Alan Connolly were the only batsmen to make more than 18 as the Australians sank supinely to defeat by 307 runs.

The last wicket partnership between the wicket keeper Brian Taber and the opening bowler Connolly was hugely enjoyed by everyone on the ground except perhaps the Australian top order as the two men put on 52 with a series of wild swings and productive edges. Eventually Connolly was caught by Richards off the bowling of Trevor Goddard, who was given plenty of overs by the slightly embarrassed captain, Ali Bacher. Goddard's bowling figures in his final match were a remarkable 24.5-16-27-3. Goddard, who had been captain of South Africa between 1963 and 1965, had announced that this would be his last series and he did not wish to be considered for inclusion in the South Africa squad for the forthcoming tour of England. The selectors chose the moment of celebration in the dressing room after victory in the third Test to tell Goddard that since he had made himself unavailable for the summer he would not play in the fourth and final Test. Goddard was much liked and all the players felt badly at the manner in which he had been so crudely jettisoned.

The fourth Test against Australia was to be the final one in the series because the Australian players were in dispute with their board over their insultingly low remuneration and a fifth Test was removed from the schedule. When the South Africans took the field in Port Elizabeth, it appeared as though the stubbornness of the Cricket Council, in its desperation to make good its invitation to SACA, would prevail and the South Africans, with the series already won, approached that fateful last match in good spirits.

The fourth Test followed the pattern of the previous one at The Wanderers with remarkable fidelity. Richards and Barlow put on 157 for the first wicket but 6-47 by Alan Connolly helped to restrict the hosts to 311. In reply, only half-centuries by Redpath and Paul Sheahan enabled Australia to get to 212 and in their second innings the South African batsmen simply took the game away from their opponents. Barry Richards made 126, Lee Irvine 102 and when Ali Bacher declared the innings closed at the fall of the eighth wicket, the total was showing 470, compiled at a rate just short of four runs an over. Needing a purely nominal 570 to win, nearly all the Australian batsmen got a start but nobody made more than Sheahan's 46 and with Mike Procter picking up six wickets for 73 runs, they subsided gently to 246 all out just after lunch on the final day, giving South Africa a winning margin of 323 runs. In the aftermath of such a convincing series of Test match victories, John Woodcock, who was covering the tour for *The Times*, noted that:

> Tactically and technically they are a side to be reckoned with
> – the best South Africa have had – and in recent weeks they
> have provided a lot of pleasure. Given a fair crack of the whip,
> they will win many friends in England.

Whether they would be allowed this fair crack of the whip was a moot point but the implication of Woodcock's words was that the tour would go ahead even if it were accompanied by the threatened demonstrations.

Neville Cardus considered and then rejected the now fashionable notion that South Africa's current team was the greatest there had ever been and sniffily referred such fools to the England side that took the field at Edgbaston in 1902 which had included such immortals as A.C. MacLaren, C.B. Fry, K.S. Ranjitsinhji and W. Rhodes. He acknowledged that Alan Knott was a better wicketkeeper than A.A. Lilley had been in 1902 but that was the only change he would have made. He also accepted the claim that Graeme Pollock was probably the most 'gallant' batsman since Victor Trumper – praise indeed. Cardus clearly shared Michael Parkinson's view of Illingworth's England which he dismissed as probably the most boring side he had ever seen. He was neither a demonstrator nor a protester and he preferred an evening listening to Barbirolli conducting Elgar rather than one spent at the hustings, but he agreed with Arlott that cricket was not a game to be watched through a barbed wire fence. Holding his nose at England's current preoccupation with seamers (Snow, Brown, Greig, Lever, Shuttleworth, Ward etc.), Cardus vowed to watch them through the barbed wire as it might make the sight more interesting. He and his readers might have pined for Lindwall and Larwood but the fact was that the England selectors could only pick from those currently available in county cricket and Australian spectators were soon to realise that John Snow was just as quick, exciting and effective as any fast bowler England had ever sent to Australia. Whether Snow and any other England player would be playing international cricket in the summer of 1970 before the party set off in its quest to regain the Ashes for the first time in 12 years remained to be seen.

In South African folklore the four-Test series against Australia and in particular this last poignant match has assumed an enormous significance. It would have been unlikely that, as they left the field, any of the players was under the impression that they would never play Test cricket again although that is precisely what happened. The MCC tour had been cancelled in 1968/69 but South Africa continued to play Test cricket against other white nations. It was believed in South Africa that if MCC withdrew its invitation to tour the same thing would happen. It is only with hindsight that the poignancy of the victory in Port Elizabeth is revealed. On a purely cricketing note, one that was willingly admitted by Peter Hain, it was a personal tragedy that such outstanding performers as Graeme Pollock, Barry Richards and Mike Procter should have been deprived of their chance to display their manifold talents on the world stage. He felt particularly badly that his actions would inevitably adversely affect one of his heroes.

> The thing that I felt most sorry about was Graeme Pollock. He
> was a left-handed batsman and so was I because my grandfather

was, though I'm right-handed in everything else. He of course was one of the greatest left-handers ever to play the game. I used to watch him, follow him in South Africa, keep newspaper clippings of him.

It didn't, however, give Hain more than a moment's pause and a twinge of regret. He knew that he was engaged on a mission that was more important than one white cricketer's Test career. Jonathan Steele reported back to *The Guardian* the divisive atmosphere in South Africa.

> White South Africans live in a crazy half world somewhere between Victorian England and the American Dream. There's the religious drinking of tea every afternoon at 4pm served by a maid, the tedious conversations about the difficulties of getting staff, the bars on the windows, the big dogs in the yard and the feeling that the masses can't be trusted and then the Puritanism of public life (bans on magazines like *Playboy*, Afrikaans disapproval of miniskirts, even suggestions recently that South African Airways should on Sundays switch its piped music in its aircraft to religious tunes). But with that go the big cars, the barbeques, the swimming pools, the emphasis on outdoor life, virility and sport, sport, sport.

Peter Hain and his friends knew perfectly well that sport was the South Africans' weak spot and depriving them of this outlet was going to make a considerable impact. Sport to white South Africans was a way of asserting their national pride which made victory doubly important because victory validated their belief in white supremacy. The disappointing results of the recent rugby tour of the British Isles could be explained away by the team having to perform under the unfair handicap imposed by the demonstrators. The glorious victory of the cricket team in its series against Australia restored that pride. It is a small step from noting the primacy of South Africa's sporting victories and their implicit belief in the racial superiority of the white race to noting the parallel with the manner in which Nazi Germany asserted Aryan supremacy through sport. No Jews were selected for the German Olympic team in 1936 for reasons which are only too obvious but, when prompted by the International Olympic Committee to explain how this happened, it was announced that no Jew had been good enough to achieve the qualifying standard. If that were indeed true it was the fact that sporting facilities were closed to Jews that made the situation of qualification impossible, not their lack of athletic ability. This was the identical situation to the one in South Africa when Jack Cheetham, to the sound of hosannas being sung in the Long Room at Lord's, had announced in December 1969 that future South African cricket teams would be chosen on merit. Sadly, it was discovered that there were no non-white cricketers good enough to be chosen to represent South Africa for the perfectly valid reason that they were forced to play their cricket on makeshift pitches and were denied any of the advantages of the first class facilities available to white South Africans.

Non-whites in South Africa assumed the position of the 'Untermensch' in Nazi Germany. It was firmly believed that black South Africans were unable to swim competitively because their pores closed quickly in the water and they therefore tired more quickly than white swimmers. The fact that black swimmers were not allowed in the same water as white swimmers in case they somehow contaminated it was safely ignored. The belief in the physical inferiority of non-whites therefore justified all the discriminatory laws that were passed. It reduced the non-white to a man and woman not only to be feared as the traditional 'other' but to have their common humanity ignored and remorselessly demolished by both law and practice.

No wonder then that in the townships, news of demonstrations in Britain and other countries against South African sport and sportsmen were greeted with cries of delight and wonder. Hain was later told by Nelson Mandela that he and the other political prisoners on Robben Island only knew of what was happening in Britain through the muttered comments and bad temper of the prison guards. It made the beatings that followed bearable. The South African media was strictly controlled and news of that nature had to be gathered by word of mouth.

Kenneth J. Costa, the president of the Students' Representative Council at the University of Witwatersrand, wrote to *The Times*, reminding its readers that the demonstrations in Britain against the rugby and proposed cricket tours were having an impact in South Africa.

> It is often argued here and overseas that the present demonstrations are aimed at the isolation of South Africa: whether this is true or not, they have had the effect here of reminding white South Africans – who would often prefer to ignore this – that apartheid is an unpopular minority view in the world context. This, for me, has been one of the most encouraging effects of the demonstrations.

Even the Africans who were not in prison knew almost nothing about the events of the rugby tour and the controversy surrounding the cricket tour. White journalists found it hard to talk to Africans because official approval had to be given to any visit to the townships and that was frequently refused. The government controlled African-language radio and many blacks were too poor to be able to afford a radio in any case. Where it was possible to speak to an African, it was usually through the good offices of a white friend who inevitably had a master/servant relationship with the black workers. It was hard to penetrate the mask in open and honest conversation but the outrage of apartheid was not difficult to find if a white person wanted to look. On previous tours to South Africa, MCC and most of its players chose not to look. When Bob Barber sneaked off at 6am to visit the townships and see for himself what they were like during the MCC tour of South Africa in 1964/65 he did not tell his captain and close friend Mike Smith because he knew the news would not have been welcomed and it would immediately have placed his good friend in a very uncomfortable position.

South Africa wasn't Russia. It wasn't that the visiting cricketers were expressly forbidden to visit the townships in this manner. Donald Carr was a popular and laid-back manager of the tour, invariably to be seen with a cigarette in one hand and a gin and tonic in the other and he certainly did not lay down the law to his players but it was generally understood that sneaking off to the townships in the early morning was not the done thing. Had the news leaked, it would have been considered 'rude' to their hosts and that would have been unforgivable. Had the news then travelled back to Lord's and the MCC officials, it would have been regarded as a breach of discipline. They were cricketers, they had come to the country at the kind invitation of SACA and politics was not their business. Better to let sleeping prejudices lie. What good could they have done anyway? Apartheid had been government policy since the Nationalists had won the election in 1948 and it was now the law of the land. A 'democratically' elected government was surely entitled to enact its own legislation and the officers of the law were entitled to enforce it. It wasn't up to English county cricketers to make public objections. It was far better to encourage sporting relations between the two countries so that South Africans would come to see the error of their ways.

By 1970 there had been more than two decades of 'bridge-building' between sportsmen from other countries and white South African sportsmen. In terms of a reduction in the iniquities of apartheid it had achieved precisely nothing. No white sportsman had publicly voiced his opposition. The cracks were now appearing because of the real possibility that South African sport would be cast into the darkness of isolation. South Africa first participated at the Olympic Games in 1904 and sent athletes to compete in every Summer Olympic Games until the 1960 Games in Rome. After the passage of United Nations General Assembly Resolution 1761 in 1962 in response to South Africa's policy of apartheid, the nation was barred from the 1964 Tokyo Games and the Games of 1968 in Mexico City. The country's tennis team was banned from the Davis Cup in March 1970 by a Davis Cup committee. British tennis players Mark Cox, Virginia Wade and Roger Taylor, at the time the decision was taken, were all competing in the South African Open lawn tennis championships in Johannesburg and John Vorster explained it to South Africans as a decision taken by communists.

Vorster's antipathy to Britain had a long history and indeed his anti-British views had been propounded with such intensity that during the Second World War he had been imprisoned by the Smuts government. The British Lawn Tennis Association had fought hard to keep South Africa in the competition, exactly like MCC, for exactly the same reasons and using exactly the same arguments to keep sporting links to South African tennis but the worldwide hostility was too great.

By lining up MCC, the LTA and the RFU on one side of the argument there is a distinct possibility that arguments in favour of the tour were the exclusive privilege of the white, wealthy, clubbable middle class. It should be remembered that the overwhelming majority of professional cricketers felt much the same way and the week before South Africa was banned from the Davis Cup, Brian Close, the respected captain of Yorkshire and former captain of England but nobody's idea of an Establishment figure, gave an address at a service for sportsmen in Bradford Cathedral in which he appealed for the tour to go ahead on exactly the same grounds as those that were used by those of a more right-wing view.

> If the South Africans see what is allowed over here, it might cause people in South Africa, people of all races, to mix together. By allowing the team to come, at least we are doing something positive. If the tour ends in a riot and they go back home, it will not affect politicians. If it goes on, good feelings will be spread and it might alter things.

Now it appeared to a sports-obsessed white minority that there would be no international competition to watch in athletics, tennis, golf, rugby and possibly cricket. It wouldn't of course change the plight of blacks in the country overnight but depriving white South Africans of their sport was perhaps the most immediate and powerful way that the rest of the world could find to let them know how widely the policy of apartheid was despised. Nobody, not even Peter Hain and the STST, believed that cancelling the cricket tour was going to produce profound changes in a country in which black inferiority was institutionalised but from their point of view it showed the depth of revulsion felt and it was better than the previous 20 years of official apathy. It wasn't, however, going to change the attitude of the South African government and, it appeared, it wasn't going to change the mind of the Cricket Council in St John's Wood.

Secure in the knowledge that their friends in England were fighting hard to maintain the integrity of the tour, the South African selectors sat down to choose the party that would tour England in what was now a shortened time frame, starting at the beginning of June. They knew they would be confronted with demonstrations and possibly the odd direct action that had wriggled free from the police protection but they knew, too, that thousands of English cricket lovers could not wait to see the South African cricketers in action. The squad they announced was as follows:

> Dr. Ali Bacher (Transvaal) captain, E.J. Barlow (Western Province) vice-captain, B.A. Richards (Natal), R.G. Pollock (Eastern Province), B.L. Irvine (Transvaal), D. Lindsay (N.E. Transvaal), H.R. Lance (Transvaal), M.J. Procter (Western Province), P.M. Pollock (Eastern Province), P.H.J. Trimborn (Natal), A.J. Traicos (Rhodesia), A.M. Short (Natal), G.L.G. Watson (Transvaal), G.A. Chevalier (Western Province). The manager would be Mr. J.B. Plimsoll.

The usual preparations for a cricket tour were under way. Official photographs were taken, plane tickets and hotels were booked, assurances of eternal friendship were re-confirmed between South African and English cricket administrators. Whatever the Stop the Seventy Tour mob had in store for them would be resisted to the last man. It would be Rorke's Drift all over again, arguably in reverse this time with the South Africans triumphant at the last.

On Saturday 28 March, Mr Victor Koekemoer, aged 39, issued a challenge to Peter Hain to fight a duel to the death with him through the good offices of a Johannesburg newspaper. He said:

'I am deadly serious in this. Let him put his courage where his mouth is and become a hero or a martyr.' Hain rejected the offer commenting shortly, 'If it had been Mr Vorster or maybe even Mr Herzog, then perhaps we could have considered the matter.'

South Africa v Oxford University at Twickenham. 5 November 1969

Wilf Wooller inspects the paint job on his car inexpertly applied by opponents of the tour. 20 January 1970

A young and rather nervous Mike Brearley addressing Peter Hain's Stop the Seventy Tour meeting in Hampstead Town Hall. 7 March 1970

Peter Hain advises against opening a bank account at Barclays

STST was a mass movement but the masses seem to be stuck in traffic

First day of the season and there are more people outside the ground than in it. Middlesex v Hampshire at Lord's. 2 May 1970

Peter Hain demonstrates against Sobers before the Surrey v Nottinghamshire match at The Oval. 20 May 1970

England v Brazil 7 June 1970. Back row (l to r) Harold Shepherdson, Brian Labone, Gordon Banks, Terry Cooper, Bobby Charlton, Martin Peters, Bobby Moore, Les Cocker Front row (l to r) Alan Ball, Francis Lee, Alan Mullery, Tommy Wright, Geoff Hurst

Harold and Mary Wilson on election day before the horse trod on her foot. 18 June 1970

The new secretary of education tells the new prime minister and Lord Chancellor how to run the country. 19 June 1970

Brian Johnston and John Arlott – colleagues in the commentary box but with very different views on South Africa

England v Rest of the World, Lord's 19 June 1970. Back row (l to r) Alan Jones, Brian Luckhurst, Derek Underwood, Alan Ward, Ken Shuttleworth, Mike Denness. Front row (l to r) Basil D'Oliveira, John Snow, Ray Illingworth, Phil Sharpe, Alan Knott

Alan Knott spent much of his life watching Sobers doing this

K.W.R. Fletcher c Murray b Sobers 0. Edgbaston, 16 July 1970

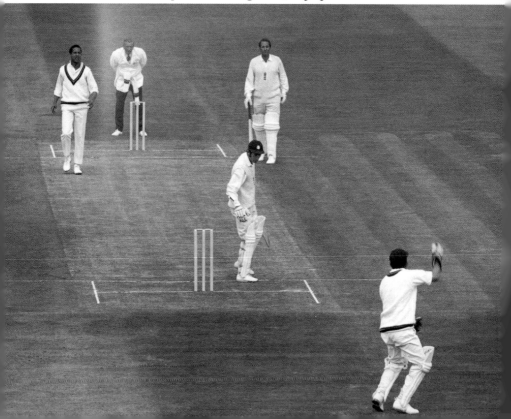

Garry Sobers thinks he doesn't need to get changed to beat Illingworth's England

Garry Sobers handed the winner's cheque by Brian Vernall, the Midlands manager of sponsors Guinness after the Rest of the World beat England by five wickets to win the third Test at Edgbaston 21 July 1970

England v Rest of the World Headingley. 1 August 1970 Back row (l to r) Brian Luckhurst, Chris Old, Tony Greig, Don Wilson, Basil D'Oliveira, Keith Fletcher. Front row (l to r) Alan Knott, Colin Cowdrey, Ray Illingworth, Geoffrey Boycott, John Snow.

Rest of the World v England Headingley. 1 August 1970. Back row (l to r) Deryck Murray, Barry Richards, Clive Lloyd, Mike Procter, Intikhab Alam, Mushtaq Mohammad. Front row (l to r) Rohan Kanhai, Eddie Barlow, Garry Sobers, Lance Gibbs, Graeme Pollock

Sobers displays the Guinness trophy at The Oval at the end of an absorbing series. 18 August 1970

CHAPTER SIX
APRIL 1970

Oh, to be in England now that April's there
And whoever wakes in England sees, some morning,
unaware / That the lowest boughs and the brushwood
sheaf / Round the elm-tree bole are in tiny leaf,
While the chaffinch sings on the orchard bough
In England—now!

ROBERT Browning's *Home Thoughts from Abroad* would have probably been the way that expats and possibly naïve South African cricketers still regarded the 'Mother Country'. In the spring of 1970 this was a very outdated concept indeed. It must be obvious by now that this book is not a conventional cricket book. The fact is that cricket, like all aspects of cultural life, cannot exist in a vacuum. Admittedly, one of its many charms is that it is possible to watch the game, whether at a Test ground or on a village green, and see in the cricketers dressed in white playing a game on green grass a sense of the timelessness of cricket. Spectators and students of the game need little prompting to watch the players in action in front of them and still see the heroes of their youth in their full pomp and majesty. Statham beating May outside the off stump, Dexter hammering Sobers through the covers, Lock in the leg trap clutching an inside edge off a sharply turning Laker off break. It is a vision that never dies and it is the 'Cucumber Sandwiches' that forms part of this book's title.

The 'Barbed Wire', however, would have reminded cricket lovers in 1970 that they were living through a different cricket season from any they had known before and they were living in an England after nearly six years of a Labour government. Reading of these events 50 years after they have happened might induce a feeling of nostalgia for the players that no longer play and for an England that is itself long vanished after 20 years of the 21st century but it is important that we place the 1970 cricket tour firmly in its appropriate cultural context. Checking how the controversy surrounding the tour was covered by contemporary newspapers, a historian is confronted by all the events of the day not just the cricket scores. It is to the reality of the England of 1970 that we must turn in order that we may fully appreciate why the events surrounding the cricket tour took the course they did.

For Peter Hain and his family, arriving in England in 1966 as exiles was difficult both emotionally and financially, particularly as they found their new country, although in no way comparable to the apartheid they had left, not to be the country of tolerance they had expected to discover.

> I found England in 1966 racist to a disconcerting degree. We had come from fighting against apartheid South Africa to discover slowly that this new society we were now living in was also racist though not in the institutionalised sense that apartheid South Africa was. It was nothing compared to that, nothing. There is an argument that says that Israel is an apartheid state but people who say that don't actually understand what apartheid was like.

Two years earlier Patrick Gordon Walker, the Shadow Foreign Secretary and sitting Labour MP for Smethwick in the West Midlands, had lost in the 1964 general election to the Conservative candidate who had utilised the slogan 'If you want a nigger for a neighbour, Vote Labour', although Colin Jordan, the best known of British Nazis, later claimed responsibility for inventing it. Following that election result, a British branch of the Ku Klux Klan was formed, and black and ethnic minority residents in the area had burning crosses put through their letterboxes. Peter Griffiths, the new member for Smethwick, made a maiden speech in which he stated that his constituency faced the problems of factory closures and over 4,000 families awaiting council accommodation which he believed were the reasons for his election rather than overt racial hatred.

Two years after they had arrived in Britain the Hains must have watched in horror as Home Secretary James Callaghan guided through parliament a Commonwealth Immigrants Bill in the teeth of vocal opposition from middle-class activists like the Hains and the liberal press. For the former, such legislation must have sounded like uncomfortable echoes of the country they had left. The Labour government felt compelled to act in response to increasing anxiety from the white working class that thousands of Asians were being forced out of Kenya and would inevitably arrive in Britain to which they had unlimited access. Their arrival would take away jobs, force down wages and deplete the housing stock, especially council housing. The bill became law on 1 March 1968 after which only 1,500 Kenyan Asians would be allowed in each year. Richard Crossman in his diary notes that Callaghan had no time for wishy-washy liberalism when he knew perfectly well what the will of the electorate really was. The fact that it broke a long-standing contract with those who had traditionally been entitled to British passports and that it clearly discriminated against a non-white minority was of no political consequence.

In this context it should have come as little surprise that seven weeks later in the Midland Hotel, Birmingham, Enoch Powell delivered his notorious 'Rivers of Blood' speech as it soon became known. He told a story of a little old white lady whose white neighbours had moved out, leaving her as the sole white resident in a street now populated entirely by black and Asian immigrants. She was alone and terrified of physical assault.

> She is becoming afraid to go out. Windows are broken. She finds excreta pushed through her letterbox. When she goes to the shops, she is followed by children, charming, wide-grinning piccaninnies. They cannot speak English, but one word they

know. 'Racialist', they chant. When the new Race Relations
Bill is passed, this woman is convinced she will go to prison.

The story was extracted from a letter sent to Powell by a woman
living in Northumberland about this defenceless, helpless old white
woman who lived in Powell's own constituency of Wolverhampton.
It was a powerful speech which caused an immediate outcry but the
story chimed uncannily with the traditional stereotypes promulgated
by racists on the far right. The press leaped into action but failed to
find either the woman in Northumberland or the helpless old lady
in Wolverhampton. Such stories emanating from the National Front
or the Racial Preservation Society would scarcely have warranted
two paragraphs in the local Birmingham newspapers. However, this
wasn't Colin Jordan of the National Socialist Party, this was coming
from Enoch Powell, the Shadow Secretary of State for Health, who
had served in the Tory Cabinet throughout the time when Harold
Macmillan was the prime minister.

Almost immediately, Enoch Powell became the most popular
politician in Britain. At the end of April a Gallup poll found that
74% of those interviewed agreed with what Powell had said. A mere
15% disagreed. Powell had dared to express the frequently unspoken
thoughts of the embattled white working class and they sang his
praises with conviction. It is the same phenomenon the country was
to see in the Brexit referendum and America experienced during
the presidential campaign of Donald Trump. It was not so much
the blatant and hateful racism as the belief that those with political
power had no understanding of their lives and their difficulties.
Three days after the Birmingham speech, the East End dockers
marched in support of Powell, carrying placards proclaiming 'Enoch
Was Right'. Many of these men would have been traditional Labour
voters but, just as Brexit was to do nearly 50 years later, the issue
of coloured immigration to Britain as it was known transcended
party lines.

It is entirely possible that they and their wives also formed part
of the staple audience for The Black and White Minstrel Show, a
light entertainment programme on BBC Television which ran for
20 years from 1958 (the year of the Notting Hill race riots) to 1978
(the year Viv Anderson became the first black footballer to play for

England). Throughout these 20 years of radical social change, *The Black and White Minstrel Show* continued to present its traditional mixture of American minstrel and country songs and show tunes with the George Mitchell Singers and dancers in lavish costumes. Indeed, with no suggestion of irony, when BBC1 started transmitting in colour in November 1969, one of its proud boasts was that audiences would now be able to watch the black and white minstrels in colour. It maintained its popularity throughout its 20-year run, reaching 21 million viewers a week in 1964 and when it was finally cancelled it was because of the embarrassment caused to the BBC by its promotion of racial stereotypes rather than declining ratings. It wasn't just a ratings success for the BBC; it also won a highly coveted Golden Rose for Best Light Entertainment Programme at the Montreux Television Festival.

The pressure on the BBC to do something about the programme grew throughout the 1960s but, such was its popularity, it was difficult for successive controllers of BBC1 deliberately to jettison one of their valuable ratings winners. In 1969 it temporarily gave way to a similar show called *Music, Music, Music* in which the George Mitchell singers appeared with their very own white faces. The replacement did well but not well enough to suppress the increasingly strident demands for the return of the original and soon *The Black and White Minstrel Show* was back on BBC1 in prime time in all its colourful glory. In fact only the men blacked up. The women remained as white as they were when they were born. It was feared that making the women wear blackface would make them less attractive to viewers.

After the murder in Alabama in 1963 of a 35-year-old white postal worker who was on a protest march against segregation in the American South, *That Was the Week That Was* performed a sketch in which Millicent Martin, dressed as Uncle Sam, sang a parody of *I Wanna Go Back to Mississippi* ('Where the scent of blossom kissed the evening breeze/Where the Mississippi mud/ Seems to mingle with the blood/Of the niggers that are hanging from the branches of the trees.') She was accompanied by minstrel singers in blackface ('... we hate all the darkies and the Catholics and the Jews/Where we welcome any man/Who is strong and white and belongs to the Ku Klux Klan'), parodying the *Black and White*

Minstrel Show's trivialisation of racism in the United States, particularly in the Deep South.

Political pressure from anti-racist organisations like the Campaign Against Racial Discrimination eventually succeeded in persuading the BBC to cancel the programme in 1978, although a stage version ran for ten years thereafter at the Victoria Palace Theatre in London. This was followed by tours of Australia and New Zealand where the show had broken box office records in the 1960s and where it still retained its popularity. *The Black and White Minstrel Show* is now widely regarded as a huge embarrassment but it must not be forgotten by those who wish to see the reality of the history of those times that it was enduringly popular and as such must be taken as a valuable indicator of the temperature of racial relations in Great Britain.

Another ratings winner on television throughout the 1960s had been the *Miss World* pageant and of course it too was being subjected to complaints that it was out of date in the era of what was generally known as Women's Lib. It was indeed a cattle market but at the time it was regarded by many women as well as men and teenage boys as 'unmissable' television. In the 1970 event, taking their cue from Peter Hain's direct action, activists from the Women's Liberation movement threw flour bombs at the host, Bob Hope. He was momentarily stunned, panicked perhaps by not having immediate access to his team of joke writers for an instant response. It was, after all, difficult for him to understand what had happened to his cultural pillars. He had been booed by the boys in Vietnam for telling them that their President wanted to bring them home as soon as possible and now in London, the seat of the British monarchy, the country of tradition and formal courtesy, he was being attacked and vilified on national television by a bunch of crazy women just for telling jokes and entertaining people who wanted to watch a parade of beautiful girls earnestly notifying the audience and judges, whilst dressed in a figure-hugging swimsuit, how much they wanted to travel and help mankind. 'Anyone who would want to break up an affair as wonderful as this has got to be on some kind of dope', was the best Hope could come up with afterwards.

The 1970 pageant had been controversial before the flour bombing. Tom Lehrer had recently sung a song of his own composition about nuclear proliferation climaxing in the line, 'South Africa wants two, that's right/One for the blacks and one for the whites'. Now the Miss World contest proudly boasted two women contestants from South Africa. Miss South Africa was white and Miss Africa South was black. It was ridiculous but one has to say that it was an advance on the South African Cricket Association's selection of an all-white cricket team that never had any intention of including a black cricketer, however talented. If it was clumsy, which it was, it could be said that Eric and Julia Morley, the husband and wife team that ran the contest, were at least trying to do their best, however small, to right a historical wrong.

Unfortunately, this brave but doomed attempt at equality, or at least impartiality, aroused no cheers from the militant Young Liberals who regarded it as neither equal nor impartial but merely yet another endorsement of apartheid which seems on the face of it a harsh judgement but then they weren't much interested in nuances. They had no comment to make on the fact that the contest was actually won by Jennifer Hosten, Miss Grenada, who became the first black winner nor on the fact that the now infamous Miss Africa South was the runner-up. As Brian Viner points out in his excellent book on television in the 1970s, Nice to See It, To See it Nice, Sir Eric Gairy, the Prime Minister of Grenada was one of the judges, which must surely have produced a conflict of interests. Sir Eric was eventually to be swept from office in a coup after being accused of human rights abuses and corruption though not necessarily for the charge of voting for his own candidate. His other claim to immortality was his gallant but vain attempt to persuade the United Nations to investigate the dangers of an invasion of the Earth by extra-terrestrials who would arrive in flying saucers. His early years had presumably been marked by regular cinema attendance when Hollywood B pictures of the 1950s were playing. On a slightly more serious note it should be noted that the Miss World contest attracted enormous viewing figures for a single programme and maintained its position at the top of the ratings for pretty much the same 20 years that The Black and White Minstrel Show was on the air. The spectacular success of both these programmes gives an insight into the reality of Britain in 1970.

For most of England the most important event of the year was its football team's defence of the World Cup. Since the heady days of July 1966 when England won the World Cup for the only time in its history, the country had revelled in the success of its sport and culture while being uncomfortably aware of the fragility of its economy. When Labour came into office in October 1964, the outgoing Chancellor of the Exchequer, Reggie Maudling, allegedly smiled apologetically at the incoming Chancellor, Jim Callaghan, and said, 'Sorry about the money, old man. I'm afraid it's all gone.' It might be an apocryphal story but it was true enough. Throughout most of the next six years the government was buffeted by one economic crisis after another, with the weakness of sterling a constant factor, the monthly balance of payments deficit invariably heading in the wrong direction, labour relations worsening and gross domestic product falling for much of the time.

A crippling seamen's strike followed within days of Bobby Moore being photographed on the shoulders of his team-mates holding aloft the Jules Rimet trophy. The following year, despite vowing consistently not to do so, the government devalued sterling from an exchange rate of $2.80 to the £ to $2.40. Harold Wilson's attempts to explain what had happened to the British people included the unfortunate but enduring phrase about the value of 'the pound in your pocket or purse' being unchanged, which was simply untrue. The Labour Party's core belief of tax and spend, of increasing public services whilst ensuring a fairer tax system for all was hard to spot as the government lurched from one economic crisis to the next. Cutting public services and pursuing a policy of austerity was anathema to Labour voters and indeed to the Labour government itself but events that were out of their control dictated otherwise. 'The spirit of 1940', otherwise known as 'the Dunkirk spirit', was invoked as the 'I'm Backing Britain' campaign gathered temporary velocity. This involved typists and other badly paid workers contributing an hour or so of their labour for no financial reward. Admirable as it was, the campaign made little impact on the balance of payments deficit.

There was something about the calendar year 1970, apart from the fact that it was the first year of a new decade, that suggested the end of one era and the start of another. Nothing better symbolised the end of the 1960s than the break-up of the Beatles. When they first emerged in their full mop top glory in 1963 and even more when they were controversially awarded MBEs in 1965, they were seen by what for the sake of argument we'll identify as those who wanted to continue to play cricket with South Africa, as being harbingers of the doom of civilisation. The barbarians appeared to be at the gates but they were wearing distinctively neat hairstyles and distinctively neat suits. Looking back at the Beatles in 1963 from the vantage point of 1970 they appeared to be harmless and family friendly. If teenage girls wanted to scream and throw jelly babies at them while they sang their tuneful melodies, as harmless as 'I Wanna Hold Your Hand', that was surely easy to indulge. By 1970 they were a disunited bunch, split by warring factions, George Harrison embracing Eastern mysticism and John Lennon seemingly every kind of left-wing protest.

They retreated from touring after playing one last concert in Candlestick Park in San Francisco in 1966. It was no longer enjoyable or creatively satisfying. Music making in the studio allowed them to experiment with different instruments and orchestrations and their music reached a new level of richness and sophistication but after a while even that palled for them. Although none of the four was yet 30 years old, they were looking for new challenges and they didn't look or sound like the group that had conquered the world in a few short months. They had gone to India in search of spiritual peace and failed to find it, they had lost their manager Brian Epstein in 1967 and they had alienated large sections of the public, particularly in America, when John Lennon announced that the Beatles were more popular than Jesus. George Harrison wanted recognition for his own songs, John Lennon was more interested in working and living with Yoko Ono than with the Beatles and Ringo Starr took a leading part alongside Peter Sellers in The Magic Christian and fancied himself as a comedy film star. They were all fed up with Paul McCartney harassing them to turn up on time at the studio and to sign contracts for future recordings and concerts as the Beatles.

The purity of the talented four music makers was tainted by these internal rows, constant disputes with and about girlfriends and the unholy mess they made of their commercial lives when, after the death of Epstein, they created Apple Corps, the company name given to a series of financial misadventures. Apple had a boutique on Baker Street which attracted vast crowds, most of whom disappeared with the stock without bothering to pay for any of it and it shut down in six months. The overall business was a mismanaged shambles with its headquarters a haven for the eccentric and the quite frankly barmy. It was a good place to drink alcohol and do drugs. In desperation the four agreed to employ Allan Klein who had made his reputation as a ruthless accountant serving the interests of the Rolling Stones. Klein immediately sacked much of the Apple staff, most of whom were friends of the Beatles.

Although the creative achievement of *Sgt. Pepper's Lonely Hearts Club Band* in 1967 saw the Beatles at the height of their creative powers, there followed the nonsense of *The Magical Mystery Tour* song and television film and a general sense that nothing was worth the effort any longer. The *White Album* in 1968 suggested a significant falling away from the previous year's masterpiece. Lennon was living in a haze of LSD and heroin-induced alienation, listening to Yoko Ono's comments when recording in the studio and not to his other three colleagues. Lennon also started to be much more vocal and aggressive in his criticism of McCartney's more traditional melodies and they all seemed to stop listening to George Martin, their talented producer at the EMI Studios in Abbey Road.

Where Cynthia Lennon had accepted that she had no place in the public life of the Beatles, Yoko Ono was not someone who was prepared to hide her light under a bushel. It was felt that the Japanese woman drove a wedge between John and the others by encouraging Lennon's potential for narcissistic self-absorption. Paul McCartney's much publicised romance with Linda Eastman put a further strain on the group's unity, particularly when it became evident that the women didn't get on and their partners felt the understandable need to support the other. It was reported that the two men came close to trading blows on a number of occasions. The other Beatles objected to seeing Yoko Ono through the glass in the recording gallery and George Harrison was reported to have objected violently when she deliberately and with malice aforethought ate one of George's chocolate digestive biscuits. It was clearly all going to end in tears. When John Lennon and Yoko Ono formed the Plastic Ono Band and performed to enthusiastic applause at the Toronto Rock and Roll Revival in September 1969 he knew for sure that his future creative life was never again going to be with the Beatles.

On 10 April 1970, the *Daily Mirror* published a feature interview with Paul McCartney (who wanted to publicise the following week's release of his new solo album *McCartney*) in which he told a shocked world that he was leaving the Beatles, though in reality he was the only one of the four who wanted to continue and the Beatles had already in effect left him first. The fans by and large blamed Yoko Ono since none of the Fab Four could ever have committed so wilful an act of desecration. *Let It Be*, which had been recorded during the making of the *White Album* the previous year, was released in March 1970; it was to be their last single and it marked the end of a unique collaboration. In January 1969 George Harrison had written in his diary an entry of Adrian Mole proportions – 'Got up. Had breakfast. Left the Beatles.' Its triteness was a relief because when it was publicly announced in April the following year this seemingly banal act inevitably unleashed a torrent of emotional over-reaction. But then the Beatles were not just a random group of four musicians.

William Mann in *The Times* accorded the songs of Lennon and McCartney the respect he would normally grant to *Die Schöne Mullerin* and *Die Winterreise*, the great song cycles of Franz Schubert. It might have sounded ineffably pretentious to many *Times* readers but their very longevity is a tribute to the way in which they revolutionised the world of popular music. Mann's equivalent in *The Guardian* was Edward Greenfield and in his obituary of the group he wrote of sitting down and listening to all their LPs in chronological order, a Liverpudlian version of Wagner's Ring cycle. He came up with much the same critical conclusion as Mann although in more restrained language. He couldn't help observing, however, that Leonard Bernstein did not stint in his praise for the Beatles and that their creativity around the time of *Sgt. Pepper* was now being 'treated with a reverence normally reserved for late Beethoven'.

It wasn't just the quality and the variety of their songs. The Beatles maintained their popularity even as their creativity was pushing the boundaries of what pop music was. The seven years they spent at the top of their profession was a lifetime in a business that frequently demonstrated its capacity to swallow and dispose of bands after one or two hits. Popular taste is fickle and to maintain the devotion of their fans in the way they did from 1963 to 1970, despite their transformation from ostensibly cheerful, smiling and uncomplicated young men from the suburbs of Liverpool to rather more controversial icons for a disaffected generation was a remarkable achievement. The official end of the Beatles in April 1970 meant for popular culture the end of the musical revolution of the 1960s.

There was a ray of comfort for devastated Beatles fans who were also football fans. The World Cup finals in Mexico were fast approaching and the good news was that England were sending there a squad of players that was arguably better than the squad that had won the cup four years earlier. The national enthusiasm that greeted the progress of the England team to the semi-finals of the 2018 World Cup in Russia exceeded the interest evoked by the England football team in 1970 but in 1970 media coverage was still in the relative Dark Ages. There was less hysterical jingoism on display and more deeply felt patriotism. The generation that had lived through the war years and austerity still formed the bulk of the population and they did not display their emotions with quite the same promiscuity as is currently apparent in public life.

Football was important in the lives of hundreds of thousands of Britons but it did not warrant the media overkill that it was eventually to attract. Cricket was still the summer game. Some boys played football in the park during the cricket season but not many. A street lamp post or a litter bin or a tree trunk served as a perfectly acceptable alternative to three stumps and from somewhere an old bat and a tennis ball could usually be found. The controversy over the South Africa tour severely embarrassed many people who loved their cricket but recognised that playing against an all-white South Africa team coming from the land of apartheid posed significant problems.

The April 1970 edition of *The Cricketer* was edited by John Arlott, as the regular editor, E.W. Swanton, was on tour with the Duke of Norfolk's XI in the West Indies. The acting editor warned that cricket and politics were now inextricably linked and the attitude of the cricket authorities was making political radicals where they least expected.

Many of the opponents of apartheid who believe they can effectively protest against that political theory by boycotting of, or peaceful demonstrations against matches of South African rugby or cricket teams, are enthusiasts for those games. For many of them cricket has now been given, for the first time, an antipathetic political image ... The Council ... has set at risk a substantial proportion of public support and goodwill not only for the coming season but for the entire future.

Clive van Ryneveld, a hero of comic book proportions, politician, lawyer, Rhodes Scholar at Oxford, selected for England at rugby union yet captain of South Africa against England on their 1956/57 cricket tour, wrote a considered piece in the same edition based on his belief that,

> senior coloured cricketers were in favour of the tour continuing. Although opposed to apartheid, and committed to the principle that rights and opportunities should be granted on the basis of merit, irrespective of race, I disagree with those who have called for the cancellation of the tour. I do not think the South African cricketers should be held responsible for the policy of apartheid. Nor do I think that calling off the tour will do the cause of multi-racialism in South Africa any good.
>
> We have an outstanding team at present, probably our best ever, and they will be coming to England with a very convincing series against Australia behind them. If the non-whites here are in favour of the tour and the Springboks are happy to play against cricketers of any colour and D'Oliveira is prepared to play against them, surely it would not be necessary to play behind barbed wire.

Van Ryneveld was a member of the Progressive Party who had long taken a principled stand against apartheid. Tour protesters, while convinced that Arlott was right, should have been aware that not all supporters of the tour were therefore white supremacists and believers in apartheid.

It was a relief for English sports lovers to turn to football which appeared on the surface to be thankfully free of such overt politics. Nobody started a campaign to prevent the England football team from playing against Soviet Russia with its lengthy list of human rights abuses and people took a quiet pride in the achievements of the England football team managed by Sir Alf Ramsey and captained by Bobby Moore. Despite being football's world champions, the England players were a modest bunch. Gordon Banks, Bobby Charlton and Bobby Moore were all world class players but, apart from the occasional advert or television commercial, their appearances in the newspapers were confined to the back pages or the sports programmes on television. If they were celebrities by dint of their considerable achievements they did not comport themselves in the manner in which modern celebrities now behave.

The 1969/70 football season was shaped to allow England as much time to prepare for the World Cup as 42 First Division games and an unrestricted number of FA Cup replays would allow. The FA Cup Final was scheduled to be played at Wembley on 11 April but the match finished in a 2-2 draw and the replay at Old Trafford could not be arranged until 29 April, such were the commitments of the two finalists, Chelsea and Leeds United. Peter Hain had always been an enthusiastic player and follower of sport which people who opposed him politically found impossible to believe. When he came to England, because he lived in West London, he had decided to adopt Chelsea as his football club. It was the days of Dave Sexton as manager who had inherited a club with promising players like Peter Osgood and Alan Hudson when he had taken over from Tommy Docherty in 1967. The telephone in the Hains' small family flat in Putney rang constantly, particularly as the start of the cricket tour approached, so it was a major decision for Hain to refuse to answer it during the infamous FA Cup Final replay at the end of April.

> I am and always have been and still am a mad keen fanatical Chelsea supporter. At the end of April 1970 when the STST was at its height I took the phone off the hook in order to watch the replay of the FA Cup Final when Chelsea beat Leeds. I didn't go to many Chelsea matches that season but I went whenever I had a Saturday off.

Leeds United had won the league championship the previous year and as England's sole European Cup representatives, they were the only side engaged in the final stages of a war on three fronts. On Saturday 21 March Leeds won 2-1 away at Wolverhampton Wanderers. On Saturday 4 April they beat Burnley 1-0 at Elland Road. In the space of those two weeks Leeds had to play a total of eight vital matches including two hard fought FA Cup semi-finals against Manchester United, five league matches as they battled with Everton to retain their title and a European Cup semi-final first leg against Celtic. That match at Elland Road on Wednesday 1 April which was lost 0-1 was followed 24 hours later by a drawn league game away at West Ham United. In the end, perhaps inevitably, they won none of the competitions they had striven so hard for over the previous eight months. Norman Hunter, Allan Clarke, Terry Cooper and Jack Charlton did well to stagger up the steps of the plane let alone play in the thin air and the brutal heat they were about to experience.

When the draw was made in the middle of January for the group stages, Desmond Hackett in the *Daily Express* was not alone in proclaiming with back page certainty 'I'm Backing England', pointing out that he had also done so in 1966 'before a foot was raised in anger'. His cheery jingoistic optimism was not entirely misplaced for English football was in rude good health. The 22 players who made up the party that arrived in Guadalajara for the first of the group games were drawn from ten different league clubs. Between 1959 and 1977 no club retained the title of league champions. In those 18 years the First Division title was won by no fewer than 11 different clubs. Ironically, cricket was more predictable. Surrey had won the County Championship seven years in a row from 1952 to 1958 and Yorkshire had won it seven times between 1959 and 1968. The discussion that accompanied the start of a new football season was more interesting than it became in the era of the Premier League precisely because the destination of the title was so difficult to predict. Alf Ramsey was frequently accused of preferring hard work to flair but the 1970 squad now contained Peter Osgood and Colin Bell as well as Bobby Charlton and Gordon Banks. It was the perfect blend of youth and experience. As the domestic season drew to an exciting climax the prospect of Ramsey's England conquering the football world again, even in a very different climate, was regarded as entirely possible.

It is ironic to think that in 1970 football offered a stable, ordered and successful image whilst cricket was being torn apart at the seams by the intransigence of the Cricket Council and its supporters on the one hand and the bellicosity and determination exhibited by those who wished the South Africa tour to be cancelled on the other. At the start of April, as the Leeds United players were staggering round the country not quite sure which opposition they were playing that day, the Young Liberals reiterated their support for direct action. Their militant chairman Louis Eaks was ousted from power by the more moderate Tony Greaves but almost immediately, Greaves and four other leaders of the Young Liberals including Peter Hain announced their intention of proceeding with their stated objective of wrecking the South African tour and warned of the hard line they were taking on South Africa in general. Greaves made it clear that his election would in no way soften their stance and that their policy was 'to stop this tour by direct action. The cricket season will be chaotic.' They would disrupt every match the South Africans were due to play by 'non-violent action'. It was still a threat. 'The abject failure of the MCC to understand the issues involved let alone respond to moral pressures leaves us no alternative,' he warned.

The same week David Sheppard set up the Fair Cricket Campaign. It was greeted by the supporters of the tour as a split in the ranks of the opposition but the fact is that there was always a broad spectrum of opinion on both sides of the argument. Hain understood perfectly well that his own tactics of direct action were not to the taste of everyone and particularly not to the taste of the Bishop of Woolwich. David Sheppard's determination to stop the tour going ahead was just as strong as Peter Hain's but he did not believe that digging up the pitch at Lord's or spray painting Wilf Wooller's car was the best way to succeed. On the other hand, Wilf Wooller and the right-wing press and their readers were much more likely to be fearful of Hain's direct action than they would be at the prospect of Sheppard's stated determination to hold a large protest meeting outside Lord's on all five days of the Test match against South Africa that was scheduled to take place there on 20 June.

The campaign has no intention of encouraging violence to further its aims. By its massive, passive demonstration outside the Lord's cricket ground on 20 June it will demonstrate to the authorities and to the wider public the strong opposition that exists among people in all walks of life who normally do not involve themselves in the more conventional type of protest.

The combination of the aggressive behaviour of STST and the Young Liberals on the one hand and the more temperate behaviour of an assorted collection of MPs and organisations like the Church and the TUC was likely to prove highly effective. This much was now becoming clear to cricket authorities.

Kent County Cricket Club solemnly announced that at the conclusion of its Annual General Meeting on 29 April, a special meeting would be held to discuss the resolution that 'The club's players shall not take part in any matches against the South Africans in 1970'. The Pakistan Board of Control for Cricket advised Pakistani cricketers playing in the County Championship like Majid Khan at Glamorgan, Asif Iqbal at Kent, Mushtaq Mohammed at Northants and Younis Ahmed and Intikhab Alam at Surrey, that they should not take the field if their counties were to proceed with their scheduled matches against South Africa.

It wasn't as if the South African PR machine was rolling along to any great effect. In early April the world got to learn that the Vorster government had now banned Africans from all white-collar jobs, however lowly, in the cities. From 3 May, Africans would no longer be able to work as clerks, typists, telephone operators, cashiers, receptionists, sales clerks and countermen. It was a ruling issued by the Ministry of the Interior that appeared to cut out the ground of the country's defenders from underneath their feet. It had been argued for some time that South Africa's industrial and economic expansion would force changes in its racial policies that would make them more acceptable to the rest of the world. A booming economy would require South Africa to offer more skilled and better-paying jobs to Africans, or so the theory had it.

Economic sanctions imposed on South Africa would cause the economy to contract and therefore remove the possibility of such employment for Africans. Increased trade would demand that some of the more onerous restrictions on non-whites would fall away

145

which meant that a booming South African economy, stimulated by trade with the outside world, would be of benefit to all South Africans. Currently, unemployment among white South Africans stood at less than 1% and indeed there was a shortage of white labour. The government was embarking on a campaign to attract more white immigration to fill the jobs it was restricting to whites only. In 1969, 40,000 immigrants from Britain, Holland, Germany, Belgium, Austria, Switzerland, Portugal and Italy arrived in the country. The impact of the new law was likely to mean the loss of over 10,000 black jobs in Johannesburg alone. The argument for retaining links with South Africa, economic, sporting or political, was getting harder to advance with any conviction.

Newspapers started to agonise as to whether they should report the tour at all. John Arlott had made his position very clear. He had not been to cover the England tours in South Africa in 1956/57 and 1964/65 after his experiences on the 1948/49 tour when he witnessed at first hand the impact of the recent introduction of apartheid laws. However, he earned what he always thought was a precarious living as a freelance journalist and after the *Any Questions* fiasco of 1950 he had never taken for granted that his position as a commentator on *Test Match Special* was automatically guaranteed.

On the other hand he had broadcast his commentary on *Test Match Special* during the 1960 and 1965 tours of England by all-white South Africa sides. In the wake of the D'Oliveira affair in 1968 and the widespread controversy over the forthcoming visit, he now had to decide not only whether or not to broadcast but whether or not to decline to cover for *The Guardian*, where he was the chief cricket correspondent, any matches played by South Africa. He did not feel secure in his seasonal employment with the BBC but recognised that much of his other freelance journalistic work depended on the continuation of that broadcasting contract. If he withdrew voluntarily there was no guarantee that he would be rehired in 1971 by the *TMS* producer Michael Tuke-Hastings, who, as his successor Peter Baxter has observed, didn't very much like cricket or John Arlott. Fortunately for him, his newspaper employer was going through similar ethical struggles. An editorial on 11 April demonstrated how it was preparing itself to act.

The tour has inevitably become more of a political than a sporting event but it must be reported as both. The demonstrators will have a prominent but deserved place in the news pages: so will their arguments which are worth support. The cricket, as cricket ought to appear, as it will, in the sports pages. To refuse to report [the matches] because one dislikes the players or detests what they stand for would be the thin end of a dangerous censorship. Cricket played behind barbed wire or guarded by police with dogs is perhaps not cricket. That is what the demonstrators want to achieve – and good luck to them. The Cricket Council should never have persisted with its invitation to South Africa ... to accept a South African team here this summer would be to condone segregation and racialism. But it would be wrong to refuse to report what happens in the matches – on the field as well as in the crowd.

This argument was not universally acclaimed even by *Guardian* readers, many of whom wrote to the editor to express their dissatisfaction with what they regarded as obfuscation. The newspaper had a long and honourable tradition of standing up for the causes in which it believed even when they were at odds with that of the political establishment and possibly the general public. It had provided no jingoistic applause for the British army's behaviour in the Boer War and, like its sister paper *The Observer*, it had taken a stance against Anthony Eden in the early days of Suez.

Arlott's negotiations with the BBC reached a successful conclusion by 17 April when he announced in a newspaper in an influential article headed 'Why I Am Off The Air' the reasons why he would not be part of the *Test Match Special* team.

For personal reasons I shall not broadcast on the matches of the South African cricket tour of England, arranged for 1970. The BBC has accepted my decision with understanding and an undertaking that my standing with them will not be affected by it. [*Here is Arlott's employment anxiety revealing itself. That sentence must have been included to remind the BBC not to break its promise when the commentary teams for 1971 were being assembled.]* Apartheid is detestable to me, and I would always oppose it …

A successful tour would offer comfort and confirmation to a completely evil regime. To my mind, the Cricket Council, acting on behalf of British cricket, has failed fairly to represent those British people – especially cricketers – who genuinely abominate apartheid.

The council might have determined, and been granted, terms which would have demonstrated its declared disapproval of apartheid. It did not do so; nor gave the slightest indication of a will to do so. To persist with the tour seems to me a social, political and cricketing error. If I were a supporter of apartheid I would feel the same. It seems to me destined to failure at all levels, with the game of cricket the ultimate and inevitable sufferer. If it should 'succeed' to the extent of being completed, what is the outcome to be: a similarly contentious tour four years hence? …

The terms of the BBC's charter do not permit expression of editorial opinion. *[The* Any Questions *scar had still not permanently healed.]* It would not be professional or polite to disagree with my fellow commentators on the significance of the tour within the hearing of listeners. It therefore seems to me unfair, on both sides, for me to broadcast about the tour in a manner uncritical of its major issues, while retaining the right to be critical of them in this newspaper.

It provoked a large postbag, a small fraction of which appeared on the Letters page of *The Guardian*, expressing a variety of views from those who would not read the reports if they were published to those who would read the reports but not go to the matches. A Research Fellow in African Economic Studies at the University of Leeds disparaged Arlott's argument, which he accused of being naïve, that the South African cricketers had demonstrated their opposition to apartheid simply by playing cricket with and against black cricketers and enjoying the experience. At no point had the Pollocks, Goddard, Lindsay and the rest actually had the courage to come out and state categorically that they abhorred the official policy of their own country. He criticised Ali Bacher's comment that as he was a Jew, people could be sure there was no hint of racial discrimination in the selection of the touring party. No South African cricketer had ever demonstrated his opposition to apartheid by refusing to take part in the all-white Test matches they played. Their failure to make any such statement or take any significant action must lead to the supposition that the Test cricketers of South Africa tacitly condone the policy of apartheid. There was some suggestion that although Arlott had not reported on the 1956/57 and 1964/65 MCC tours to South Africa he had still managed to bring himself to report and broadcast on all the tours previously made to England by an all-white South African side. Where was the consistency in his attitude?

Most of Arlott's own postbag was more sympathetic to his plight but he did receive letters criticising him severely. According to Arlott's son, Tim, the most unpleasant of them was written by the former England captain Peter May, a sorry state of affairs indeed for those who held different political opinions but still recalled with nostalgic affection the power and grace of May's on drives. May was held in great regard by many people, not just for his self-evident skill at the crease but for his decency as a man. On the issue of South Africa he appeared to become uncharacteristically intemperate, as his attitude to both John Arlott and David Sheppard revealed. His father-in-law was Harold Gilligan, who, like his brother Arthur, played for Sussex and England. Gilligan was a man who, to put it politely, was a man of right-wing views and it is entirely possible that May's response to Sheppard and Arlott was influenced by Harold Gilligan's support for South Africa.

The *Jewish Chronicle* joined the list of those publications to voice direct disapproval of the tour. In an article headlined *Jew Boycott Jew* it called on Jewish cricket fans to stay away from matches in which South Africa was to take part. Given the fact that the captain of the South African side, Ali Bacher, was Jewish, indeed, the first ever Jew to captain any Test side, this entailed a major sacrifice from Jews who did not have the opportunity very often to see any of their co-religionists playing top level sport. 'Peaceful abstention will demonstrate our disapproval of apartheid in sport and may induce South Africa's leadership to reconsider their racial policies.' Presumably, Jeremy Corbyn's copy of the *Jewish Chronicle* wasn't delivered that week.

Journalists of all shades of political opinion found the issue of whether or not to report the tour troubling. At their meeting in Harrogate, the National Union of Journalists, while expressing unanimous opposition to apartheid, decided by a large majority that they would go ahead and report the tour. No motion was tabled calling for the tour to be cancelled but one that sought to boycott such reporting of it had been proposed by Paul Foot and backed by the Book and Magazine branch and the Central London branch which were the two largest branches in the union. The ironic parallels with the public agonising by the Cricket Council seemed to be lost on them at the time. However, the fundamental precept was that the news had to be reported. To decide deliberately not to cover the tour would be to condone self-censorship which was anathema to all journalists. The divisions in the union were symptomatic of the wide diversity of opinions on what to do about the tour, despite the general condemnation of apartheid.

Meanwhile, the Stop the Seventy Tour campaign was promising direct action at cricket games in which the South Africans were not playing. On 5 April Peter Hain announced that the first games of the three-day County Championship season, which were to start as was traditionally the case on the first Saturday in May, would be targeted. Demonstrators would be found outside Lord's for Middlesex's game against Hampshire and outside The Oval for the match between Surrey and Northamptonshire. Hain had despaired of ever getting the cricket authorities to see the South Africa tour as a moral issue and decided that he would have to cast the net wider and attract the support of traditional cricket enthusiasts who would attend County Championship matches as a matter of course, particularly on a Saturday, and who might be persuaded to join the campaign against the South African tour. If traditional cricket supporters with their *Wisden*s, binoculars, flasks of tea and fish paste sandwiches started to let MCC know that the tour should be cancelled on moral grounds, it would be harder for the cricket authorities to pretend that the protesters were simply a bunch of long-haired, dissolute, unwashed student layabouts.

STST was joined by the West Indian Campaign Against Apartheid Cricket. Its spokesman, Jeff Crawford, said that the most important thing was to offer the West Indian cricket supporters a choice. They could shout themselves hoarse outside cricket grounds or they could simply refuse to watch the South Africa Test matches on television. Learie Constantine, now Baron Constantine of Nelson (for whom he had played with such distinction in the Lancashire League during the 1930s), and a member of the Race Relations Board, called on all West Indians living in Britain to support the demonstrations against the tour. 'I think the MCC were wrong to invite them back. I could support any action against the tour. It could be disastrous for race relations in this country to invite the South Africans.'

At the same time, David Sheppard and his followers were firmly separating themselves from both the Stop the Seventy Tour and the Anti-Apartheid Movement because they did not agree with the proposed objective which would interfere with the right of cricketers to play matches against whomever they liked. Sheppard told the press on 14 April at the Travellers Club that he would host a meeting of all sides of the opposition to the tour. These included Jack Straw, then president of the National Union of Students, immigrant leaders, government ministers, Vic Feather, the general secretary of the TUC and the director of the previous year's film version of *Oh! What a Lovely War*, Richard Attenborough. It was truly a ministry of all the talents.

The widening of the protest movement in this way increased the likelihood of violence for all the fact that Hain had been consistent and explicit about his own lack of enthusiasm for direct action that involved violence. However, he also knew from his own experience to say nothing of the experience of the Civil Rights protesters in the United States that passive non-violence did not preclude violence perpetrated by the outraged opposition. While it was unlikely that Gubby Allen and Billy Griffith would be found on the streets of St John's Wood wielding baseball bats against people peacefully carrying placards, everyone knew what had happened on the recent rugby tour and there was a strong likelihood of civil disorder of some kind. For a government that was planning an election to be held in the near future this was not a welcome prospect.

On 16 April, Harold Wilson was interviewed by a panel of journalists for the weekly Thames Television current affairs series *This Week*. During the course of the programme the question of the South Africa tour came up and Wilson, possibly to the surprise of other politicians who expected him to hedge his bets, let it be known that if the tour went ahead, he believed that 'people should feel free to demonstrate against it although not by sneaky things like shining mirrors in the batsmen's eyes'. He criticised MCC for issuing the invitation and called the decision of the Cricket Council's decision in February to proceed with the tour 'very ill judged'. 'It is not the first time I have said that if the South Africans behave as they do with apartheid in the matter of sport, they really have put themselves outside the pale of civilised cricket and civilised everything else,' although he conceded that they should be allowed to play their matches and not be disrupted by violence or digging up pitches. In answer to a question asking if he would be going to any matches he replied, 'Good heavens, no!' It was a remarkably bold statement in the context of the times but Wilson had always felt strongly about the iniquities of apartheid, hence his stand against selling arms to South Africa despite its obvious economic benefits to a fragile economy. Dennis Brutus, president of the South African Non-Racial Olympic Committee (SANROC) described the Prime Minister's statement as a heartening encouragement which cleared the way for non-violent demonstrations and recognised the moral justice of the anti-apartheid campaign.

The impact at Lord's of the Prime Minister telling the country on ITV that 'the Cricket Council should not feel they are being subject to blackmail' but then doing exactly that was immediate and antagonistic. The gentlemen in the Long Room had previously prided themselves on the impeccably restrained manner in which they had conducted themselves. They had sought counsel's opinion to establish that they were proceeding lawfully and they had explained that very courteously to the Home Secretary. They believed that they had every right to expect that the government would support the maintenance of law and order when protesters were using violence to disrupt it. To be publicly chastised in this way on television by a man for whom they were never going to vote anyway was felt to be an outrage.

A letter to the *Daily Telegraph* on 20 April from Brigadier E. Rait-Kerr of North Warnborough in Hampshire gave vent to these feelings.

The Government should tell us what advice, if any, it gave MCC prior to the decision being made to hold the tour. If, as I believe, no advice was offered, surely it would be far better from all points of view, if Government spokesmen, particularly Ministers, were to refrain from comment at this stage. According to your reports the Prime Minister then went on to advocate demonstrations. We are only too well aware how easily peaceful and lawful demonstrations can degenerate into hooliganism and if this occurs (I nearly said 'when') I submit, Sir, that Mr Wilson cannot escape his share of blame.

Brigadier Rait-Kerr was no doubt related to Colonel R.S. Rait-Kerr who had been Secretary of MCC from 1936 to 1952.

The reaction from the Rt Hon Sir Peter Maudslay Hordern, the Conservative MP for Horsham, was predictably similar. He accused the Prime Minister of inciting demonstrators to interfere with the peaceful enjoyment of millions by saying that the MCC had made a big mistake by inviting the South African team. He went on to ask a perfectly reasonable question.

How is it that we can give such an effusive welcome to an official Russian delegation and allow the choir of the Red Army, that instrument of the suppression of freedom, to perform here? If there is one thing worse than racial discrimination, of which Russia, Kenya, Uganda and South Africa are all guilty it is hypocrisy and Mr Wilson is guilty of that.

Richard Crossman, writing his diary, entirely approved of the Prime Minister's actions. 'Harold and Jim have handled this issue extremely adroitly in a way that is simultaneously liberal, fair minded and pro-sport.' Mr Wilson himself did not bother to respond to the accusation. He had other matters on his mind.

The Budget of 14 April 1970 was expected to be a conventional piece of pre-election grandstanding. Traditionally, Chancellors of the Exchequer, most recently Derick Heathcote-Amory in 1959 and Reginald Maudling in 1964, had courted popularity with a Budget that gave all voters something to feel positive about before they cast their ballots. Roy Jenkins, presumably with the agreement of the Prime Minister, decided not to do that. The economy was only just starting to show signs of strength after the traumas of devaluation in November 1967 and he would therefore not stoop to what the media always called a 'give-away Budget'. He made few significant changes apart from raising the personal allowances above which people started paying tax, which benefited two million of the most poorly paid. He reduced bank rates from 7.5% to 7% which marginally helped mortgage payers but otherwise the expected pre-election bonanza of tax cuts on alcohol, tobacco, petrol and vehicles failed to materialise.

It irritated Labour MPs but perhaps more importantly from Wilson's point of view it puzzled the Tories who had been prepared to issue a withering condemnation of the fiscally irresponsible Budget they had been expecting. The Tory press labelled the Budget an afternoon of anti-climax and disappointment. The *Daily Express* moaned,

> Oh what a let down! Here was the Commons assembled like a happy family waiting to hear something from its rich Uncle Roy Jenkins. What was it to be? A bottle of vintage port for Dad? A string of pearls for Mum? A load of shiny new toys for the kids? Alas for the illusion. The gift, when the Chancellor unwrapped it, was nothing like that. No port, no pearls, no toys. Just a fusty old promissory note tied up in strings an inch thick.

Maybe it was because the country was on that day gripped by the drama surrounding the fate of Apollo 13. After the triumph of the walk on the Moon nine months earlier this subsequent flight had gone wrong ('Houston, we have a problem') and the world held its collective breath as the three astronauts (not including Tom Hanks) struggled to return to the Earth's atmosphere. Maybe the country was infected with the relief that was felt all round the world when the astronauts splashed down safely in the sea.

To the surprise of most commentators, the political result of Jenkins's cautious non-election Budget was positive for Labour. The Budget, as measured by a Gallup poll conducted a week after it was delivered to the House of Commons, was judged the most popular for 15 years and in a Harris poll published in the *Daily Express* the same day, Labour was showing a lead over the Conservatives for the first time since devaluation in November 1967. Although Wilson had never lost his personal battle with Heath, the strangely asexual sailor with a love of music and a smile of bared teeth, the Labour government had recently won the support of only 35% of those polled by Harris compared with a 52% share for the Tories. Although that enormous lead had been gradually slipping over the previous 12 months there had been a marked swing to Labour in the past few weeks, greatly aided by Jenkins's studiedly non-partisan Budget. Now Marplan was predicting an overall majority for Labour of 20 seats if Wilson went to the country soon. It was by no means unanimous. A Gallup poll carried out for the *Daily Telegraph* was still showing the Conservatives with a respectable lead of 4.5% although that figure was down from the previous poll, and a National Opinion Poll in the *Daily Mail* at the end of April also showed a lead of 1.9% but that was 5.6% down on the lead the Tories had held seven weeks earlier and further confirmation of a trend that was showing a pronounced swing towards Labour. At the same time, Ted Heath's personal popularity also fell five points in the same time frame whereas Harold Wilson's own rating was at its highest since devaluation in November 1967.

The choice for Wilson's government was between an election either in June or in October. The danger of October was that while his standing in the polls might be rising, so, almost certainly, would be prices and the cost of living. It would give the Tories longer to counteract the current slump in their poll rating and the attendant danger of a summer of strikes would offset the gain that would come Labour's way by virtue of the fact that the 1970 election would be the first at which people aged between 18 and 21 would be permitted to vote. The balance of payments, the difference between what was received for exports and what was paid out for imports, could turn into a large deficit and people who had currently received the impression that the economy was finally stable might not be feeling so sanguine about their economic prospects in the autumn.

There were three negatives if the government opted for June. One was that the situation in Ulster, which had been in crisis for nearly a year, might deteriorate which would certainly be a problem for the government. The second was the World Cup. Harold Wilson, a long-time supporter of Huddersfield Town, was very aware that June was the month of the World Cup finals in Mexico and a bad performance by the England team would not aid his cause. The final was due to take place on 21 June. An election on the previous Thursday, 18 June, would take out the danger of England losing in the final but not losing in the quarter-finals or semi-finals, both of which were due to kick off on the Wednesday at 4pm. It couldn't take place on Thursday 11 June because that was the day England would be playing Czechoslovakia in the last of their group matches.

Although they had been drawn in the same group as Brazil it was anticipated by everyone that England would be able to dispatch both Romania on 2 June and Czechoslovakia to assure themselves of a quarter-final spot even if they were to lose to Brazil in the match on Sunday 7 June. Richard Crossman, the Secretary of State for Health and Social Services, wrote in his diaries, the first to be published with such candour by a recent cabinet minister, that Wilson was constantly badgering the Cabinet about the consequences of the World Cup and its impact on the date of the election. 'The risk of June is the World Cup, the risk of October is rising prices,' he wrote. It seems absurd now that the government was becoming as dependent on the scoring prowess of Francis Lee and Geoff Hurst as it was on ensuring the stability of wages and prices but that would be to ignore the fervent atmosphere that was building in the country throughout that spring. Until the week of the semi-final and final the atmosphere in the country in 1966 for the World Cup played on home soil was less fanatical than it was in the last two months preceding the start of the World Cup in Mexico in 1970.

The other problem for the government was the South Africa cricket tour. The tour matches were due to start at the beginning of June. Two weeks of violence and mayhem on the streets and outside and inside cricket grounds and pictures of police with riot shields in open combat with hundreds of demonstrators, replayed nightly on the BBC and ITN television news programmes, would be a disaster for the government. It would show the country that it hadn't the faintest idea how to maintain law and order or, alternatively and, equally damaging, it would convey the impression that it was condoning apartheid by the use of force, creating an unfortunate echo of the real events in South Africa itself. Either way it was an open goal for a Conservative Party that was licking its wounds after the revelation of the opinion polls and desperately looking for a way back into the race for political supremacy in an election that was fast approaching, whichever date the government finally decided upon. In fact it decided to wait until after the results of the local elections in May before coming to an irrevocable decision. If it was to be 18 June as many were speculating, England needed to still be in the World Cup which meant they had to be in the final for the government to gain from any reflected glory. It was a good job Alf Ramsey didn't know the detail of Cabinet discussions on the timing of the election date. He still had to reduce his squad from the 28 players announced at the end of March to the 22 who would fly to Mexico. And Harold Wilson thought he had problems.

CHAPTER SEVEN

APRIL/MAY 1970

O N St George's Day, 23 April 1970, the 1970 Cricket Tour Fund was launched by Lieutenant Colonel Charles Newman, VC, OBE, TD, DL, a hero of the commando raid on St Nazaire in the Second World War for which he was decorated with the Victoria Cross. In addition to these honours he was also a member of both Kent and Essex County Cricket Clubs. It was exactly the right time for such an Englishman to stand up and proclaim his belief in the traditional English virtues of patriotism, free speech and Test cricket divorced from the ugliness of the politics and life on the street in 1970.

His distinguished list of patrons included the Duke of Norfolk, the Duke of Beaufort, Viscount Portal, the Bishops of Bath & Wells and Leicester, Lord Wakefield, Judge Sir Carl Aarvold, Sir Peter Studd, the war hero Douglas Bader, Tony Lewis, captain of Glamorgan, M.J.C. Allom the president of MCC, A.V. Bedser, the chairman of the England selectors, (but not E.A. Bedser), Rachael Heyhoe, Gareth Edwards, the Welsh scrum half, Dai Rees the former captain of the British Ryder Cup team, Colin Cowdrey, the recently departed captain of England and Brian Close who had been rather more forcefully ejected from that position. Cowdrey charged with using blackmail those countries who threatened England with a sports boycott if the tour went ahead. Close spoke of coloured cricketers who had been warned they would not be allowed to return home if they played against South Africa. Much to this author's dismay, the list also included Joe Mercer, the manager of Manchester City.

Field Marshal Lord Montgomery, hero of El Alamein and a patron of Hampshire County Cricket Club, on the other hand refused to allow his name to be added to the list of patrons of the Tour Fund despite Newman's assurance that a quarter of the money raised would be set aside to foster cricket 'regardless of race, creed or colour', wherever it is played. Five others, presumably of similar distinction but whose names were not revealed, had been approached and had similarly declined.

The Fund declared two aims: to raise £200,000 to support the tour by providing resources to pay for police protection and stewarding arrangements and to utilise whatever was left in the fund after the conclusion of a successful tour to further the cause of multi-racial cricket in South Africa. Whether Newman was merely the front man for the cricket authorities or whether it was entirely his own proposal was never disclosed. What was immediately apparent was that the Cricket Council welcomed the initiative with open arms, particularly as it had already been forced to take out an expensive indemnity policy earlier that month which would provide £140,000 of cover should the tour be called off. The threat from the Labour government to force them to cancel the tour by saddling them with huge policing costs might be forestalled if Newman were to be successful. The largest early contribution was one of £3,000 donated by Geoffrey Poore, the erstwhile managing director of BSA motorcycles. His accompanying letter was typical of others which arrived at Lord's accompanying donations which were considerably smaller.

> I enclose this cheque in the knowledge that the cricket authorities, with the best of motives, have landed themselves in a lot of trouble, first with D'Oliveira and now because they quite rightly insist on going ahead with cricket against South Africa. I hope my donation will serve to bail you out, if only to buy a few miles of barbed wire.

MCC let it be known that thousands of small donations from the 'man and woman in the street' were pouring into Lord's on behalf of the 1970 Cricket Fund. After five days' post nearly 3,000 letters containing an estimated £15,000 had been received from these sources at Lord's alone. An over-excited press office babbled that such a sum took no account of monies handed into branches of banks all over the country or to individual county clubs. Equally excited, a press release informed supporters that the volume of correspondence had caused the Fund organisers to enlist the help of extra staff.

> Response to the Fund has come from every walk of life and every shade of opinion, including housewives, clergymen, teachers, old age pensioners, students etc. The aim of individual donations has ranged from well-wishers who want to make a contribution however small, to the largest donations received so far of £250. Lord's switchboard has been inundated with callers wishing to know where to send their contributions.

The general pattern of correspondence received with donations indicated to a proud MCC that contributors had strong views against racial discrimination and felt just as strongly that everyone in this country should be free to pursue a lawful activity without interference. The press office released some sample quotes from the letters that accompanied the cheques and bank notes.

> My reply to the left wing bias of BBC – particularly *The World at One*

> A great pleasure to counter the objectionable and unwarranted intrusion of politics into sport

> I spent many happy hours at Lord's and The Oval when my husband was alive. Wish I could send more

> All lovers of cricket and freedom must contribute – however much they dislike apartheid

> I care little for cricket but much for toleration

In the MCC archives there is a copy of a particularly unpleasant and racist pamphlet issued at this time by an organisation calling itself The Immigration Control Association which was based in Maidenhead, Berks. Headlined THE GREAT BETRAYAL: FACTS ON IMMIGRATION it suggested that words were used as weapons in a war directed against the Anglo-Saxon race. It lined up various phrases and castigated them as fiction, offering a factual 'translation' of them alongside. In its opinion the Race Relations Board would be better named the Agency for Coloured Aliens. 'Racial integration' was fictional and its factual equivalent was the 'Imposition of Coloured Aliens on the Defenceless British Native'. There was plenty more of the same but it cannot be emphasised too strongly that on both sides of this increasingly fractious and emotional debate there was a broad spectrum of opinion.

If that was the extreme end of one of the spectrums there were considerably more who occupied a position of tolerance, of 'live and let live', who just loved their cricket and living in a country where the vicious degradations of the reality of apartheid were almost unimaginable, they did not see the harm of playing against a friendly country's talented cricketers. None of these people approved of apartheid but they did not believe that sending South Africa into sporting isolation would lessen the iniquities of the policy whereas building bridges and maintaining such links might do so. John Woodcock puts it mildly.

> I thought that if we didn't keep going there and they didn't keep coming here nothing would ever change. Even the rebel tours helped to bring about the end of apartheid because the South Africans all felt so strongly about their sport.

Robin Marlar puts it a little more forcibly.

> From my point of view it was quite simple. I loathed the system but I knew the people who were trying to amend it and I felt they needed all the support, financial and otherwise, that could be given and outright opposition seemed to me to be totally negative and totally self-absorbed. I had a full-scale contempt for that brigade who believed in cutting off all contacts.

Like David Sheppard and many others on the moderate side of the opposing spectrum they abhorred violence of any kind. Whatever merits direct action had, however strongly people felt about apartheid, there was simply no excuse for protests on the streets that turned into violence or the sort of destructive actions which had taken place on county grounds in January and which were threatened as soon as the South Africans came out to play their first match.

Unfortunately, every time the Cricket Council took a step forward proclaiming that they were representing 'the will of the people' something happened that forced it to retreat. This time the blow really hurt because it emanated from Buckingham Palace which let MCC know that the Queen would not be making her traditional visit to Lord's to greet the players of both sides who lined up in front of the pavilion to shake hands. It was the only time a woman was allowed into the pavilion as MCC did not permit women to become members. The South African players would not receive their traditional invitation to attend the Queen for tea at Buckingham Palace either. No doubt there was a reluctance to embroil the Queen in politics as there always is when a contentious issue arises in which she is involved by virtue of her position as the monarch but the very fact of her refusal to meet the South Africans would have appalled the supporters of the tour who were almost certainly monarchists to a man and woman. This seemed to line the Queen up against her most loyal supporters and place her on the same side of the argument as the demon Hain.

The Queen has always taken her role as head of the Commonwealth extremely seriously and South Africa's decision to secede from the Commonwealth in March 1961 must have caused her some distress. The secession took place after a referendum was held in South Africa in October 1960, in which the all-white electorate was asked if it wished the country to become a republic: 52% replied in the affirmative. Dr Verwoerd, the Prime Minister of South Africa, wanted to honour the result of the referendum despite a wider desire to remain within the Commonwealth. He flew to London to make his case in front of the Conference of Commonwealth Prime Ministers in which he gave formal notice of his country's imminent intention of turning from a monarchy to a republic but was told in no uncertain terms that if South Africa no longer wished the Queen to be its head of state it could not remain in the Commonwealth. No backstop was proposed.

MCC tried to cover its embarrassment over this decision by the Palace by claiming it was their idea in the first place which, considering the Queen had never missed a Lord's Test in the previous 18 years of her reign, was hard to credit. Billy Griffith said, 'The committee does not wish to embarrass the Queen by suggesting that Her Majesty should come to Lord's and be a witness to a display of bad manners outside or even inside the ground.' Traditionally, MCC would approach the Palace and ask whether, should an invitation be issued, Her Majesty would be pleased to accept. Clearly on this occasion the answer was clear that she wouldn't be pleased which at least enabled MCC to claim, technically correctly, that they had not issued the invitation in the first place. The Queen had indicated where her sympathies lay before Christmas the previous year when she had also refused to attend the England v South Africa rugby Test at Twickenham so she was spared the awkwardness of watching the two men attempting to handcuff themselves to the goal posts. Who knew what Peter Hain had in store for her should she emerge from the pavilion at tea on the fourth day? MCC shuddered at the prospect and reluctantly forewent the honour of hosting their royal visitor.

Everyone tried to claim the moral high ground. When asked why the South Africans weren't coming to the Palace for tea and cucumber sandwiches a spokesman said simply that there would be no point as the Queen hadn't been invited to attend the match so a reciprocal invitation was not called for. In addition, the invitation to tea was not issued as a matter of course to every touring team and there the conversation ended. Meanwhile, Granada Television announced that it would not broadcast any matches played by South Africa to which the Cricket Council replied with a marked irritation that such moral grandstanding was beside the point since only the BBC had the broadcast rights to cover the Test matches. Granada had indeed transmitted live coverage of some recent Roses County Championship matches (not terribly well) but this virtue signalling was essentially a result of the tour controversy. On the other hand, when the shop steward of the Association of Cinema and Television Technicians followed Granada's line by threatening that his BBC cameramen would not agree to work on the Test matches if South Africa played England, MCC were compelled to take such threats seriously, particularly when they were supported by Vic Feather, the general secretary of the TUC. The BBC did hold the broadcast rights and cricket was very reliant on the more than £50,000 that such rights raised in vital revenue for cricket.

The Queen's bold move encouraged other African nations. On the very day that the Fund was launched, the Supreme Council for Sport in Africa, which was the representative body for 36 African countries, announced that after a meeting of all its members in Cairo if the cricket tour went ahead in June, 13 African countries who were members of the Commonwealth would withdraw their athletes from the Commonwealth Games due to take place in Edinburgh in July 1970. It called on the British government to act decisively on the matter. As the government pondered the pros and cons of intervening directly and ordering the Cricket Council to withdraw its invitation to South Africa this was clearly another con. Kenya had already made it clear that no athlete from its country would be permitted to compete against any athlete from any country that had competed against South Africans in any sporting competition within the previous three years. The idea of a major athletics meeting without the participation of Kipchoge Keino who had won the gold medal in the 1,500 metres at the Mexico Olympics two years previously and Wilson Kiprigut, the 800 metres champion, was unpalatable. The same could be said if the Ghanaian and Ugandan boxers stayed at home. The Games which were designed to celebrate the sporting achievements of the Commonwealth would be reduced to a series of meaningless running races between the home countries and those of Canada, Australia and New Zealand with scarcely a black face or body to be seen.

This threat provoked the more extreme supporters of the tour to outrage. An undated anonymous letter in the MCC archive scribbled on The Churchill notepaper warned that: 'If the forthcoming South African tour is cancelled through the efforts of the African and Asian and the nigger loving scum of this fair land, drastic and serious action will be taken against Team members of all and every country and state and organisation concerned during the Commonwealth Games.'

The Cricket Council was far from cowed by the threat, however, and requested a meeting with Alastair Ross, the chairman of the Commonwealth Games Committee. The Council did not want the Games to be called off but made it clear 'politely but firmly' that their business was cricket and if the 13 countries were threatening to withdraw their athletes the Cricket Council was not going to respond to that kind of blackmail. The Council's job was to look after cricket and that is what they thought they were doing. The politicians who controlled the athletes had to be made aware that such bullying tactics were not consistent with the smooth administration of any sport. If English cricket changed what it considered to be its excellent protocols and governance because of the unreasonable (as they saw them) demands of another sport it would be an open invitation to anarchy and chaos.

It can be suspected, however, that it was the Council that leaned slightly on Lt Col Newman to modify his original claim for the tour Fund to insist that the money raised would be used entirely in Britain and the words South Africa were largely deleted. The Fund became a means of supporting cricket in his own country and was therefore divorced from the specific reason it had been started and enthusiastically welcomed by its supporters, i.e. to enable the tour by an all-white South Africa side to go ahead and not to be derailed by a lack of money for policing. The backtracking by the Fund intensified in the light of the telegram sent to Whitehall by the Supreme Council for Sport in Africa. No contributions would be accepted from South Africa or from companies or organisations with links to South Africa. Desperately, Newman added that the Fund would be administered from Lord's and that great efforts would be made to seek out the funds that had South African connections. Wherever they were discovered the money would be returned to the donors. The tour, however, would proceed as planned.

In the middle of April 1970 those South Africans who were permitted the vote went to the polls in an election called by John Vorster a year before he needed to do so in order to demonstrate to the world that the policies of his Nationalist government received the overwhelming support of the country. He had been disconcerted by the growth of a new party that was more right wing than his Nationalists. This was the HNP, a splinter group that was set up in much the same way that the Brexit Party suddenly arrived to challenge traditional Tories. HNP believed that in opening tentative trade negotiations with certain black countries to the north, Vorster had deviated from the strictly orthodox line of complete racial segregation that had been the major platform of Dr Hendrik Verwoerd, the previous South African Prime Minister who in 1966 had been stabbed to death in parliament by a Greek-Mozambican communist. Vorster was attempting to buy off outside support for the guerrillas within South Africa by making those countries clients within South Africa's economic orbit. It was also a recognition that economic sanctions were forcing the country to widen the markets for the sale of their manufactured goods as they were going to be the main source of export earnings. The HNP was appalled at this (relatively) open policy and claimed that the Afrikaners had sold out to the English – which would have come as a surprise to Harold Wilson. They were also fiercely opposed to the immigration from Southern Europe of Roman Catholics who had arrived as part of the government's plan to import more white labour. If Vorster had any intention of appearing marginally more moderate to the outside world the emergence of this new political threat from the right prevented it.

Perhaps this pressure from the extreme right wing disconcerted Vorster, who was not used to having to prove his right-wing credentials. Certainly the results of the election were disappointing. Although the HNP fielded 80 candidates it only attracted 3.5% of the vote and wound up with a very UKIP-like number of seats – precisely none. Vorster's Nationalist Party retained power comfortably, winning 117 of the 165 seats on offer but they had returned with nine fewer MPs, the first time that had happened since 1948 when the Nationalists first came to power. The official opposition as it were, the United Party, increased both its share of the vote and its number of MPs although it believed just as strongly in white supremacy as the Nationalists. It was seen as the party of business and, as more Afrikaners deserted their traditional farms for life in business, the United Party rather than the National Party aligned with their interests. Helen Suzman remained the sole member of the Progressive Party, but she increased her majority in the affluent white suburb of Johannesburg from 700 to over 2,000. It looked, the day after the election, that white supremacy would have to be a little more flexible but if it did that it would probably help to strengthen rather than weaken the system. Despite the fall in the National Party's share of the vote, black Africans had little to celebrate in the result.

The swing away from the Nationalists suggested of course to the supporters of the cricket tour that their policy of building bridges with white South Africa and gently pointing out the error of their ways was making progress. It could, of course, be argued with equal conviction that such a swing was the result of the increasing fear of South Africa's sporting isolation and that was undoubtedly the result of direct action, however uncomfortable the liberals were with it at as a tactic. Meanwhile, the 16 million non-whites of voting age in the country continued to be both voteless and effectively voiceless. The Anti-Apartheid Movement distributed a poster that left a lasting impression on many of those who saw it. It showed a photograph of a policeman beating defenceless blacks in a township outside Durban. The caption read: 'If you could see their national sport you might be less keen to see their cricket.'

The *Daily Telegraph* in London sent its former editor Colin Coote to report on what he found in South Africa. In three feature articles he articulated a different viewpoint to anything a *Guardian* journalist might find.

> The Bantu homelands policy of the South African Government has been so far the only sincere effort to educate the Bantu for self-government and independence.
>
> And this is an advantage which is even greater than their living standard, which is higher than in countries under African rule.

Following his unexpected electoral reverse, gleefully reported in most countries, the Prime Minister John Vorster issued a response aimed more at foreign observers than his own countrymen who needed little reminding of the philosophy underpinning apartheid. In a radio speech, deliberately recalling those of Churchill in 1940, he proclaimed the willingness of South Africa to stand alone against the world in defence of its sacred birthright. He explained the basic idea of apartheid in the most calm and logical tone he could summon.

> Separate development is not the denial of the human dignity of anyone. The basis thereof is also not the suppression of anyone or the deprival of anybody's rights or land. On the contrary, separate

development guarantees the inalienable right of everybody to be and remain himself. This applies to the Whites as well as to the non-whites, and no pressure from whatever source or of whatever nature will force the Government to abandon this standpoint.

It was of course exactly the same reasoning behind the 'Separate but Equal' policy which permitted segregation in American schools. That had existed in the United States until the landmark Supreme Court decision of 1954 in the case of *Brown versus Board of Education of Topeka*. It was pernicious nonsense in both cases. Segregation adversely affected black schoolchildren. Apartheid gave legal justification to a system that encouraged oppression of non-white races. By 1970 some of the key aims of the Civil Rights movement had already been achieved. In South Africa in that year apartheid was as securely entrenched as at any time since 1948.

That knowledge continued to motivate the opponents to the 1970 tour. The Stop The Seventy Tour Special Action Group fortuitously discovered the existence of an underground train tunnel which ran underneath Lord's and from which a dramatic entrance could be made which would entirely defeat the presence of the dogs, the burly, well-armed security guards and the barbed wire. Preparations continued to be made to greet the arriving cricketers at Heathrow (now only five weeks away) with the sort of chorus of disapproval that had been given to the departing rugby players three months earlier. STST were also joined by sympathisers who had nothing to do with the organised movement. Hain answered his front door one day to be greeted by two model aeroplane enthusiasts who told him they could interrupt play by buzzing the pitch with planes operated from the flat of an aunt which overlooked Lord's. In the days before drones this was an ingenious and original plan.

Another imaginative wheeze involved unleashing a plague of locusts on the Lord's pitch although no plans for the killing of the first born of all MCC members had been devised despite the close proximity to the Grace Gates of the St John's Wood Reform Synagogue. David Wilton-Godberford was an entomologist and a strong opponent of apartheid living in Colwyn Bay who set about breeding 300,000 locusts for use during the tourists' matches. 'They will ravage every blade of grass and green foliage,' he told suitably awed reporters. He was hoping for a hot summer as apparently locusts do their best work, like West Indian cricketers were supposed to do, when they could feel the sun on their backs. The locusts would be starved for 24 hours before being released on the pitch. Presumably, Derek Underwood would then be able to bowl into the locusts' footmarks.

> It takes 70,000 hoppers twelve minutes to consume one hundredweight of grass. The crack of a solid army of locusts feeding on the grass will sound like flames. The South Africans are going to dread this trip.

A rival entomologist, however, was sceptical of the plan. He believed that the locusts needed not just a period of sunshine but temperatures in the nineties Fahrenheit, a highly unlikely occurrence in the days before climate change was thought about. Additionally, he pointed out that plagues in Africa involved literally billions of locusts and the damage that would be inflicted by 300,000 locusts on a cricket field would be minimal. 'Most of them', he added encouragingly for Gubby Allen and Billy Griffith, 'would be likely to keel over before they get near the grass. Most of them would be dead within a day.'

In this atmosphere of religious fervour, stimulated by late-night readings of the Book of Exodus, possibly accompanied by a small glass of dry sherry, the Bishop of Gloucester, the Right Reverend Basil Guy, sent out a diocesan letter calling on Christians to pray for rain to wash out all the tour matches. He called MCC 'blind' to arrange such a series of matches that would inevitably be distasteful to many people and seriously damage the cause of good race relations in Britain. He warned that:

> We have been led into a situation from which no good can possibly come and we must address ourselves to the repair of the damage.

He acknowledged that nobody had the right to disrupt the tour by violence but he insisted that many opponents of the tour, presumably including himself in this category, were not hooligans.

It was impossible to prevent the controversy surrounding the tour becoming involved in the party politics of a country heading for an election. David Steel, the Liberal MP who had been front and centre during the rugby tour, observed that if the old saw had it that the Church of England could be regarded as the Tory Party at prayer the Cricket Council could now be fairly seen as the Tory Party at play. Steel was particularly disheartened by the realisation that the 1970 Tour Fund was being supported by both the Bishop of Leicester and the Bishop of Bath and Wells, who, he thought, needed lessons in Christian charity from Lord Montgomery of Alamein, John Arlott and Granada Television. The Bishop of Gloucester was unfortunately not name-checked. He pointed out that the result of the recent elections in South Africa, despite the minimal amount of policy change that might result, was evidence that the wide-ranging nature of support for the cancellation of the tour was having an impact.

It comes as a surprise to read that distinguished churchmen were supporters of the tour. In addition to Leicester and Bath & Wells there was an allegedly witty letter to the editor of *The Guardian* written by the Bishop of St Andrews who wondered why so much attention was being given to a cricket tour which should be allowed to proceed unmolested. It produced a furious response from Mr L.E. Weidberg of Templewood Avenue, NW3 who wondered why the Anglican Church had blessed with their silence previous all-white cricket tours of this country.

Mr Weidberg, it should be explained at this point, was my mother's brother and the man responsible for introducing me to cricket when he took me as a five-year-old to my first Test match at Old Trafford – against the South Africans in 1955. Uncle Laurence as he was known familiarly also took me to watch the South Africans in the Lord's Test match of 1965 where we marvelled at the manner in which Colin Bland ran out both Ken Barrington and Jim Parks. No doubt he also lectured me on the iniquities of apartheid and indeed he wanted the 1970/71 tour of Australia to be cancelled because of the way in which the Australian government treated the Aborigines. Despite his many personal inconsistencies (he was a key official in the Socialist Party of Great Britain who drove a Bentley and lived in the most expensive road in Hampstead) he made me understand that at some level all activity, even cricket, is a political event.

David Steel, who might well have agreed with Uncle Laurence on many issues, castigated too the reluctance of Ted Heath and the Conservatives to declare that they would have no truck with the all-white government of Southern Rhodesia led by Ian Smith after the Unilateral Declaration of Independence which had happened in 1965. Ted Heath was being coy which suggested he would have no problem re-establishing diplomatic contact, just as he would lift the embargo on arms sales to South Africa. At least Harold Wilson had always made his opposition to apartheid, to the Nationalist government and to arms sales to its armed forces abundantly clear. It seemed logical to Steel that the pressure on the government was now overwhelming following the threat to the Commonwealth Games in Edinburgh. Significant sums of HM Treasury money had been invested by the government and by the ratepayers of Edinburgh, so to see the Games collapse into a meaningless parody of a truly Commonwealth event was a waste of such a public investment. Steel warned that a Conservative government would be a boost to the governments of John Vorster and Ian Smith – but then he was writing in *The Guardian*, few of whose readers would be likely to vote for their local Tory candidate.

On 21 April, to the great relief of all cricket lovers, the English domestic season opened, as was traditional, at Fenner's with a match between Cambridge University and Warwickshire. At the end of the game, won by Warwickshire by an innings, their players returned to Edgbaston to continue their preparations for their first County Championship match of the season against Nottinghamshire at Trent Bridge and the students cycled off to the University Library to put in some token work for their exams which would start in a month's time.

Other Cambridge students, including this author, were also preparing for Finals and in a university town which had been a hotbed of student radicalism during the previous two terms the traditional concentration on the approach of examinations seemed to draw a vast blanket over the contentious issue of the South Africa tour. A huge sigh of relief by the university authorities greeted what appeared to be the return of normality.

The Annual General Meeting of the members of Surrey CCC took place at The Oval in the middle of the match between Cambridge University and Warwickshire in which a motion was put to the members that the county should not play the visiting South Africans. It was resoundingly defeated. 'Cricket, cricket and be damned' roared one red-faced member at the county's most heated and best-attended AGM in living memory. The proposer of the motion, Mr M. Loosley, mildly pointed out that national feeling was clearly running heavily against entertaining the South Africans in Britain while apartheid prevailed in their homeland as a national policy. He added that the Trades Union Congress had earlier that day called on its nine million affiliated members for a total boycott of the tour.

When he suggested that some people seemed to think that cricket was above moral and ethical issues he received the instant and almost unanimous response to the effect that it certainly was. Loosley countered by citing that in addition to the TUC, the British Council of Churches, the United Nations Association, the Prime Minister and John Arlott had all voiced their opposition to the tour. From the response of the Surrey members it was clear that not even John Arlott commanded enough respect to alter the mood of the meeting. Harold Wilson and the other organisations elicited nothing but intemperate cat calls. Mr Loosley concluded his address by reminding the audience that they were meeting in Kennington at the very heart of a large and vibrant West Indian immigrant community who would be extremely upset if the South Africans were playing in their midst. After he sat down to muted applause the chairman of the meeting reminded members that important as the issue they were discussing was, the fact remained that dinner was about to be served and he urged the seconder of the motion to be as brief as possible. Mr T.R. Gibson said simply, 'I hate apartheid but I also hate the idea of cricket being played behind barbed wire and rows of police constables. And that, gentlemen, is what is going to happen.'

Shudders ran round the room as police and protestors and disruptions and demonstrations were mentioned. Raman Subba Row, a former opening batsman for the county, then put the case for opposing the motion, using the well-rehearsed arguments for the continuation of the tour advanced by MCC and the Cricket

Council. 'We are concerned with cricket, not the internal politics of South Africa. We have been told that the South African Cricket Association intends to select teams on a multi-racial basis in future. Let us help them make progress. Let us play cricket.' He sat down to thunderous applause. The cheers were positively deafening. A vote was taken, the motion was heavily defeated and everyone adjourned to the dinner table. Like the current Brexit debate it was clear that neither side was going to grant its opponents the courtesy of a considered hearing. Positions were adopted, attitudes entrenched and neither side could find in the other's argument a shred of logic or credibility. As in the 2019 House of Commons, each side had its foot pressed down hard on the accelerator and was simply driving headlong towards the onrushing car with its headlights on full beam and its horn blaring, each expecting the other to brake first.

Even in the car bearing all the opponents to the tour there was dissension in the ranks. The letters page of *The Guardian* in the days after Arlott's announcement that he would not be commentating for *Test Match Special* was getting increasingly heated, particularly with what was perceived as the wishy-washy ineffectual self-serving attitude of *The Guardian* itself. One letter from a reader in Maidenhead asked pointedly where the broadcast revenues would go. Would they go to defray the costs of policing and the purchase of barbed wire? Would they go to the South Africans to help them with the expenses of their tour? The writer's point was that BBC revenues were gathered from the licence fee paying public and therefore should not be used for overtly political purposes. If the tour had to go ahead it would be far better if the BBC withdrew its entire planned coverage on radio and television and MCC met the costs out of its own pocket.

A letter from Leigh on Sea noted that even if all the South African cricketers were lined up against the wall and shot it wouldn't cause John Vorster too much distress. The only way to force his government to abandon the policy of apartheid would be by disrupting trade with South Africa, which would hurt the British economy. To put this into context, British exports to Southern Africa rose from £298million in 1968 to £326million in 1969. The book value of direct investments there stood at £740million, a not insubstantial sum.

173

In the end cricket was only a symbol of the racial problem. Multi-racial sport in South Africa could only be achieved by changing South African society. At least one correspondent retained his sense of humour. Writing from Fareham in Hampshire, Mr P.E. Reid suggested that *The Guardian* should not cover the tour in any way. Nor, he added, should it ever mention the Vietnam War, Wilson, Heath, Powell, the Common Market, Strikes, Pay Rises, Price Increases, Violence, Starvation, Sickness etc because of the number of people with strong feelings against them. 'I suggest you publish 20 pages of blank paper', he concluded, 'and let us make up our own news about the things we want to read about.'

As the county cricket season approached, each of the grounds which were scheduled to host a match featuring the tourists was required to demonstrate that its barbed wire and other security measures were functioning properly. Peter Hain and the STST decided to put these measures to the test by 'playing' a match with multi-racial teams on the hallowed turf of Lord's. The plan was to drive a van, with all the players crammed into the back of it, through the North Gate showing as identification the card of an MCC member who was in sympathy with the aims of the campaign. The van driver and his passenger would tell the gatekeeper that they were going to use the squash courts for which they had booked a starting time and the North Gate would get them into the ground where they could park alongside genuine squash players and users of the indoor nets. Trial runs proceeded smoothly but on the day, with the players huddled in the back, the gatekeeper, now under instructions not to admit any van, refused admission. The MCC member, standing on his dignity, insisted the gatekeeper ring the appropriate office to get approval. The phone rang without reply so the gatekeeper, using his initiative, said he would admit the van but he would have to look in the back first. As soon as the van's back door was opened the jig was up.

A dozen young men in white cricket clothes jumped out and set up a wicket of sorts in Wellington Place just off the busy Finchley Road. A television news crew, that had been previously advised that it might be worth their while coming to Lord's that day, arrived and started filming this impromptu game which of course was causing more than normal traffic congestion in NW8. The ball, as anyone who has ever played in the street knows was inevitable, was soon driven underneath a 159 bus thundering its way down to the Lord's roundabout on its way to Lewisham. Irritated car owners who tried to get past the cricketers by driving straight at them were forced to halt as the players simply lay down in the road and dared the drivers to continue. It didn't need to last long for the campaigners to make their point. There were no injuries, there was no damage to property but the attendant publicity helped to make the point that STST and other campaigners opposed to the tour had a variety of methods to cause havoc and the South Africans hadn't even arrived yet.

On Monday 27 April the BBC devoted its entire 50-minute weekly *Panorama* programme to a discussion about the tour with Peter Hain, John Arlott, David Sheppard and Dennis Brutus on one side lined up against the usual suspects from MCC on the other. Sir Peter Rawlinson, the Shadow Attorney General and Brian Walden – still a Labour MP before his elevation to the office of presenter of LWT's *Weekend World* – appeared to give appropriate political balance. Inevitably, after 50 minutes of the airing of all the arguments that had been presented in other forms many times before no conclusion was arrived at. Each side walked away from the studio believing it had made an overwhelming case and many new converts had been gained.

What was certainly true was that it was impossible that anyone in the country was unaware of the principles of each side. That was probably a small gain for the anti-tour side as it was difficult for anyone to take the side of apartheid South Africa. The response for many viewers would have been to think that David Sheppard's principled opposition to the tour which disdained the use of direct action tactics would be the one the majority of *Panorama* viewers would have found the most convincing. When he asked Maurice Allom, the President of MCC, if Allom had bothered to consult any expert in community relations with regard to the possible impact the tour might have, Allom was forced to admit that he had not. Even the shortened tour involved matches in Birmingham, Nottingham and at The Oval in the heart of London's West Indian community. If the tour went ahead the likelihood of protests spilling into violence on the streets was strong. MCC of course cared only about what might happen within the grounds. It was a blinkered view which Sheppard easily exposed.

The Labour MP for Ilkeston, Raymond Fletcher, was equally unimpressed. He confessed to a dislike of cricket and a refusal to believe in the healing powers of international sport. He dismissed the claims of Baron de Coubertin who had famously stressed before the rebirth of the Olympic movement in 1896 that 'we should preserve in sport those characteristics of nobility and chivalry which have distinguished it in the past'. For him a stated intention not to attend any cricket match played by South Africa would entail no sacrifice at all but then as he pointed out what de Coubertin wished to preserve did not appear to him to exist in sport any more. On the other hand he did object to the policy of apartheid but what really got his goat was the hypocrisy of the Cricket Council. In that notorious *Why the '70 Tour?* pamphlet, the Council declared that it would not be dictated to by a militant minority – by which it meant of course the Stop the Seventy Tour. Fletcher, who had spent some time in South Africa, pointed out forcefully that during the Second World War, Vorster and 'his fellow conspirators' were a militant minority who were hostile to Britain, actively opposed to it and sabotaged efforts to help the British war effort wherever they could. They came to power as a militant minority and they remained a militant minority that was currently dictating to the Cricket Council. 'The South Africans, particularly the Afrikaners, have hated Britain since the days of Paul Kruger. They are an inadequate people and their almost morbid craving for international sporting honours is a measure of their inadequacy.'

Fletcher was convinced that sport was simply an exercise in the deployment of tribal passions. He wasn't at Old Trafford the night that article appeared in print to watch Chelsea play Leeds United in their FA Cup Final replay. Had he been, he would have witnessed his theory triumphantly vindicated. Mick Jones had put Leeds United in front seven minutes before the interval but Peter Osgood had equalised for Chelsea 12 minutes from time. The game was won by a David Webb goal which looped past David Harvey off Webb's shoulder from a long throw-in by Ian Hutchinson after fourteen minutes of extra time. It was a scrappy, unsatisfactory way (except for Peter Hain and other Chelsea supporters) to end a season in which Leeds United had played 63 games and Chelsea 57, both of them utilising squads of 15 or so players in the days before the idea of rotating players to preserve their physical health had even been conceived.

The game has gone down in football history as an infamously bad-tempered one. The blatant hacking and kicking, pushing and fouling was so all-pervasive that it was something of a surprise when a game of football broke out. Fifty years later in a different refereeing climate, it is doubtful if more than a dozen players would have been on the field at the end of the 120 minutes. Mr E.T. Jennings of Stourbridge, however, saw the exhibition of all-in wrestling as meriting one booking, that of Ian Hutchinson for pushing over Billy Bremner. In the circumstances, Hutchinson must have considered himself somewhat unfortunate. At the foot of the television screen during extra time a strap line read Manchester City 2 Gornik Zabrze 1. With a goal by Neil Young and a penalty converted by Francis Lee, the club from the other side of Manchester had won the European Cup Winners' Cup in a torrential downpour in front of a crowd estimated at 4,000. For some opponents of the South Africa cricket tour, it was indeed a night off and a night to be long remembered.

Presumably the letter Peter Hain wrote to the editor of *The Guardian* had been posted long before the BBC began its coverage of the Cup Final 45 minutes before the kick-off because it appeared the following morning along with Eric Todd's distinctive match report from Old Trafford. Todd wondered why the Leeds United players had not been presented with statuettes of a blindfolded Justice. Hain, no doubt revelling in Chelsea's first ever FA Cup win, was more concerned to keep the focus on Lord's because there was a danger that the issue of racialism, which was the whole point of STST, was becoming obscured by the increasing emphasis being placed on the law and order issue. Hain suspected that the Conservative Party was looking for the law and order issue to become a central plank in the Tory manifesto at the next election. Hain was clearly anxious to switch the debate back to one about morality and apartheid. To that extent Lord's was in the dock, he wrote.

Is cricket prepared to bear responsibility for poisoning race relations in this country; for intensifying a politically motivated absurdity about law and order; for precipitating a split in international sport; for sacrificing the Commonwealth Games; and above all for capitulating to racialism? All this in order to protect an apartheid regime which will be laughing at Britain's discomfiture? This is a time for courage, not for retreat. In cancelling the racialist cricket tour, even at this late stage, the Cricket Council will have shown a dignity worthy of the game itself.

Hain's own courage was never in doubt for one of the more remarkable aspects of the letter was that Hain included and *The Guardian* published his address – 21a Gwendolen Avenue, Putney, London SW15. No doubt as chairman of the Stop the Seventy Tour committee Hain's contact address was a matter of public record but in view of the fact that he had become a serious figure attracting what would now be termed 'hate crimes' and indeed was sent a parcel bomb a couple of years later, it seems brave to the point of recklessness. His point about the likelihood of race relations being poisoned was shared by another letter writer on the same page. A relatively calm and reasoned letter written by the president of the Association of Commonwealth Teachers pleaded for the government to call off the tour because of the very real danger of it inflaming racial tensions. The temporary disappointment caused to cricket lovers would be lost in the general relief felt in the rest of the country that the relations between the races in Britain would not be sent back to the days of the Notting Hill riots. It was a view publicly supported by the Association of Community Relations Officers.

The next day United States troops invaded Cambodia. On television that night President Nixon explained to the American people that American armed forces accompanied by the South Vietnamese People's Army were forced to take this action in order to disrupt the supply lines of the North Vietnamese. Whilst they were there American B52 bombers would increase the number of unofficial air strikes that had been taking place in Cambodia for some weeks in order to destroy Viet Cong base camps. Nixon had campaigned for the presidency in 1968 on the basis of 'Vietnamisation'; in other words following the policy of withdrawing American troops in order to allow the South Vietnamese to fight their own war. It was a policy that would have shifted enough votes to Nixon to make the difference in a close race with Hubert Humphrey, the Democratic Party candidate. The feeling of disillusion with the war in Vietnam and in particular with the President which had been growing since the Tet offensive began in January 1968 was approaching outright rebellion. It was hard for Americans to remember a time in the country's history when a wartime President was so unpopular, harder still to remember when so many Americans believed their President simply lied to them. The feelings of solidarity which bound young people of different countries and different races together were getting stronger.

During Nixon's television address he lost his place in his prepared script. If he had a teleprompter he never looked at it as he shuffled the papers in front of him desperately searching for the place to resume. There was a silence that lasted for only four or five seconds but the broadcast was live and the lens of the television camera is unforgiving. For those who supported Nixon it was evidence of the terrible strain under which the man was living. For those who loathed him it was evident that he had lost his grip on his office. It was as if Nixon were being punished, publicly embarrassed and humiliated for committing such a flagrantly immoral if not illegal act.

Students across America and the Western world did not have to be politicised to any great degree to come out and campaign against the war. The older generation, epitomised by the Nixon administration and the military industrial complex as it came to be called, were simply the enemy. In America the two great causes were the war in Vietnam and Civil Rights. For students in England the anti-war protests meant just as much even if Harold Wilson had successfully negotiated with Johnson and Nixon to keep British students out of the jungles of South East Asia (for which they gave him no credit). For them the other cause where they could show their opposition to the right-wing orthodoxy and bourgeois values of the middle class was the South African cricket tour.

Cricket lovers resolutely looked at their membership cards with their familiar fixture lists and noted in their diaries Saturday 2 May as the start of the cricket season and the return of everything they looked forward to during the long, dark winter months. Originally of course it had been the date on which the South African tour would begin with the traditional match against Worcestershire at New

Road but that match had disappeared in February when the tour had been shortened. For STST it was the start of the final campaign to harness ordinary cricket supporters behind their cause and to ensure that these sensible people saw the moral necessity of calling on the cricket authorities and the government to take the appropriate step of cancelling the tour. The first-class domestic season opened on time with the usual attendance figures. Hain and the STST picketed outside Lord's and The Oval ready to place pamphlets explaining their point of view into the hands of the milling spectators. As it transpired there were more STST campaigners than there were cricket lovers desperate to get into their usual seats at the Nursery End or behind the arm at the Vauxhall End. The English cricket season was up and running but for how long?

CHAPTER EIGHT

MAY 1970

COUNTY cricketers took the field at the start of May 1970 thinking about things other than cricket. Many of them had been the unwilling recipients of hate-filled anonymous letters. The spectrum of behaviour of those opposing the tour ranged from the gentle persuasion of David Sheppard to these anonymous letter writers who concentrated their efforts on those who were likely to play for England and had not made themselves unavailable for selection against South Africa. Keith Fletcher was one of the recipients.

> The impending arrival of the South Africans had stirred the anti-apartheid demonstrators to one of their most forceful protests and I was one of a number of England players to receive anonymous letters threatening violence against myself and my family and calling me a 'bastard' for playing against the all-white tourists. I did not exactly walk around in fear of my life but I could see that the future of the tour was probably short-lived. It was probably the players who were likely to play for England so I don't know how widespread those letters were but they said things like, 'Be careful when you walk outside your front door' and all that sort of crap.

Fletcher might not have been impressed by the threats but some of the counties were. Lancashire's two overseas players, the Indian wicket-keeper Farokh Engineer and the exciting West Indian Clive Lloyd and their families were threatened with violence if they did not publicly announce that they would not play for Lancashire or the Northern Counties side against the South Africans. The threats came in anonymous letters and phone calls. The phone call to Engineer was taken by his wife who was upset to hear the threats issued against not only her husband but also herself and their little daughter. The unmarried Lloyd soon learned that his family in Guyana had also been threatened if he played in the match. When Lancashire announced that neither player would be asked to play in the county's match against the South Africans, scheduled for 3 August, both players described themselves as relieved. Peter Lever, who had taken a principled stand as early as January not to play against the tourists, was nevertheless also the recipient of unpleasant letters from the other side.

A lot of them said that it was nice to see that someone in the cricket world has got principles and then I got a lot of them the other way that said I was supporting the black man. Two or three of them called me the usual thing 'niggerlover'. Silly things like that had no effect on me whatsoever. I never felt at any point that there would be people coming up to me from behind to give me a good hiding. I wasn't going to mention the ones that said they knew where my children went to school but I had a few of those too. I also had letters from people questioning why I was playing against the Rest of the World when there were South Africans playing for them. But of course Pollock and Richards were playing for a multi-racial team. They hadn't been selected on apartheid grounds. That's what I was trying to do – to get everyone playing for the same team – black, white, it didn't matter. All cricketers were of the same opinion – they just wanted to play with a bat and ball but before that 1970 season started nobody that I knew of stood up. I just did what I felt was right and I felt sorry for the white cricketers in England who didn't have the balls to stand up and do something about it. I got a letter off Peter Hain saying well done and did I want to go on a march through the streets of London.

At the same time Warwickshire announced that it would not ask Rohan Kanhai, Lance Gibbs or Billy Ibadulla to play in their match against South Africa to spare the players any embarrassment. The Birmingham Anti-Apartheid Committee filed a complaint against Warwickshire for this decision but the Race Relations Board ruled that its refusal to select the three players was not a breach of the Race Relations Act.

The Test and County Cricket Board took the unusual step of writing to all those players who were likely to be selected for England or for the Northern and Southern Counties sides informing them that they would have their lives insured for £15,000. The TCCB insurance policy also included £3,000 for blinding in one or both eyes, £3,000 for total loss by severance of one or both hands or feet, £30 a week for 52 weeks for total disablement and of course there was the big star prize of £15,000 for death. Really, could professional cricketers have genuinely considered themselves under-valued in 1970?

On Saturday 2 May, the first day of the season, a crowd of 100 demonstrating against the tour picketed Lord's during the Middlesex v Hampshire game. Extra police were called but released when it was realised they were not needed. The placards contained such inoffensive demands as 'Hit Apartheid for Six' and 'Knock Vorster's Bails Off'. A sharp-eyed reporter observed that there were four people of colour in the ground. One of them was the Hampshire fast bowler and later umpire, John Holder.

On the day that real three-day County Championship cricket broke out at county grounds across the country, Sir Edward Boyle, MCC member, schoolboy scorer for the Eton Cricket First XI, Minister of Education in the last Conservative government and now the newly appointed vice-chancellor of the University of Leeds, joined David Sheppard's Fair Cricket Campaign as one of two vice-chairmen. The other was Reg Prentice, who had recently been the Minister for Overseas Development in Harold Wilson's Cabinet but who had resigned on a point of principle over the cuts in overseas aid. He was later to cross the floor and join the Conservatives when faced with de-selection by left-wing activists. A few days later a second Tory MP, Sir William Robson Brown, the member for the safe Surrey seat of Esher also joined. He was due to stand down in the forthcoming election so he was not subject to the prospect of de-selection by his constituency party in the heart of the Surrey 'blue belt' and free to follow his conscience. 'Much as I love watching cricket', he said as he made his announcement, 'the threatened violence and the unusual tensions the tour will create between coloured people and our own far outweigh the benefits.' Splits were starting to appear in the Conservative Party's previously sustained unanimous support for the tour.

Harold Wilson intensified his own campaign to persuade the cricket authorities to abandon the tour without the need to issue a specific government directive. On the last day of April, only two weeks after he had appeared on ITV's *This Week* programme to clarify his own personal position, he was a guest on *Sportsnight with Coleman*, the weekly sports magazine programme on BBC1. It seems likely that Wilson had asked the BBC to make an appearance as it was unlikely that the editor of the programme would have issued such an invitation without some prior indication that it would be accepted. He said almost exactly the same things that he had said on ITV but there was an added sense of urgency as now there was only just over four weeks to go before the South African cricketers would be disembarking at Heathrow.

Wilson began in polite mode by asking MCC to think again. He said that if MCC were to withdraw its invitation nobody would regard the organisation as being weak or that it would lose face by such a climb-down. He hoped that the Council would not feel that it was being blackmailed into cancellation by fear of the threatened demonstrations.

> I think everyone would respect and honour them. After all, we always respect a sporting declaration. We all respect the man who starts walking towards the pavilion without waiting for the umpire's finger.

He repeated his hope that all those who wanted to demonstrate would feel free to do so although he warned that the police would deal severely with any who abused that precious freedom to demonstrate. If the tour went ahead spectators were entitled to watch the match in peace and the police would ensure that they would be able to do so.

Wilson then raised the possibility of Scotland being deprived of the Commonwealth Games if the African countries and others carried out their threats to boycott them if the tour went ahead but he still stopped short of saying the government would tell MCC to withdraw their invitation. However, he conjured an image of Great Britain presiding over a Commonwealth Prime Ministers' conference attended by a rump of white nations. The Cricket Council might have believed sincerely that politics should be kept out of sport but decisions like the one to invite South Africa had political consequences and besides, he argued, it was South Africa that had introduced politics into sport in 1968 when it banned Basil D'Oliveira from entering its territory. Wilson was desperate to learn that the South Africa tour would be called off but he was clearly very anxious indeed that it was done with no overt government pressure. Of course, the pressure that this interview imposed on Lord's was all too obvious.

The assistant secretary of MCC, Jack Bailey and Raman Subba Row, an equally influential figure at Lord's, composed between them an instant reply in the face of press enquiries and their inability to contact Billy Griffith. It later transpired that the secretary of the Cricket Council, anticipating the barrage of press enquiries, had retired to bed and taken the phone off the hook. In time for the last editions of the following morning's newspapers the two men released a statement which dared Wilson to go further and cancel the tour himself, thereby appearing to be giving in to the violent protesters and making his government look weak, let alone losing the vote of everyone who was looking forward to watching Barry Richards, Mike Procter and Graeme Pollock.

> In his broadcast this evening, the Prime Minister referred to the right of all people to demonstrate freely during cricket matches against the South Africans this summer. He also mentioned that the Cricket Council should not feel that they are being blackmailed. It is for the Prime Minister to decide whether incitement to demonstrate constitutes blackmail, just as it is for the government to decide whether law and order can be maintained in the face of public demonstrations. If, for these or any other reasons the Prime Minister feels that the tour by

BARBED WIRE AND CUCUMBER SANDWICHES

the South Africans should not go ahead, then he should come
out and say so to the South African government.

Bailey and Subba Row noted with satisfaction that the reaction
to this statement amongst 'supporters' was enthusiastic and an
allegedly cowed government was noticeable for its lack of response.
Duncan Sandys, Conservative member for Streatham and a member
of Conservative governments stretching back to the time when
Winston Churchill was Prime Minister, told *The Times* that Wilson
had now dropped the moral argument and was urging cancellation
on the grounds that if the tour went ahead African countries might
boycott the Commonwealth Games.

> He is thus advocating a grovelling capitulation to blackmail by
> countries which are themselves practising racial discrimination
> of the most blatant kind. Whatever views one holds about
> apartheid – and I have always condemned it – there can be no
> question of retreating even if the retreat is led by the Prime
> Minister.

John Jackson, the chairman of the newly formed Support the 70
Tour Committee, snidely referenced Harold Wilson's troubled trade
union reform bill *In Place of Strife* which had failed in 1969. 'Because
the Prime Minister is a pushover does not mean that the sporting
public can be blown over quite so easily.' Peter Rost, the prospective
Conservative candidate for South East Derbyshire, urged county
clubs who suffered loss of gate money or damage to county grounds
to sue Harold Wilson for restitution on the grounds that it was
Wilson's inflammatory words that would be the prime cause of such
'hooliganism'.

South Africans reacted with disgust to Wilson's appeal to the
Cricket Council to withdraw the invitation to the Springbok side.
They had previously believed that British 'good sense and fair play'
would prevail but it was now widely perceived that the tour was
doomed.

A SACA official said, 'We concede that Mr Vorster interfered in
sport by barring an MCC side which included Basil D'Oliveira. But
surely Mr Wilson subscribes to the theory that two wrongs do not

make a right?' Over on ITV, Thames Television was compensating for ITV's traditional incompetence in its cricket coverage by returning to the cricket tour yet again. The same night that Wilson was on the BBC granting his approval for peaceful demonstrations, the weekly political programme *This Week* invited Ted Heath to rebut everything Wilson had said. In a rehearsal for the general election campaign which was shortly to kick off, Heath dismissed Wilson's belief that apartheid was best opposed by sporting isolation. Instead, Heath argued that the best method was to take every opportunity of mixing with supporters of apartheid to show them how they too could have the same perfect race relations Britain had. Because others were intolerant he saw no reason why the British people should display similar intolerance by cancelling the tour.

Also on the night of 30 April, Hain and Wooller squared up to each other again, this time in a debate in the Oxford Union which Wooller surprisingly won. The motion was 'This house would disrupt the South African cricket tour' but it was lost by 400 votes to 391 amid scenes of general outrage at a corrupt voting system that would have been regarded as transparently corrupt by the Soviet Praesidium. Afterwards, two tellers from St Catherine's and Hertford were censured for 'nodding through', fined £5 each and banned from vote counting for the rest of the term. It was not reported whether a career at Conservative Party Central Office was awaiting them.

Hain and Wooller did not achieve any measure of personal friendliness as Wooller, triumphing in the 'result', maintained his hard line stance and deeply felt desire to see his opponent across the dispatch box in prison. During the debate, Wooller claimed Hain was friendly with a man responsible for a bomb outrage which killed a woman and mutilated several children. At that most of the 1,000 students in the Union erupted with protests to the chair. Wooller then withdrew the remark. Hain said that non-violent action need not lead to a bloodbath as the rugby demonstrations had shown.

An editorial in *The Times* reiterated the paper's belief that the tour should have been cancelled shortly after John Vorster had declared Basil D'Oliveira *persona non grata* in his own country in 1968. It defended the Cricket Council's determination to press ahead with the 1970 tour only on the grounds that it was legally fully entitled to do so and opposition to that decision, however morally justified, ran counter to the toleration that had been a principle long fought for and precariously preserved throughout Britain's long civil history. It argued that the debate had moved on from a discussion as to whether cancelling the tour would have a major impact on South African domestic racial policy to a more serious question for Britain to consider. Did the anti-tour protesters have the right in their attempt to strike a blow for the oppressed non-whites in South Africa to employ violent and dangerous means to do so? *The Times*, edited by William Rees-Mogg, believed that would substitute mob rule for the rule of law. In his opinion if STST and the anti-apartheid campaigners were to cause violence on the streets it would indeed be bad for race relations in the country and would adversely affect exactly those people for whose cause they were theoretically fighting. Therefore, drawing entirely the wrong conclusion, the best thing they could do would be not to demonstrate and ignore the tour and everything to do with it. ·

A Freedom Rally in Trafalgar Square on 1 May held by the Conservative Monday Club was attended by 1,000 people. One of the speakers, the MP Julian Amery, was greeted by a fanfare from a brass band. Amery blamed communists 'who never had any sense of humour' for bringing politics into sport. 'They have now been joined by a bunch of cranks, crackpots and sanctimonious fellow-travelling clergymen.' Uncle Laurence, who never had any time for sanctimonious clergymen of whatever denomination, nevertheless had a sense of humour though it was one that MCC failed to appreciate. He reiterated his demand that they call off the forthcoming Ashes tour on the grounds of the host's treatment of its Aboriginal population. He wasn't necessarily joking as he strove to highlight the hypocrisy the South African tour had generated on both sides of the argument.

Ali Bacher, the captain of South Africa, worried that if anti-apartheid demonstrators broke up the tour there would be serious repercussions not just in South Africa but elsewhere. If a small minority group could succeed in stopping the tour others might regard it as a precedent and there would be dire consequences. He did not specify what those consequences might be and marooned as he was in South Africa, being drip fed news by a government determined to control its dissemination, he could not possibly have known how widespread the opposition to the tour was becoming. 'We are not politicians,' he concluded, 'we are going to Britain to play cricket.' Peter Pollock, South Africa's main strike bowler, spoke to the press on Sunday 3 May. Coming in off his long run (in 1965 he had bowled beamers at Geoffrey Boycott until physically threatened by Boycott's opening partner, Bob Barber) he let fly in an outburst that read as though it had been written for him.

> I see these demonstrations and riots as part of a Communist-inspired idea to smash the vital links which have for years forced the Western nations firmly together. We cannot afford to give them [the demonstrators] the scent of victory. A principle is involved and any measure of success for this kind of defiance would see the idea spreading far beyond the realms of sport.

In *The Cricketer* magazine, the distinguished BBC football correspondent, Bryon Butler, contributed a regular column called *In The Press*. In the May edition Butler recalled a story written by E.M. Wellings, the somewhat irascible cricket correspondent of the London *Evening News*, who had held his nose sufficiently long enough to have interviewed Peter Hain who, he alleged, had told him that he knew the Pollock brothers and that although they paid lip service to multi-racialism while in this country, they were pro-apartheid when they were at home in South Africa. 'This is totally untrue,' thundered Wellings. He had checked with the Pollock brothers and discovered they could not remember ever meeting Peter Hain. He continued to thunder:

> Both Peter and Graeme used to play with Africans as youngsters and now give all their kit to Africans at the end of each season ... the Pollocks were actually accorded a reception at an African township near Port Elizabeth. Hain may claim they are pro-apartheid but the black Africans themselves know otherwise.

As in the Brexit 'debate', nobody was actually bothering to listen to anyone else who might express a view different from their own.

The views expressed by Pollock, Bacher and Rees-Mogg were much appreciated at Lord's because however temperately Harold Wilson might have felt that he had expressed his views on *Sportsnight with Coleman*, within MCC and the Cricket Council there was outrage that this Labour government, which most of them never voted for and probably despised, would stick its nose into a business which they still felt was a matter for them and for nobody else. They would have been relatively relaxed about David Sheppard and the Fair Cricket Campaign. There were enough people inside Lord's like Doug Insole, who took his secrets to the grave, but it is safe to conclude from what he did do and say that he had a reasonable response to those who disapproved of the tour going ahead. He might have been in a minority on that side of the fence but the problem now was that the days of non-violence were numbered and while 200 people holding a silent vigil or placards outside the Grace Gates would be a nuisance there was nothing to fear from them. Wild, uncontrollable hoodlums who lived at the far end of the activist spectrum and were intent on digging up the pitches and constantly interfering with play, however, were another matter entirely, especially if they managed to commandeer the news media in a way that the Cricket Council was incapable of doing.

On the other side STST and the Young Liberals, the key movers in the direct action campaign blamed, the narrow and unprincipled attitude of British sports authorities which necessitated the switch to militancy. They believed that the tactics of polite and reasonable persuasion did not work and never would, hence the need for direct action, despite the fact that David Sheppard and the Bishop of Stepney, Trevor Huddleston, had managed to convert to their way of thinking the wife of R.A. Butler, now Master of Trinity College, Cambridge. She said that she would be quite prepared to march round Lord's before the start of the Test match in June carrying a banner although she would not be persuaded to do anything violent. All places on the spectrum of anti-apartheid feeling believed that the evil of apartheid was greater than the unfortunate consequence of crowds who came to watch a cricket or a rugby match being deprived of the pleasure of watching a good game. It was increasingly obvious that apartheid could only be defeated by militant action.

The threat of violence and general mayhem increased as the May days slipped past and the prospect of the South Africans landing at Heathrow grew nearer. *'We need another Home Guard'*, reads one letter in the MCC archive, *'but on this occasion the enemy is within – the Quislings of 1970.'* A letter from The Old Rectory, Staplegrove, Taunton (but not from a cleric) told MCC that the author was giving 25% of her pension to the fund to keep the tour going. This admirable old lady then rather blotted her copybook with the closing remark that *'one immigrant student* [presumably Peter Hain] *has started this campaign and our niggerloving bishops and MPs will have made England the laughing stock of the world.'* Another elderly lady wrote what appears initially to be a sweet reminiscence, recalling her days as a bus conductress in the First World War, when her husband was away fighting in Mesopotamia. Her regular route was the number 53 from Plumstead Common to West Hampstead via St John's Wood. When the bus was on Finchley Road she would make a point of collecting fares on the upper deck so she could see the cricket in play from the open top. Unfortunately, she then launches into a diatribe against the 'wicked threaterous [sic] Zionist V signers' who apparently are behind the attempts to stop the tour of the loyal South Africans who came to our aid to fight Nazism. Having relieved herself of her deeply felt anti-Semitism she then apologises for her spelling and the fact that she shakes now that she is 75 but doesn't blame the Jews for it. Another letter also refers to the anti-tour protesters, 'many of whom emanate from Eastern Europe'. Maybe the author had been sitting next to Uncle Laurence.

In America, non-violence was losing its appeal even before Martin Luther King, its supreme champion, was assassinated in April 1968. Ralph Abernathy, who succeeded Dr King as president of the Southern Christian Leadership Conference, lacked King's charisma and the disheartened black population, particularly the younger element, increasingly turned to the blandishments of Stokely Carmichael, Huey Newton, Angela Davis and the Black Panthers, all of whom were considerably more militant than Dr King and his supporters had been. They were fed up with the beatings, the dogs, the water cannon, the wrongful imprisonment and the rest of the discrimination suffered under the Jim Crow laws. It was time for direct action and it was this action that caused tremors among the white population and accounted in part for the election of Richard Nixon.

In Britain, the carrying of placards, however admirable, seemed to belong to the early days of CND, to the days when Bertrand Russell and John Osborne might be arrested at a demonstration for a nominal breach of the peace, held in a cell overnight, appear before Bow Street magistrates the following morning and be fined minimally. It was a game in which nobody got hurt and the issues were raised in the press to be argued about democratically. 1968 had changed the rules of the game. In 1970 it was now believed that, in order to be effective, protest had to involve direct action. It was two years after Grosvenor Square, two years after the Tet offensive and LBJ's decision not to run again. It was nearly a year after the Stonewall riots in New York City when young gay men had finally had enough of being abused and humiliated by the straight world and were finding the courage to fight back. 1970 was the year when the Women's Liberation Movement showed a sceptical male world that they were no longer willing to be taken for granted and that they were now prepared to act in a physical demonstration of their determination to right an historical wrong.

Once the political heavyweight Sir Edward Boyle had joined David Sheppard's Fair Cricket Campaign, Peter Hain and STST deliberately went quiet. It was their opinion that the moderate and responsible FCC must be allowed to make its appeal to the wider British public, something the militant supporters of direct action would have found difficult. Speaking on *The World This Weekend* on Radio 4 on Sunday 3 May, Boyle acknowledged that Rees-Mogg's leading article in the previous day's *Times* should be given due consideration but he still felt that 'the predictable consequences of the tour would be wholly bad – bad for race relations, bad for cricket, bad for sport generally, for relations within the Commonwealth, for law and order in this country and for civil liberty'. Perhaps to justify his view Mr Ken Taylor, not the fine Yorkshire opening batsman, brilliant fielder and useful change bowler but the Ken Taylor who gloried in the title of the prospective National Front candidate for the constituency of Enfield, declared that MCC and Scotland Yard could rely on the brave loyal members of the National Front to preserve law and order on the streets of Britain if there was going to be any trouble from left-wing organisations during the tour.

This of course was exactly what the left-wing organisations were hoping to hear, as it alienated the moderate apolitical cricket supporters who were disinclined to line themselves up alongside British Nazis. They were also helped unwittingly of course by Richard Nixon's decision to invade Cambodia and the tragic aftermath on the campus of Kent State University. On 4 May members of the Ohio National Guard, a hastily mustered collection of civilian reservists, were called on to the campus at Kent State in response to a request by the university administration to help to quell the unrest which had followed the President's television announcement that American troops had seriously escalated the war in South East Asia by invading Cambodia. The demonstration on campus was unruly but not violent. The response was cataclysmic. Twenty-eight guardsmen started firing into a crowd of unarmed students.

The Adjutant General of the Ohio National Guard later claimed that they had come under fire from a sniper whose identity was never discovered. Eager to avoid the blame, he also claimed that the guardsmen had been told to fire in the air. It appeared that some did but others certainly did not. In the event, two young men and two young women were shot dead immediately, and a further nine were seriously wounded including one who was left permanently paralysed. Some of those who were shot were not demonstrating at all and had simply been walking nearby or observing the protest from a distance. It should be added that these students were white which, realistically, added to the sense of national outrage. One can only wonder whether the same level of outrage would have been felt if the lives that were so cruelly and senselessly terminated had been black.

Nevertheless, there was a significant national response to the shootings in which hundreds of universities, colleges and high schools closed throughout the United States in response to a strike of four million students and the event further affected public opinion, at an already socially contentious time, over the war that was becoming more unpopular with every passing day. For President Nixon such demonstrations in the universities were a betrayal of the privileges the students had been granted.

You see these bums, you know, blowing up the campuses. Listen, the boys that are on the college campuses today are the luckiest people in the world, going to the greatest universities, and here they are burning up the books, storming around about this issue. You name it. Get rid of the war there will be another one.

Such inflammatory words increased the anger and frustration of the anti-war protesters of all ages but Nixon knew that the electorate that had voted him in 19 months previously would be cheering such sentiments.

It undoubtedly helped to spread the anti-war protest to the parental generation but it re-emphasised to the student population that they were in open conflict with the ideas and values of the people who wielded power over them. It may seem a long way both in distance and culture from Ohio to St John's Wood but there was a sense among British students who were demonstrating against apartheid that they were engaged in the same battle as American students protesting against the war in Vietnam. What American students felt about MCC and the South African cricket tour was never publicly expressed but no doubt had the issues been explained to them they would have conveyed a mutual solidarity. Their parents had fought a world war to defend liberty and democracy and now they were engaged in another war to deprive their children of what those children felt were precisely those rights.

In Washington, the American equivalent of the NUS, the National Student Association, called for a nationwide university strike in protest against the extension of the war into neutral Cambodia. Having taught for many years in a British university I am all too aware that it doesn't take much effort to persuade students not to attend lectures but the reality in May 1970 was that the war in Vietnam was a constant and serious concern. The editors of 11 student newspapers on the East Coast agreed to run the identical article condemning Nixon's decision to invade Cambodia. Senator George McGovern, who would win the Democratic nomination in 1972 to run against Richard Nixon in that year's presidential race, introduced a measure into Congress to deny the President access to any further funds for the war in Indo-China as it now became known, other than for use in bringing the troops home. McGovern asked for help from the students which was readily forthcoming and he became the man who picked up the torch borne by Eugene McCarthy and Robert Kennedy in 1968. In Parliament, Michael Stewart, the Foreign Secretary, refused to condemn the action of the Americans to the consternation of the left wing of his party led by Michael Foot. Six weeks before a general election would be held this kind of split in the Labour Party was precisely what he was trying to avoid.

The one element in public life that appeared to elicit only a positive response from the country was the fate of the England football team. Twenty-seven players and their support staff flew out to Mexico City on 5 May leaving behind Francis Lee, whose wife was in hospital but who rejoined the squad a few days later. There was enormous and justifiable confidence that the World Cup, which had been won so dramatically at Wembley in 1966, could be retained in the less congenial atmosphere engendered by South Americans who appeared to be openly resentful of England's colonial past. In fact, the antagonism the England party discovered when they arrived in Mexico City had originated in one of the few emotional sound bites ever uttered by Sir Alf Ramsey. Speaking shortly after England's 1-0 victory over Argentina in the quarter-final of the 1966 World Cup, Ramsey had called the Argentinians 'animals' after they had kicked and fouled and cheated their way through the match. It appeared that he had offended not just the people of Argentina but the entire continent of Latin America, who had neither forgotten not forgiven Ramsey's outrageous and offensive slander.

At Heathrow, on boarding the plane to Mexico City, Ramsey let it be known that he considered it would be his fault alone if England did not retain the cup, such had been the thoroughness of their preparation. The previous summer Ramsey had taken the England team on a tour of South America to give them some experience of the heat and the problems of playing at high altitude which they would face the following year. After a 0–0 draw with Mexico, the party flew to Montevideo where they beat Uruguay 2–1. It was an excellent result, the gloss of which was tarnished when it emerged that the England players had refused to eat any of the food at the barbecue laid on by the host football federation. Jack Charlton had tried to digest something which turned out to be sheep's kidneys and was vomiting for the whole of the following day. Finally, in Rio, against the team who would be their main rivals in Mexico, England lost somewhat unluckily, having held on for most of the game to a 1–0 lead given them early on by Colin Bell. The Brazilians scored twice against an exhausted England in the last few minutes. Ramsey was by no means dissatisfied.

Mindful of the horrors of the food in Brazil in 1950 and the unfortunate confrontation in Montevideo in 1969, Ramsey ensured that his 1970 World Cup squad would eat and drink nothing but food that had been shipped to Mexico from England. Ramsey's most recent biographer, Leo McKinstry, revealed that 25,000 bottles of Malvern water were sent ahead of the team and Ramsey negotiated with the frozen food company Findus to transport 140lb of beefburgers, 400lb of sausages, 300lb of frozen fish and ten cases of tomato ketchup. Unfortunately, the Mexicans got wind of the importation because Findus were too keen to boast of their part in England's future success and the hosts were predictably insulted. The Mexican authorities refused to allow any meat or dairy products into the country and the England team doctor had to go down to the quayside and watch his carefully planned supplies of steak, butter, sausages and beef burned in front of him. It might have been done on the grounds of public health but it must have felt like a 20th-century version of a 16th-century religious persecution. At home the news was regarded as confirmation that foreigners could not be trusted. The United Kingdom was two and a half years away from joining the Common Market but the deep residual xenophobic feelings that would emerge fully formed as the Brexit Party were already in evidence.

It would be another three weeks before England would kick off their first game in the group stage against Romania. As long as everyone stayed fit there seemed no reason to expect that anything would happen in the friendly games against Ecuador and Colombia that would prevent England starting that match against Romania with their strongest team and expecting to reach the final. The newspapers and television were also prepared to slake what appeared to be an unending public thirst for stories about the best footballers in England. There was a firm belief that England was a better side in

1970 than it had been in 1966 with the addition of Mullery, Labone, Cooper and Lee to replace Stiles, Jack Charlton, Wilson and Hunt. There were no problems with football, a subject on which the nation was united. The problems were all with cricket.

CHAPTER NINE

MAY 1970

I N the 6 May edition of the *Daily Telegraph*, E.W. Swanton previewed what threatened to be a stormy Annual General Meeting of MCC.

> Although the probability is that most members of MCC, like most members of the public, still want the tour to proceed, I suspect that many, reluctantly or otherwise, would like to see it cancelled, if only on the ground that protesters have raised the temperature to such dangerous levels.

Swanton was edging closer to the point of view of David Sheppard, who was still trying hard to persuade MCC to change its mind. After several fruitless meetings with members of its Council, the bishop spoke out against the tour at the AGM but as far as MCC was concerned, considering what had happened in 1968 and the dangers of a possible repeat, the meeting actually passed without much trouble. The MCC press office issued a statement declaring that the club was pleased to note that the feeling of the meeting closely followed what it believed was the majority view in the country, that the tour should proceed. There was ample evidence, it claimed, of the strength of this feeling both from the flood of letters received since the opening of the 1970 Cricket Fund, as well as from recent opinion polls.

Echoing this sentiment in an article in the May edition of *The Cricketer*, John Woodcock wrote:

To hear both past and present officers of the non-white cricket authority saying that South Africa's isolation could be the death-knell of their own cricket, was to realise that we have a moral obligation to see the thing through. This is something which can most easily be understood by those who have been to South Africa.

It is no use demanding that South African cricket should forthwith become fully integrated. To make that a condition of maintaining contact is hopelessly unrealistic.

However, in a letter written to Billy Griffith the day after the AGM, David Sheppard took issue with MCC's stated position that, although no vote was taken, the feeling of the meeting 'closely followed the majority view in this country that the tour should proceed'. He, Mark Bonham Carter, the chairman of the Race Relations Board and Sir Edward Boyle had emerged from the AGM to tell journalists that in their opinion there was still a chance that MCC would see sense and call off the tour. They were encouraged by the number of members who had previously opposed them but that day had spoken in their favour. They had also delivered a letter from Frank Cousins, the former trade union official and Labour government minister, who, in his capacity as the chairman of the Community Relations Commission, pleaded with MCC to cancel the tour. The pressure was building but the government had not ordered them to do so and as far as MCC was concerned their members, the counties, cricket supporters and the majority of the public wanted them to stand up to the pressure exerted by politically motivated left-wingers. They would continue to do so.

One item of AGM business that MCC thought would be uncontroversial was the succession to Maurice Allom as its president by Sir Cyril Hawker. Hawker was chairman of the Standard Bank, which had the Standard Bank of South Africa as its subsidiary. He was to become president of MCC and *de facto* chairman of the Cricket Council on 1 October. Peter Hain was disgusted by the appointment.

This will provoke scenes which none of us wanted. I cannot see the MCC's reason for making such a provocative appointment.

This only confirms what many of us suspected, that the MCC
is influenced by very strong business links with South Africa.

Just as Swanton was starting to agree with Sheppard about
cancellation, the letters to the *Daily Telegraph*, a bellwether of tour
supporters, began to include those from people who had started out
from different positions but were all heading towards the recognition
that cancellation was inevitable. L.P. Hartley, the author of *The Go-
Between* which had been dramatised by Harold Pinter and was about
to start filming its famous cricket match in Norfolk that summer,
wrote on 9 May quoting Lord Macaulay's well-known observation
'We know of no spectacle so ridiculous as the British public in one
of its periodic fits of morality.' He added:

> Why do the Springboks want to visit a country where, from
> the Prime Minister downwards (or upwards), they are so
> unwelcome? Why don't they stay at home knowing they are
> the best team in the world and could wipe the floor with us?
>
> Some years ago we 'owned' and ruled at least one-fifth of
> the Continent of Africa; nor did we pause to ask ourselves if
> minority rule was a 'good thing' provided it was good for us. ...
> Since then we have had a change of heart; we insist on 'majority
> rule' and have handed over Nigeria to its tender mercies. The
> results we know though we do not blame ourselves.

He goes on to recall the concentration camps of the Boer War and the
inhumane treatment of Cetewayo and the Zulus and concludes that:

> The Springbok tour will give much encouragement to
> hooligans, whether of Church or State, and tie the hands of the
> police who will be mustered in thousands to safeguard cricket
> pitches. The only people who will benefit by the tour... are
> the criminals who will take advantage of the enforced absence
> of the police.

Not all *Telegraph* correspondents had changed their minds
though. Underneath Hartley's letter was one from Wilf Wooller,
complaining that 'alien organisers' (presumably a euphemism for

Peter Hain) 'have the art of suspending laws which apply to the natives of Britain'. He called for the Public Meeting Act to be obeyed which logically would lead to Hain being tried before a judge and jury and, if (inevitably) found guilty, would be subject to 12 months' imprisonment, a £500 fine or both. Wooller's passionate desire to see Hain behind bars had not diminished with time. Three days later, on 12 May the monocled former Surrey captain Percy Fender wrote that the Prime Minister's stated opinions on demonstrations should have laid him open to prosecution for inciting public disorder.

> More people dislike Communism than South Africa yet Mr Wilson did nothing when the Red choir came to do more than sing a few songs. Yet Mr Wilson sees fit to incite a smaller minority to demonstrate against a few cricket matches between England and a friendly State.

It would have been a relief for Harold Wilson to turn his attention from the bitterness of cricket to the relative calm of the local elections, which would be a significant factor in the Cabinet's decision if it were to call a general election. When the results were announced, there had been a massive 10% swing to Labour which made the desirability of a June general election much stronger. The polls had been heading Labour's way since the Budget, but polls, even in 1970, were known to be not entirely reliable. Nobody could argue though with the evidence of the ballot box.

At Lord's it was not clear what this political climate meant for them. If Labour was returned to power, as now seemed likely, it would not be until after the South Africa tour had started, in which case they would be unable to do anything, in the sense that they would be unlikely to insist on an abandonment in the middle of the tour, unless there were large-scale and violent disturbances. If the Fates smiled on Lord's and the Conservatives regained power then all would be right with the world though again it would be too late for the Conservative Party's approval of the tour to have any impact, particularly if the incumbent Labour government had already insisted on cancellation. The only thing that mattered was the attitude of the government between early May and the beginning of June when the tourists would have played their first matches amidst tight security and presumably in the face of vocal opposition outside and possibly inside the grounds.

They believed their case was strengthened when Jack Plimsoll, the appointed manager of the tour, announced in Johannesburg that his squad was eager to play against any team in the world, regardless of politics or colour and he was certainly not against the idea of mixed sport in South Africa. Left unspoken, of course, was the reality that his government was dead set against it and as long as it remained in power, which with the voting system operating as it did, was likely to be for the foreseeable future, the chance of any mixed sport happening in South Africa was non-existent.

Supporters of the tour welcomed Plimsoll's 'bold' statement enthusiastically. Opponents just saw it as the same old empty words. And with just cause. The same newspapers which carried Plimsoll's words also reported on the case of 22 Africans currently languishing in South African jails although the Vorster government was silent as to where they were being held. The men had been arrested under the Suppression of Communism Act but found not guilty. However, instead of being released they were re-arrested on emerging from the courtroom whilst the South African authorities tried to think of another charge that would stick. Following a noisy meeting of 2,500 undergraduates from the University of Witwatersrand, 150 students marched 12-abreast down the streets of Johannesburg in support of the 22. They had defied a ban on their protest and were, as expected, confronted by police. The students sat down, sang 'We Shall Overcome', the anthem of the Civil Rights movement, and were duly arrested and taken to jail. The South Africans might have been uncompromising in their condemnation of and fight against communism but they had created a police state that dealt with 'dissidents' in exactly the same manner as the Russians so notoriously did.

Public opinion was certainly starting to swing behind the idea of cancellation although it was impossible to tell to what extent with any precision. On a small scale it was noted that the Professional Cricketers' Association were starting to have a change of heart. When their members had been asked at the turn of the year whether they were in favour of the tour going ahead the answer was almost unanimously positive. In the middle of May the PCA committee took another vote and although it supported the tour the resolution passed by a majority of just one. The eyes of the cricketers were being opened. Maybe it was not possible to take refuge in the traditional stance that politics should be kept out of sport and that they were just cricketers who were only interested in playing cricket. As the atmosphere in the country became more frenzied their easy retreat from the fray was no longer tenable. Some of them at least started to recognise that this was a moral issue not a political one and as human beings they had a responsibility at least to think about the morality behind the tour. Once they did so, it wasn't too far to travel to a position in which they recognised that the tour would have to be cancelled.

In New Zealand the forthcoming tour by the Springbok rugby team, who had returned home from Britain chastened at the end of January, was beginning to come under threat. The Prime Minister, Keith Holyoake, was adopting the now familiar governmental position that the tour was a matter for the rugby authorities in New Zealand and they should come to their own decision free from interference or a direct order from the government. Like the Cricket Council, the NZRFU was of the opinion that the tour should go ahead. What happened in South Africa was none of their business. As in Britain, the country, which cared greatly about the All Blacks, was several steps ahead of its government.

Although STST was temporarily adopting a low profile, preparations were still going ahead for activity at the first three matches now scheduled for Lord's, Trent Bridge and Headingley. In addition, just as they had chased the Springboks rugby team out of the country, they were planning an equally aggressive 'welcome' for the cricketers by mounting a blockade of Heathrow airport. The announced arrival day was 1 June but STST officials had been tipped off that there would be a last-minute switch in arrangements of some sort and they were determined not to be outfoxed. Matches were mostly all-ticket as the authorities sought desperately to control the flow of tickets so that they went to genuine cricket fans. The problem they faced was, 'What did a real cricket fan look like?' A middle-aged Australian woman managed to persuade the ticket office at Lord's to give her 25 applications, each of which permitted four tickets. However harmless she appeared, she was in fact working for STST and by the end of the exercise Lord's looked like it was going to be filled mostly by anti-apartheid campaigners.

It wasn't just well-organised white supporters who were making their feelings known. Black teenagers had set up an enterprising group for what they termed 'Explanation Day'. In other words they wanted an explanation from MCC as to why this benighted tour was going ahead. They issued a leaflet which stated that on 30 May, the day before the South Africans were due to arrive,

> young West Indians, Pakistanis, Africans and Indians plan to march from Hyde Park Corner to Lord's to ask MCC why they are insulting us in this way.... Black people in this country continue to suffer mockery, discrimination and insult. When the MCC invites an all-white South African team to this country it is condoning racism and insulting the Black Community yet again. In ten years' time British sport will be grateful and probably dependent on black sporting talent and skill – but at the moment they don't give a damn about us.

It is hard to disagree with any of those propositions. Roland Butcher the black Middlesex batsman, made his debut for England in the first Test match against the West Indies on the 1980/81 tour. In 1977 Viv Anderson of Nottingham Forest became the first black footballer to represent England in a full international. And until such players as these came forward and made a major impact for a British sports team, British society by and large did not give a damn about them.

Wherever the cricket authorities looked in the middle of May 1970, apart from into their own heartlands of mainly Tory-held constituencies in the South of England, they found opposition. It would have been entirely understandable if at any point after 19 January when the county grounds were attacked, making a strong statement about what was to come, the Cricket Council had made contact with SACA and called off the tour. However, they had clearly seen Michael Caine and Stanley Baker at the battle of Rorke's Drift in *Zulu* and decided they were going to barricade themselves into the Lord's pavilion and repel all attempts at infiltration. In this enterprise they would at least have been able to rely on the staunch help provided by the pavilion gatekeepers in linen jackets singing *Jerusalem*, rather than *Men of Harlech*, who would have taken one look at the improperly dressed hordes and sent them packing to sit in the free seats at the Nursery End with the rest of the hoi polloi.

They must, however, have been aware that a meeting of the ICC was planned for June which was to take place as usual at Lord's. The ground would be surrounded by barbed wire and the representatives from all the Test-playing countries plus those of Ceylon, Malaysia, Fiji, East Africa and the United States would be making their way to the meeting through a police cordon, with a view out of the window not of old Father Time but of a concentration camp. Surely they must have feared that India, Pakistan and West Indies would tolerate no longer the inequitable system in which South Africa was allowed to play cricket only against other all-white teams.

India and Pakistan were both due to tour England the following summer and West Indies would return in 1973. The cricket boards of Pakistan, India and West Indies had all been somewhat intimidated by England and Australia, the traditional powers behind the ICC. South Africa had been a republic since 1961 and just as the country had also been forced out of the Commonwealth at that point, it was also then told it could no longer be a member of the Imperial Cricket Conference (which became the International Cricket Conference in 1965), the organisation it had founded with England and Australia in 1909. It did, however, continue to send an observer to ICC meetings without provoking any objection from the subcontinent or the Caribbean.

If the tour were now to go ahead as planned in June, the white nations must have been anxious that they would end up playing cricket only against each other in future seasons. The Cricket Council's policy of building bridges to South Africa and maintaining dialogue would then become instantly redundant. There was some thought that had Sir Frank Worrell not died of leukaemia in 1967 at the tragically young age of 43, he might have been the perfect candidate to broker some sort of accord between the two sides separated by the issue of colour. In July 1961 the first ICC meeting had taken place after South Africa's departure from the Commonwealth. The West Indies, unwilling to rock the boat, sent, as was their wont, two white representatives. MCC made all representatives aware, to the evident satisfaction of the South African observer, that nothing that happened in the realm of politics in the wider world was going to prevent England continuing to play South Africa away in 1964/65 and hosting them at home in the English summer of 1965. No objection was raised. Australia also confirmed that it would host a South African tour during its 1963/64 season. These matches would clearly be between all-white teams.

By 1970 these attitudes were widely seen, even within the reactionary world of cricket politics, as antediluvian and the Cricket Council was confronted by a change in social attitudes and behaviour that it was incapable of understanding, although it was also apparent that it was making little attempt to do so. The Test and County Cricket Board had introduced the very popular John Player Sunday League which attracted families to county grounds for a 2pm start with play guaranteed to finish by 6.30 allowing time to get home, make the children's tea and to ensure they were in bed in time for school the following morning. It had taken to heart the calls for brighter cricket from the press and the public and had earnestly sought a solution to the problem of declining attendances at county cricket matches which had begun in the early 1950s after the initial post-war boom had petered out and had continued to spiral downwards ever since. In 1962 the anachronistic class difference between amateurs and professionals had been abolished and the following year the first knockout competition with a single innings for each side, limited to 65 overs for its first year, had been successfully inaugurated. Cricket authorities had moved with the times faster than the FA in football, the LTA in tennis, the RFU in rugby union, the Royal & Ancient in golf and the AAA in athletics. They had, however, been outflanked by the social changes.

The problem now was the use of violence as a political weapon. It had started in America where both the anti-war movement and the Civil Rights movement had elicited supported from middle-class idealists throughout the decade. By 1970, however, there was a realisation that liberal attitudes, marches on Washington by concerned mothers, the burning of draft cards and the American flag were never going to be enough. Martin Luther King had been assassinated; Richard Nixon had escalated the war by invading Cambodia. Protests on a university campus had led to the deaths of the innocent. A previously moderate and peaceful university student in Madison, Wisconsin explained in May 1970 in the wake of a new wave of student strikes and violence across the country,

> We've tried peaceful ways of stopping this war for five years: it doesn't work. The blacks tried peaceful means of ending their poverty: it didn't work. Rioting brought the blacks more money. We hope rioting will bring us peace. I won't join the riots but I won't condemn them. We have to be violent to get on the news screen.

Peter Hain might not have been supportive of violence either but he would have understood exactly what this student was saying and why. He was doing a quite remarkable job as chairman of STST, particularly bearing in mind that he was at the time an undergraduate at Imperial College reading Engineering and he was effectively co-ordinating a national campaign from a phone box in college during the lunchtime break from lectures.

He was, however, incapable of halting the flow of people to the ranks whom he might have considered unhelpful to the cause. A leaflet that was circulating in London at this time urged skinheads to 'work out your aggro against apartheid and racist sport'. The leaflet was published by the Derby branch of the hitherto unknown Skinhead Mobilisation Group. It was the end of the football season and it suggested that 'Paki bashing', which was one of its core group activities, could be suspended during the close season whilst member skinheads could join STST and stop the tour with their own unique brand of political persuasion.

Younis Ahmed and Intikhab Alam, the Pakistani players who had made a successful transition to county cricket, now told Surrey that they did not wish to be considered for the county's match against South Africa or for selection for the Southern Counties. The straightforward nod of approval which the PCA had given the tour in January was now replaced by a much more nuanced view as overseas players in particular, who had almost universally been welcomed by county supporters and had responded with stirring deeds on the field, realised that this was no longer a question in which politics could be separated from the sport where they earned their living. If they had anxieties previously about raising their heads above the parapet for fear of the antagonistic reaction it would provoke they now had no reason to fear such a response. Everyone could understand why they might have ethical problems playing against an all-white South Africa team and they would not jeopardise their futures with their new counties if they quietly withdrew.

The national debate reached Westminster. Philip Noel-Baker, the Labour MP for Derby South, a former Olympic athlete and a Nobel prize-winner to boot, was due to retire at the next election but he persuaded the Speaker, supported by other Labour and Liberal MPs, to allow an emergency debate on the issue in the House of Commons on 14 May. When he spoke he cited the much repeated warnings on relations with the Commonwealth and race relations at home and that the squad of cricketers due to arrive in two weeks' time had effectively been selected by John Vorster. Opposing the motion calling on the Cricket Council to withdraw its invitation, John Biggs-Davison, the Conservative member for Chigwell, reiterated his own many times repeated unqualified support for white rule in South Africa and Rhodesia. The Deputy Leader of the Opposition, Reginald Maudling, made the point that 'banning Russian athletes from entering this country would not help the Czech people'. Edward Boyle, rising to speak from the Opposition benches, took a very different line from the majority of his party. Boyle had seen every South Africa tour since 1935 and loved watching them. He felt that the links of sport and particularly cricket were among the most valuable links binding the Commonwealth together. He also thought those who advocated disruption and violence were the people who were responsible for harming race relations in Great Britain.

Later in the debate, the Sports Minister, Denis Howell, said that it would be a 'serious error' if the government went beyond persuasion and interfered directly. The Home Secretary called on the Cricket Council to do the decent thing and stop him from having to issue that direct government order. He too had become aware of a whiff of 1940 in the counsels of the Council.

> There seems a lurking belief, that I detected in the Cricket
> Council when they came to see me, that they are a lonely band

of heroes standing against the darkening tide of lawlessness. I can relieve them of that burden. What we are discussing here is the judgment of the Council in inviting a team here in the face of an unparalleled crescendo of opposition … it is not unfair to the Cricket Council to throw responsibility upon them. They invited the South Africans and they can uninvite them if they choose to do so.

They did not choose to do so. Observing the debate upstairs in the Strangers' Gallery were representatives of the Cricket Council who tucked away the information that the Home Secretary was admitting that the police force could deal with demonstrations and protests that became violent. 'There need be no fear in anyone's mind', confirmed Callaghan, 'that the police are incapable of handling this kind of demonstration.'

The following week, on Monday 19 May, the Council was due to meet at Lord's amidst growing expectation that it could no longer hold back the tide that was now flowing relentlessly towards it. Peter Hain, on being asked his opinion, declared cautiously that he was hopeful the Cricket Council would see sense but he would reserve judgement until after the meeting. He would have been aware that the previous day SACA had issued a statement confirming their preparations for the tour. The squad was now gathering for a week of practice in Durban before leaving for England. Dr Ali Bacher told the South African press that he believed it was important that the tour went ahead. On being asked why he thought it was important he replied, 'There are a number of good reasons for it but I do not care to go into it in detail at this stage.' When he was questioned as to what he and his team expected to find in England in the way of demonstrations and possibly violent protests he replied enigmatically, 'What will be, will be.' He then produced the standard mantra of all cricketers.

My attitude is that we are going to play cricket and not make speeches. Whatever I say is my viewpoint as a player and I don't want to indulge in politics in any shape or form. Politics are outside my field.

Bacher had turned down offers from England to fly out ahead of the team and conduct press, radio and television interviews. He proclaimed his willingness to leave the future of the tour entirely in the hands of MCC which is probably why Hain did not feel confident of success when the Cricket Council announced the outcome of its deliberations of 19 May.

In the days leading up to the announcement the *Sunday Times* kept up its pressure for cancellation. Michael Parkinson announced that he would not report on the tour and he wouldn't watch any cricket at all in 1970. He also warned of the long-term consequences of the actions of a blinkered cricket establishment.

> The game would have far more attraction for a lot of young people if it did not appear to be an exclusive club run by middle-aged reactionaries for middle-aged reactionaries. It might upset the Marylebone Clodpoles Club to even contemplate the thought that those long-haired kids who demonstrate against the white South Africans belong to a generation that cricket has to appeal to if it can survive as our summer game.
>
> Those members of the Cricket Council and the TCCB who invited the white South Africans to this country are to my mind more deserving of contempt than the 13 apostles of apartheid who so gratefully accepted the invitation.

However, a pained letter the following week, the day before the announcement, took Parky to task.

> He calls the South African cricketers '13 apostles of apartheid' Why? He might with equal justice call members of the Bolshoi Ballet 'apostles of the invasion of Hungary and Czechoslovakia', members of the US Davis Cup team 'apostles of the war in Vietnam and segregation in the South'; members of the Australian cricket team 'apostles of the white Australian policy'.

Kenneth Lawrence, writing from Shaftesbury, added:

> True sportsmen in this country resent the introduction of politics into sport and Parkinson must realise that he is

condoning the very thing that he condemns in South Africa
– intolerance.

Parkinson's editor, Harold Evans, gave solid support in the same
edition in an editorial headed *Forget the demos, the tour is wrong.*

> Two conflicting rights are in conflict – the right to invite South
> Africa and watch the games and the right to protest peacefully.
> There is no place here for Government intervention. It cannot
> and it must not ban the tour. The contention that we must
> accept South Africans because we accept the Red Army choir
> does not wash; the Russians do not select teams racially and
> Russia has never been known to turn down a visiting team
> because it did not consist entirely of Communists.

Meanwhile, there was a cricket season already in full swing. On
Saturday 16 May as Lord's prepared for its version of the Gunfight
at the OK Corral, Surrey visited New Road, Worcester where,
under the benign shadow of the great cathedral, John Edrich scored
a magnificent 143. Writing about it in the following day's *Sunday
Telegraph*, Wilf Wooller tried to evoke the eternal glory of cricket
and by implication why it must be preserved but still couldn't resist
a dig at Peter Hain.

> The gentle warm sun, the fresh green of the flowering
> chestnuts, the russet brown of the copper beech, the leisurely
> movement of white figures, and the soft impact of leather on
> willow carried a reassuring tradition of permanence. Players
> from India, Pakistan, West Indies and South Africa graced
> this typical English scene which one felt would endure when
> the long-haired demonstrators had gone bald.

For the record, approaching the age of 70, Peter Hain has a fine
head of grey hair.

It turned out to be a superb match. Worcestershire dismissed
Surrey for 370 and then declared two runs behind when D'Oliveira
was bowled by Roope for 101. The visitors in turn declared, setting
the home side 219 in just over two hours on the third afternoon.

Worcestershire finished six runs short with Surrey needing just two more wickets to win. There was no politics, just hard fought cricket played in glorious sunshine in front of an appreciative crowd.

The climax of the tour controversy took place in London as Ron Headley and Glenn Turner set off in pursuit of that 219. Matters had been significantly complicated by the impending announcement about the election. The day before the Cricket Council was to deliberate on the issue for what it hoped would be the last time, the government, to very little surprise, announced that a general election would be held on Thursday 18 June. Harold Wilson had decided that going to the country with the Labour Party ahead in the polls and seemingly stretching its lead was more important than worrying about the fate of the England football team and its possible impact on voting patterns. Everyone now felt comfortable that England would at the very least reach the final which meant that if they were to lose to Brazil, the pre-tournament favourites, at that point they would still be in the competition when the country went to the polls. If they were to lose to Brazil in the final Wilson would already be back in Downing Street.

Thursday 18 June was for cricket administrators an equally important day for it was the first day of the first Test match against South Africa, scheduled to be played at Lord's when all the anti-apartheid forces would coalesce from Lady Butler to the Birmingham branch of the Skinhead Mobilisation Group. For Hain and the Anti-Apartheid Movement generally, the coming election was seen as a good thing. Even if riots inside and outside cricket grounds would be bad for the current government and therefore bad for Labour, if the Tories won they would have to pick up the pieces of a horrible social mess as the tour would continue for the first two months or so of a new Conservative government. It therefore appeared to STST and their fellow campaigners that the likelihood was that the tour would be called off. Already, men like E.W. Swanton and Robin Marlar, both of them sitting on the right-hand side of the press box, had changed their stance on the tour, believing that if it went ahead the game of cricket would suffer. The latter said recently:

> The price of the tour was going to be too high in terms of money and people getting hurt and bad publicity for the police.

By then I was 100% behind the cancellation. I had changed. It's like Brexit. You can take a point of view but events change it.

As the Cricket Council gathered at Lord's, the *Daily Telegraph* printed an editorial in flat contradiction of the views of its senior cricket correspondent. It wrote of the fear of serious disruption which,

> is the means by which the Stop the Seventy Tour committee hope to enforce their will on the great majority of cricket lovers and of the general public. If the Government wishes to surrender to its lawlessness and disorder, let it take the responsibility itself. The Cricket Council should stand firm.

On the evening of 19 May, the London evening newspapers carried headlines proclaiming the inevitability of cancellation. Brian Johnston on the other hand, the BBC cricket correspondent and a strong supporter of the tour, had other information. Peter Baxter, his long-time producer, recalled:

> Johnners always claimed that as the BBC cricket correspondent he had one scoop in his entire career. There was a big meeting at Lord's in May 1970 in which it was to be decided whether the tour could go ahead or not. Johnners had a mole on the MCC committee and that was how he found out and he went to *The World At One* and told them that yes, the tour was going to go ahead, which indeed it was at that time.

A few hours later at a press conference in the Long Room, it became clear that Johnston was right and that Hain had good reason to be dubious about the certainty of cancellation, as Billy Griffith announced that the Cricket Council had decided 'by a substantial majority' that the tour should proceed as planned. This indicated some shifting of the ground since previous decisions had always been arrived at 'unanimously'. The substantial majority indicated that at last there was a breach in the wall. Defending the cricket authorities against the inevitable attacks that would follow in the wake of its decision, Griffith added that this would be the last occasion on which SACA would be allowed to select an all-white team to tour England. In future, Griffith promised, there would be 'no future Test tours between South Africa and this country until South African cricket is played and teams selected on a multi-racial basis in South Africa'. In other words they seemed to admit they knew that what they were doing was amoral but could they please have this last night of passion with an old lover before redefining the relationship as platonic?

As in many such relationship break-ups, neither party was pleased and the divorce threatened to become very bitter very fast. The protesters were astonished that the tour was going ahead in the face of all the opposition that had been gaining such momentum in the past few weeks.

Tour supporters were equally annoyed that the Council's lily-livered statement was a negation of a fundamental principle for which they had believed they were all fighting – the right to play cricket against whomsoever it pleased. The Council confirmed that it had re-assessed its responsibilities and felt that they related exclusively to cricket and cricketers throughout the world as well as 'the other sports and sportsmen' although how that could be the case, when they were effectively cocking a snook at all the sportspeople in the world who did not wish to play against South Africa for the perfectly comprehensible reason that South Africa discriminated against them because of the colour of their skin, was not immediately apparent.

The Council had apparently discussed its now notorious policy of building bridges to South Africa and it had reached the decision that, 'It was agreed that in the long term this policy was in the best interests of cricket and cricketers of all races in South Africa.' There was no suggestion of cynicism here, merely an extraordinary conviction that they were right and the rest of the world pretty much was wrong. The statement continued:

> The question of the Commonwealth Games in Scotland had been discussed. The Council expressed deep regret at the attitude of those countries who threatened to withdraw if the tour took place but it hoped that in view of its statement about the future those countries would think again.

The Council sympathised with those boards of control which had been put under considerable pressure with regard to this tour, but felt that the long-term effects on cricket could be disastrous if they were to succumb to similar pressure. In other words, the Commonwealth Games could go hang. On the question of community relations the Council recognised that there was 'a growing concern with the unacceptable apartheid policies of the present South African government'. The Council said that it shared that concern but it wished to

> re-emphasize that cricket has made an outstanding and widely acknowledged contribution to the maintenance of good relations between all people among whom the game has been played.

On the question of law and order, the Council took the Home Secretary at his word. They had heard him tell the House of Commons that the police could handle whatever trouble erupted inside and outside the cricket grounds so they fully expected that they could rely on the local constabulary to keep order. It made a nod to the STST movement and its supporters but it pointed out the dangers of a small minority being allowed to take the law into their own hands through direct action.

> However distasteful to this minority group, the South African tour this summer is not only a lawful event but as shown by the outcome of recent opinion polls it is clearly the wish of the majority that the tour should take place.

In the Fuhrerbunker in Berlin in April 1945 as the Red Army approached the Chancellery and Adolf Hitler was ordering non-existent armies into battle, the German Chancellor showed more awareness of what was happening in the outside world than the Cricket Council managed in May 1970.

Billy Griffith was a nervous, sensitive man, whose health during the last six months had been noticeably fragile. His increasingly nervous public appearances suggested that he was feeling the pressure of the position in which he found himself. According to Jack Bailey, the assistant secretary of MCC, who was supporting

Griffith at the conference, the assembled journalists included Peter Hain who had sneaked in, surprisingly undetected by the pavilion gatekeepers who must have been impressed by his shoes or else he just sidled in with the rest of the unkempt hacks. Peter Hain himself has written that when the decision came through he was actually at the BBC waiting to go on camera for a live interview. It may very well be that by this time Hain had become such a menacing figure to the cricket establishment that he was being spotted everywhere, much in the manner that Lord Lucan was soon to be seen in every part of the globe.

Those reporters who were actually there at the time listened with growing incredulity as Griffith expounded the reasons for the Council's decision. They had expected the tour to be cancelled and they could scarcely believe the bare-faced effrontery with which the Council had treated the requests for cancellation. When they began to question Griffith, the secretary of the Council became uncharacteristically short-tempered.

The first questions concerned the exact nature of what the Council meant by its promise not to play against all-white teams from South Africa on future tours. He was asked if the South Africans in future played only Test matches and didn't tour in the accepted sense of the word would he still expect a multi-racial side to be sent? Griffith declined to answer. When asked how the Cricket Council would decide if the South African side was multi-racial enough and what criteria would be used he again side-stepped the question.

He did recognise that there was going to be a problem as the general election would coincide with the date of the first day of the Lord's Test and he accepted there would have to be a change from the traditional Thursday start. Griffith's disgust with the Labour government was only too apparent. He left none of the journalists in any doubt that the Cricket Council had no intention of carrying any political cans for it and he threw down the gauntlet by implicitly challenging the government that if they didn't like the tour they could cancel it. They had the power to do it but cricket was not going to be bullied into doing it itself. Five hundred telegrams allegedly poured into Lord's, Griffith told the next day's press. All of them were supportive.

In South Africa there was jubilation. Jack Cheetham, the president of SACA said, 'I am delighted that the tour of Britain is still on. I never had any doubts that we would be going to England.' The white sports-obsessed part of the country greeted the decision with relief after the recent hurtful expulsion from the Olympic movement. The joy was tempered by the dawning realisation that this was likely to be the last tour before the end of traditional all-white cricket teams representing South Africa. If their friends at Lord's were insisting they sent multi-racial teams in future the likelihood was that they were facing the reality of sporting isolation. Ali Bacher's response was to re-emphasise that the problems stemmed from the government's insistence on apartheid and not from any prejudice among the players. He said that he was always prepared to play cricket against anyone from any race anywhere. In the medical profession he had worked with many non-European doctors and they had always co-operated extremely well. He saw no reason why that should not apply to the world of sport.

In England reaction followed predictably along party lines. Mark Bonham Carter, the chairman of the Race Relations Board, 'very much regretted the decision of the Cricket Council' whereas Colin Cowdrey welcomed it, declaring that he had never agreed with the idea of placing South Africa into sporting isolation. Cowdrey said the decision made 'bold and Christian good sense'. Ray Illingworth pronounced himself 'absolutely delighted' with the decision, believing that 'demonstrators should not be allowed to disrupt matches'. Brian Close was equally pleased, telling the press that the Yorkshire team wanted to play against one of the finest sides in the world and he personally did not like politics invading the cricket field.

Peter Hain, who had cautioned his colleagues and supporters against premature celebration, found that his emotions were a mixture of sadness and a total lack of surprise. Nothing in his dealings with Lord's had led him to believe that the Cricket Council would experience a sudden Damascene conversion. Only a combination of direct action and political pressure from the government would achieve their ends.

It is a great pity that the Cricket Council has seen fit to retreat into this entrenched position of stubborn backwoodsmanship.

> During the past few months there has been a phenomenal
> swing against the tour. It is the cricket authorities who are now
> in the minority. If the Council really opposes racialist sport
> how can it go ahead with a racialist tour this summer?

He informed journalists that STST would make a statement about
its future plans in two days' time.

The response to the decision the following day was overwhelmingly
negative no matter how many telegrams Lord's claimed to have
received. The West Indian Campaign against Apartheid Cricket
announced that any West Indian cricketers playing in English
county cricket would be 'pilloried' if they took part in matches
against the South Africans. Apart from the previously mentioned
Clive Lloyd, Rohan Kanhai and Lance Gibbs, these would have
included John Shepherd, Garry Sobers, Alvin Kallicharran, Deryck
Murray, Vanburn Holder, Keith Boyce and Bernard Julien amongst
others. There would be demonstrations against them not only at
cricket grounds but outside their homes. They were not kidding.
During the Surrey v Nottinghamshire match which was taking place
at The Oval on the three critical days between 20 May and 22 May,
a group of anti-apartheid protesters carried pickets castigating Garry
Sobers, by common assent the best all-round cricketer in the world,
as an Uncle Tom. It was an unpleasant insult but it didn't seem to
affect the great man unduly. In Nottinghamshire's first innings he
made 160 out of a total of 281 and in the second innings he scored
103 not out before declaring and setting Surrey 222 to win which
they did comfortably by seven wickets. It was the first time he had
scored two centuries in a county match and the first time he had
been castigated by his own countrymen for political reasons rather
than for declaring at Port of Spain in 1968 and offering Boycott and
Cowdrey the chance to win the Test match, which they had taken.

Meanwhile, the Cricket Council's decision sent the ratepayers
of Leeds into an uproar. The third match of the tour after games
against Southern Counties at Lord's and Northern Counties at Trent
Bridge was scheduled to be against Yorkshire at Headingley. It was
now believed that 1,400 police officers would have to be employed
to control the expected disturbances. This was estimated to cost
£105,000 of which half would be paid by the Home Office which left

£52,500 to be charged to the ratepayers. The council made it quite clear that they thought that Yorkshire CCC had a cheek to make their ratepayers pay so they could get free policing. Yorkshire folk don't take too kindly to unnecessary expense at the best of times and expecting ratepayers to pay for what had previously been provided for free wasn't going to be a vote-winner.

As it transpired this all became irrelevant on Wednesday 20 May when Callaghan contacted the Cricket Council and told them to be in his office first thing in the morning and to make sure their shoes were polished. Clearly Callaghan and Wilson had run out of patience with the stubborn refusal of the cricket authorities to make the decision that the government had been seriously hinting to them for nearly six months. A note of the record of a telephone conversation between the two men gave evidence that they did not expect much of a fight from the Cricket Council. At Callaghan's request Sir Leslie O'Brien, the governor of the Bank of England, had approached Sir Cyril Hawker, the president-elect of MCC and the Council to see how his committee would respond to a direct request from the government. Now that the much debated election campaign was up and running there was no point in employing diplomatic niceties with the Cricket Council. Callaghan made the substance of the discussions that would take place very clear to the public, now known as the voters.

> I want to hear from them their reasons for going on with the tour, after deciding that future tours should be cancelled. We shall have a very full discussion into the possible consequences. There have been many requests to me from trade unionists, teachers, church leaders and others to intervene and I would be failing in my responsibilities if I did not meet them.

At the meeting Callaghan called their bluff. The Cricket Council had long maintained that their responsibilities extended only as far as the outer reaches of cricket. Once cricket was caught up in a political maelstrom they were no longer competent to judge what was important and what was not. It was a crass and rather idiotic argument and Callaghan had absolutely no time for it. He pretty much told them in the meeting to go home and cancel the tour. The letter he sent to them afterwards left no room for further discussion or prevarication.

> You emphasized that although the Council were naturally concerned with various other matters of a public and political nature ... they feel that these matters fell outside their responsibilities and that it was beyond their competence to judge what significance to attach to them ... The Government have come to the conclusion that on grounds of broad public policy they must request the Cricket Council to withdraw their invitation to the South African Cricket Association and I should be grateful if you would put this request before the Council.

On receipt of the letter on Friday 22 May, just ten days before the South Africans were due to land, the Cricket Council called another committee meeting followed by a press conference and this time the message given by Billy Griffith, flanked by Raman Subba Row and Jack Bailey, was the one most people had expected on Tuesday evening. The tour was finally and irreversibly to be called off. The blame for the cancellation was laid firmly at the door of the government. The committee had met for 90 minutes to discuss Callaghan's letter and had reluctantly agreed that there was no way round it. Consequently, the decision to cancel the tour was taken 'with great regret' because the Council 'were of the opinion that they had no alternative but to accede to the [government's] request'. The new statement added,

> The Council are grateful for the overwhelming support of cricketers, cricket lovers and many others and share their disappointment at the cancellation of the tour. They regret the discourtesy to the South African Cricket Association and the inconvenience caused to many people. The Council deplore the activities of those who by the intimidation of individual cricketers and threats of violence have inflamed the whole issue.

The Cricket Council and MCC were sorry to have let down their good friends in South Africa and what they doggedly believed was that the majority of British people still wanted the tour to go ahead. South Africa would not play cricket in England again until 1994, although many fine South African cricketers would play on English cricket grounds in the intervening years. On the morning of the press conference, Friday 22 May, the *Daily Telegraph* had published the latest Gallup poll revealing that 46% of those polled were in favour of the tour going ahead, 36% were against with 18% of no opinion. Submitting to a direct request from the government rather than cancelling the tour of its own volition, the Council had saved face but lost its insurance premium.

In eventually arriving at the right decision, albeit for the wrong reasons, MCC and the Cricket Council had shown themselves impervious to the moral argument which had precipitated the crisis in the first place. In not mentioning the alleged triumph that 1970 would have been the last time an all-white South African team would tour, it became quite clear that not even they believed that to be the case or that it was anything other than a desperate attempt to keep the tour on.

If Lord's did not learn from the mistakes it had made the crisis was not ended but postponed. Lord's believed itself to be the centre of world cricket but the reality was that the men who lived and worked there had shown an astonishing lack of awareness of what that world genuinely thought. Of course, it could be argued that as far as they were concerned, the view from the West Indies, India or Pakistan was simply worth less respect than the view from Sydney or Pretoria.

As in the Brexit victories and defeats, each side responded with exultation and anger whenever a decision appeared to have been arrived at that the tour was still on or, as it clearly was now, decisively off. OUT! was the headline in the *Daily Express*, with the sub-heading, 'England bowled Callaghan 0'. It recognised that Callaghan and the protesters would claim victory but it was 'BLACKMAIL, said Tory Mr. Quintin Hogg, supported by the rest' although whether that was the rest of the Tory Party, the rest of the country or the rest of the world was not immediately clear. For Hogg it was 'a sad day for British freedom'. He reiterated that the Tory Party was opposed to apartheid but claimed that wasn't the issue here. Callaghan and Wilson had bowed to threats and yielded to blackmail. He had a point, depending on how one defined the word 'blackmail'.

Certainly, as soon as the cancellation was confirmed, all the African countries that had threatened to withdraw their athletes from the Commonwealth Games announced that they would now all take part. The semantic backlash of disappointment included not only 'blackmail' but 'mob rule' and 'giving in to the forces of anarchy'. It was clearly heading down the path that would lead to 'traitors', 'betrayal', 'the Surrender bill' and 'Enemies of the People'. The right-wing Monday Club decided to call the chairman of STST 'Fuhrer Hain' and his triumphant supporters 'campus bums' – in an echo of Richard Nixon and his opinion of student protesters.

E.W. Swanton, who had started as an advocate of bridge building but who had come to accept that a tour of England by an all-white South Africa side playing under armed guard would be bad for the game, was simply relieved by the final cancellation.

> From the viewpoint of cricket this must be for the better, enjoyable and exciting as the Tests might have been in different circumstances. Our cricket fields will not now be a political battle ground. The barbed wire can come down and cricketers and administrators can sleep more peacefully at night.

He had written his editorial for the June edition of *The Cricketer* on the day before the decision to cancel was officially announced. It was headlined *Prelude to an Ordeal* and in it Swanton laid bare his agonising. He again pleaded with his friends at SACA and the Cricket Council at Lord's to invite all the non-white South African boards to a meeting in London to set up one multi-racial body to oversee all cricket in South Africa to show they were more enlightened than the politicians and on that basis he was sure South Africa could be readmitted to the International Cricket Conference.

While the front pages of the newspapers proclaimed the end of the South African tour the back pages revealed that there would be a replacement series of five Test matches to be played on the dates originally scheduled for the South African Tests apart from the first Test at Lord's which would now start on Wednesday 17 June with the second day's play continuing as had been scheduled for the original

Test series on Friday 19 June. This left the whole of Thursday 18 June for the England players to vote in the general election. Subsequent Tests would take place at Trent Bridge, Edgbaston, Headingley and The Oval. The England team was to be selected by the men already appointed to choose the team that would have played South Africa. It was also announced that full England caps would be awarded. This would become a bone of contention when that decision was controversially reversed, thus denying Alan Jones of Glamorgan what would have been his sole Test cap. All counties had agreed to release their players if chosen for either side, although, as we shall see, this was an issue that was to provoke intense irritation at some county grounds.

England's opponents would be a Rest of the World side including some Springboks. Barry Richards and Mike Procter were already in England playing for Hampshire and Gloucestershire respectively and were likely to be joined by Graeme Pollock and Eddie Barlow. Other overseas stars from West Indies, Pakistan, India and Australia were likely to present England with a very difficult challenge. Billy Griffith, announcing this new series, denied the accusation that it would be like matches at the end-of-season Scarborough Festival, which players and crowds alike enjoyed but usually did not take particularly seriously. There was an exception in 1967 at Scarborough when Basil D'Oliveira, in an unbeaten innings of 72 against a Rest of the World XI, launched a vicious assault on the bowling of Peter Pollock. It could have been a coincidence of course but the watching reporters did not think so. Now the England players would be playing for their places on the forthcoming tour of Australia and besides, players from each side would be earning £100 a match. Sponsors were being sought to defray the large costs created by such an ambitious enterprise.

Swanton was not initially convinced that this replacement series was a particularly good idea. 'Anything of an exhibition kind would fall disastrously flat. Whether interest in such a rubber could be maintained at an acceptable level over 25 days is surely doubtful.'

A series of Tests against the Rest of the World had not been the only alternative plan to be discussed by the Test & County Cricket Board as cancellation became a real possibility. In the files at Lord's there is an undated memo that was probably written in December

1969 or January 1970 to the effect that they might bring forward by a year the twin tours by India and Pakistan which were scheduled for 1971, although the preference had always been for a shortened tour by South Africa 'restricted to defensible grounds'.

When it was clear that only a Rest of the World series was practicable, calculations were immediately made as to the financial implications. The estimated income for five such Test matches was £235,000 based on the assumption that the average Test match ground admittance was 10 shillings. Each Test was individually estimated as follows:

1 Lord's: income £29,000, leaving a profit of £21,000

2 Trent Bridge: income of £20,500 leaving a profit of £12,500

3 Edgbaston: as Trent Bridge

4 Headingley: income of £27,000 leaving a profit of £19,000

5 The Oval: income of £26,500 leaving a profit of £18,500.

The total profit for the entire Rest of the World series was estimated at £83,500. Unfortunately, as we shall see, such estimates erred on the side of optimism.

There was of course satisfaction to be gained by everyone who opposed the tour in the substitution of this series in place of the toxic one that had been scheduled against South Africa, but the extent of the spectrum of that opposition was illuminated by the responses from the different ends of it. The Reverend Graham Smith (no relation one has to assume to the South African captain of later years) writing from St John's Vicarage in London SW9 attributed the victory to the numerous moderate voices of opposition, led of course by the Bishop of Woolwich. From across the river in leafy Templewood Avenue, Hampstead, Mr L.E. Weidberg, who was clearly spending more money on stamps for letters to *The Guardian* than he was on presents for his younger nephew, took, predictably, the opposite view. He attributed victory entirely to Peter Hain and the STST's tactics of direct action and not to the feeble words of the 'trendy Bishops' and certainly not to the feeble words of the editor of *The Guardian*. In his opinion, even the cancellation of a cricket tour would make no difference to the desperate plight of the Bantus in South Africa on whose behalf the campaign had begun but who had now been entirely forgotten. He was scathing about what he regarded as the overrated importance of everyone enjoying the Commonwealth Games. (Uncle Laurence had no time for any sports apart from cricket and rugby league to which he devoted his life when he wasn't listening to classical music or writing angry letters to *The Guardian*.) He does point out with some justification, however, that India and Pakistan were not sending athletes to the Games because of their mutual hostility and that Kenya would send its black athletes but discriminated against its brown ones. Life with Uncle Laurence was never easy for anyone.

On the spectrum occupied by the now defeated supporters of the tour there was, as with the result of the 2016 referendum, absolutely no sense that they were prepared to admit that they were wrong, to offer an apology to the anti-apartheid campaigners or to stop demonising Peter Hain. On Friday 22 May, as soon as Billy Griffith had informed the world that the South African tour was definitely cancelled, a barrister called Francis Bennion decided to bring a private prosecution against Peter Hain for seditious conspiracy. He was a somewhat eccentric member of the Bar but he had done his bit during the war, serving as a Coastal Command pilot for RAF Squadron 221 before going up to Oxford where he had read Law at Balliol. Five days later, on Wednesday 27 May, he published a short pamphlet for public consumption which was titled 'Why I Am Prosecuting Peter Hain'. The pamphlet started by quoting an article written by Hain in March 1970 and printed in *Challenge*, the magazine of the Young Communists. In it Hain sets out the aims of the Stop the Seventy Tour movement and specifically asks for help from workers and Young Communists. This was, appropriately enough, a red rag to Bennion's bull. Hain continued:

> In the final analysis though this campaign will be won on the strength of our commitment to direct action.
>
> STST's basic organising tactic has always been to stop the games. We have not been prepared to continue with the tactic of patient petitioning and polite protesting.

There was nothing in what Hain wrote that was subversively different in this article from the thousands of words he had written and spoken elsewhere on the aims of STST. However, to Bennion and his supporters they betokened criminal activities.

> The invitation to the South African cricketers was lawfully extended by the MCC four years ago. Arrangements were made for them to play twenty eight matches in a stay of four months. Many thousands of people would have attended these matches; millions would have watched them on television. All these activities were entirely and undoubtedly within the law of this land. They were prevented from taking place by the unlawful activities of Mr Hain and his associates.

Bennion goes on to state categorically that he is opposed to apartheid and quotes as proof his meeting in West Africa with a man who he admits was his intellectual superior, a classical scholar who was the first black African to be elected as a Fellow of All Souls College Oxford, 'that pinnacle of English intellectual achievement'. Apartheid, however, was not the issue here, which was the same argument used by Quintin Hogg. Bennion acknowledges that Britain has a proud and distinguished record as a bastion of liberty and free speech and anyone is entitled to get up anywhere in the land and proclaim his belief in anything, although there are limits to that freedom.

> Any methods of persuasion are lawful and rightly so provided they do not go *beyond* the lawful, provided they do not defame the innocent and inflame the gullible. So it follows that I am not against demonstrations – not even when they are carried out by youngsters with long hair and exotic dress.

Bennion is keen to establish that he has nothing against young people. Indeed, the idealism of young people and their unselfish dedication to noble causes at some considerable costs to themselves should be a constant reminder to older people that they should examine their own beliefs in case they get too set in their ways. So far so admirable one might think were it not for the fact that for the remainder of the pamphlet Bennion castigates those same youngsters and reveals that he is prosecuting Hain in order to teach young people a lesson.

> This generation suffers from a peculiar form of arrogance, which is that the truth is whatever liberal intellectuals feel intuitively in 1970 is true. The fact that sincere intelligent people believed in the recent past that quite different things were true is dismissed or not even thought of.
> The eternal verities are not to be discarded so easily.

Bennion denies membership of the right-wing Monday Club and is happy to laud the importance of courage, unselfishness, sympathy, tolerance, truth and justice which remain, as they always have been, the basis of any civilised society. In his last two paragraphs Bennion's intolerance makes its presence clearly felt. Agitators must not be allowed to interfere with the lawful rights of others. These agitators include not only Peter Hain but also extremists shouting down the Foreign Secretary in the Oxford Union, a 'gang' of students occupying the administration buildings of Southampton University, and Welsh language militants interfering with the work of the High Court itself. He concludes that:

> Our young people must be taught the meaning of the Rule of Law. If it is thought to be wrong to invite South African cricketers to play in Britain the answer is to persuade parliament to pass a law making it illegal to do so. We are a democracy. We elect our representatives by an elaborately fair process. It is for them to decide whether to outlaw a particular activity. Unless and until they do so it is a dangerous impertinence for the Hains of this world to take the law into their own hands. What a nerve they have – what colossal cheek! Someone must, for the sake of us all, take the initiative in checking the spread of such presumption.

It was believed by many STST supporters that Bennion was backed by the right-wing Society for Individual Freedom and benefited from help from BOSS, the notorious Bureau of State Security in South Africa.

The wheels of the law turn slowly. It wasn't exactly Jarndyce versus Jarndyce but Hain heard nothing about the intended prosecution which Bennion had claimed would start on Tuesday 27 May 1970 until the middle of the following year, when he was served with a summons for criminal conspiracy when he was at Heathrow airport about to board a flight for Australia where he was going to involve himself in the planned demonstrations against the Springboks' rugby tour there. He was summoned to appear at Bow Street Magistrates' Court in October 1971 and was sent to stand trial in August 1972 at the Royal Courts of Justice where he was eventually found guilty on the charge of interfering with the Davis Cup match in Bristol for which he was fined £200 but not guilty on the more serious charges connected with the rugby and cricket tours.

It is interesting to note that just as Bennion wanted to take down Hain on behalf of the thousands of people who were frustrated by the cancellation in 1970, so Gina Miller and John Major had recourse to the courts in a private prosecution in an attempt to call Boris Johnson's prorogation of parliament in September 2019 also unlawful. In both cases the courts were being asked to pronounce a political as well as a legal judgement. Hain received numerous threats during the STST campaign and Bennion revealed that the day after he announced his intended prosecution his wife answered the telephone at their home in Warlingham in Surrey to be greeted by an anonymous voice threatening her husband with violence. The fault line running through the country that divided Leavers and Remainers in Britain after June 2016 is not far removed from the line that divided those who supported the tour from those who exulted in its cancellation in 1970. Somehow, rational argument was no use when attitudes were so deeply entrenched. In civilised, liberal Britain violence continued to remain an option for those who held their views too passionately.

Bennion's intended prosecution made for a small item on all the front pages that carried the news of the cancellation. The back pages of those same editions all carried the story of Alf Ramsey's second pronouncement that England were going to win the World Cup. The first one, made shortly after he took charge of the England team in 1963, had proved famously prophetic. This second one was hedged with the proviso that his players would first have to show that they could overcome the heat of Mexico and problems with altitude caused by playing at 8,000 feet above sea level. After the bitterness of the Springbok tour debates and the inevitable conflicts induced by a general election campaign, the country would be united once more by the shared passion for football and the desire for a second consecutive World Cup win. Warm-up games against Ecuador and Colombia were won comfortably and stylishly but, as the country settled down to anticipate similar results against Romania, Brazil and Czechoslovakia in the group games, news reached London that genuinely shocked the nation. In Bogota, Bobby Moore, England's talismanic captain, had been arrested for stealing a bracelet from a hotel gift shop.

CHAPTER TEN

JUNE 1970

ON Monday 25 May, all the newspapers led their front pages with the story of Bobby Moore's arrest which was written by their news teams. Ironically all their back pages or sports pages were triumphantly proclaiming that the England team had won all four of its warm-up games, scoring 11 goals and conceding only one. The players (minus Moore) and the football journalists who had written that story were on the plane to Mexico from Colombia when it was noticed that the England captain was missing. When the story of the arrest was revealed the football writers were incensed. It was clearly a major story and they were helplessly entombed in an aeroplane. Moore was equally devastated that Ramsey had taken the rest of the party off to Mexico, thereby abandoning him to an unknown fate.

Thanks to the efforts of the British Consul in Bogota, Moore was allowed to remain under house arrest at the home of the director of the Colombian FA rather than languishing in a Colombian prison. Ramsey was outwardly calm but inwardly raging at what he was convinced was a Latin American stitch-up designed to hinder England's chances in the competition, particularly when it emerged that Bobby Charlton was now suspected of acting as Moore's accomplice in the theft. He felt he had no choice but to proceed as planned with the rest of the squad. When the plane had taken off from Bogota, most of the passengers believed that England's preparations could not have gone better. By the time the plane landed in Mexico City it seemed as if those preparations were in total disarray.

At home, Harold Wilson was of course in the middle of a general election campaign. The idea that the England football captain would be dragged through a foreign court like a common criminal might have done untold damage to Britain's prestige and the government's popularity. He had been worried that the Labour Party would in some weird way be held responsible by the electorate if the England football team were knocked out of the World Cup before the polls opened. Now he was worried that the government would somehow in the popular imagination be implicated in a jewel robbery. Wilson remained in close contact with Lord Harewood, the president of the FA, and even offered to telephone the President of Colombia. Moore, who never lost his dignity throughout the humiliating process, was eventually released three days later because of a lack of evidence, although the case was not closed for some years, much to his silent fury. When he arrived in Mexico City on an Argentine Airlines flight from Bogota he was greeted by 200 jostling reporters and photographers, only a few of whom were English. Moore maintained his cool and smiled his brief clichés of gratitude for his release. There was no more relieved man in Mexico than Alf Ramsey when the unflappable but mentally exhausted Moore walked into the Hilton hotel on the morning of Friday 29 May to rejoin the England party. Unfortunately, the affair of the 'Bogota bracelet' meant that, despite four years of careful planning, England were going into their first game in the 1970 World Cup against Romania on Tuesday 2 June in a highly disconcerted state.

Whatever sympathy that might have been flowing England's way in Mexico after the realisation that Moore had clearly been falsely accused disappeared abruptly the following day when Ramsey bitterly criticised the bumpy state of the pitch at the Jalisco Stadium in Guadalajara where England were due to play their group games. Mexicans did not take kindly to such criticism, particularly from a former colonial power. During the opening ceremony at the Azteca Stadium in Mexico City where the final would be played, the flags of all the competing nations were on display, carried round the ground in a procession by Mexican children. Fifteen of the 16 flags were greeted with loud applause. The 16th, the Union Jack, was roundly booed by the 107,000 happy spectators as it was dipped before the Presidential box. England's sporting teams in post-colonial times tended to pay a heavy price for what their imperialist forbears had done. The Union Jack could not have been more roundly disparaged had it been carried by Enoch Powell and Gubby Allen. It was a particularly unfortunate experience for those poor Mexican children who, through no fault of their own, had been allocated to carry the British flag.

The Bobby Moore bracelet controversy temporarily drove both the election and the various stories associated with the cancellation of the tour off the front pages. The cancellation had finally separated Peter Hain, the STST committee and the Anti-Apartheid Movement from Billy Griffith, Maurice Allom and the Cricket Council. STST was formally disbanded but its triumph empowered its key officials to expand its activities. Hain told the press that he would be liaising with anti-apartheid campaigners in Australia to stop the Springbok rugby tour to that country scheduled for 1971. He also let it be known that British firms which traded with South Africa would be subject to many of the same actions that had been a fundamental part of its STST campaign. Company headquarters would be picketed very shortly at which Anthony Barber, the Conservative MP and shortly to be Chancellor of the Exchequer, bristled, demanding to know if Harold Wilson supported this demonstration as he had supported demonstrations against the cricket tour. Wilson loftily dismissed the accusation, flicking it off his pads for four through square leg.

The positive outcome of the cancellation was immediately apparent when the South African wicketkeeper Dennis Gamsy made an open passionate appeal to his government to set up a commission of inquiry to investigate ways in which racially mixed sport could be introduced into the country which had just made its feelings abundantly clear by disallowing a visa for a Chinese scrum half who had been selected by the University of Southern Rhodesia for its forthcoming tour of South Africa. The tour was immediately called off. South Africa's sporting isolation was assuming a worrying reality for its international players. Gamsy said:

> In my own mind there is no doubt that we should have mixed sport here in South Africa. The time has come for us to examine more closely the policies which make South Africa

so repugnant to the outside world. What has happened [in England] is only the thin edge of the wedge. If we turn back into the laager because of it, our position can only worsen, not only in sport but also economically. We are only four million Whites in a continent of several hundred millions of Blacks. If we go on the way we are, we could find ourselves being sacrificed to rid the world of one of its niggling problems. I know that mixed sport at home has been against government policy. I know that it is against apartheid. But the time has surely come when we must figure out a way in which we can allow mixed sport to be played in South Africa.

The South African Prime Minister's blunt response to a political intervention by a mere cricketer was issued the following day. John Vorster claimed astonishment that the British government, which he blamed for the cancellation, had given in to blackmail and as a consequence had mortally wounded the forces of law and order in Great Britain. There was now no end to the demands a blackmailer could make on the British government. In answer to Gamsy's request for a commission of inquiry, Vorster replied that he saw no need to change the policy of apartheid at all. In the short term, he admitted, the outlook for his country's sports team to play against other international sides might be bleak but in the long term he was not at all despondent.

The question was then raised as to whether he would permit the All Blacks to tour South Africa if they included any Maoris in their side. Vorster claimed that his government had never interfered in the make-up of foreign sides (which made no sense given the events surrounding Basil D'Oliveira's late inclusion in the MCC side in 1968) and that he had always welcomed sides from New Zealand even if they included Maoris. To make his protestations a little more convincing the New Zealand rugby selectors had chosen a squad which included the three lightest-skinned Maoris. Whether they had been chosen strictly on grounds of ability and it was just an unfortunate coincidence that the dark-skinned Maoris had not been selected was unclear.

The cricketers themselves were saddened and unhappy with the cancellation and they did not initially appear at all appeased by its replacement with the Rest of the World series. Ali Bacher and the two Pollock brothers all declared that they would not play for the Rest of the World team if they were selected but in the light of subsequent events one cannot help but feel that the players had come under considerable pressure from official sources to respond in that way. Certainly, when the Rest of the World team took the field at Lord's in the first Test, Graeme Pollock trotted out quite happily alongside compatriots Barry Richards, Eddie Barlow and Mike Procter. His brother Peter remained an unselected member of the Rest of the World touring party until the third Test.

Ali Bacher, who was not selected, was working as a doctor at the 'Non-European' Baragwanath Hospital in Soweto and said he would welcome multi-racial cricket in South Africa 'as soon as the Government finds it practical'. It was a desperate attempt at painful fence-sitting, but when he was interviewed on Radio 4's *The World This Weekend* on Sunday 24 May he continued to toe the official line very firmly. He claimed the cricketers had been used as pawns by what he implied were unscrupulous politicians. 'Mr Callaghan', he said, 'had manoeuvred the MCC into a position of checkmate.' He was sure that the sadness and disappointment felt by the players was felt equally by the whole of South Africa and the great majority of the British people. He praised MCC who, he thought, had done extremely well and had been forced into the situation in which they had had to call off the tour.

To reinforce Bacher's belief that the principle of the tour had been supported by that vast majority of the British people he was convinced about, an organisation was formed called the Anti-Demonstration Association which had been designed to take on STST. Now it threatened to adopt STST's tactics to disrupt the Commonwealth Games. They wanted all 13 countries who had threatened not to attend the Games if the tour went ahead to be banned from competing in Edinburgh or else....

Aware now that the tour controversy had been hijacked by the sort of people later called 'a bunch of fruitcakes, loonies and closet racists' by a British prime minister, Ali Bacher continued the debate a few days later but now it is possible to see that the mood, certainly among the players, was starting to change. He doesn't directly challenge his own government in the way his wicketkeeper had done but he acknowledges that there has to be a way to keep South Africa in international sport even if that means a slight shift in the government's previously immovable stance on racial segregation.

> We in South Africa in 1970 must broaden our attitude towards white and non-white sport. It's not a question of appeasing demonstrators and their kind but of doing what is best for South African sport in 1970.

Peter Pollock, who a month previously was angrily denouncing international communism for being behind the demonstrators who would bring about the destruction of Test cricket and Western civilisation, was now starting to change his tune significantly. On 31 May he gave an interview to the Johannesburg *Sunday Times* in which he openly blamed his own government for a 'dogmatic attitude' that would lead inevitably to isolation from international competition for all South African sportsmen. He made it clear that he was in favour of multi-racial sport in South Africa and, having ascertained that the tennis player Cliff Drysdale and the golfer Gary Player felt similarly, he urged all sportsmen to declare their solidarity with this idea openly. He reserved his most scathing comments for the Minister of Sport, Frank Waring, who had rejected any attempt to introduce any aspect of multi-racial sports into South Africa. The worst possible way for South Africa to respond to the current crisis for its sportsmen was not, Pollock concluded, echoing Gamsy, 'to creep back into the laager'.

His views were endorsed by Alf Chalmers, the president of the South African Lawn Tennis Association, who now expected to be expelled from the International Federation of Lawn Tennis Unions when it met in Paris in July. He saw the tide of sporting isolation about to sweep over his country and he pleaded with the government to soften its stance.

> South Africa must change its outlook with regard to international sport. If the attitude is not broadened we won't be able to save anything. We are not fighting the government, but let's face it – our policies do not suit the rest of the world.

It was a considerable shock to them when, because of those policies, white fans of Percy Sledge were forbidden to attend the concerts given by the American soul singer when he performed in Cape Town. Sledge was granted a visa by the Department of the Interior but on the condition that he appeared only in front of black audiences. Such was the general admiration felt for Sledge that he was allowed to stay in a suite of four rooms in the all-white President Hotel on the Cape Town beachfront. However, Sledge's latest record had sold 100,000 copies which made him as popular as Elvis and Jim Reeves had been. Outraged white supporters of the Nationalists and their policy of apartheid were astonished that it could also disadvantage them and complained bitterly but to no avail. The one thing the Nationalist government did not want was teenage white girls fainting in the aisles, overcome by the sexual charisma of an African American.

The initial rejection of the whites led to some utterly ludicrous attempts to circumvent the ruling. Many white men 'blacked up' or wore fezzes to convince the doormen that they were Muslims. It must have looked more like a Tommy Cooper tribute night. The white women wore saris and covered their faces with veils. Few of these wheezes were successful. 'There aren't any blonde Indians', said one of the aggressive doormen as he pulled a white woman out of the queue. Extra doormen had to be hired such was the demand. Thirty-shilling tickets were changing hands for up to 12 times their face value. One Sledge enthusiast who had travelled from Johannesburg to Cape Town to see his favourite entertainer perform was stopped at the main entrance and forced to sell his ticket to a non-white. White audiences who did not think the laws of apartheid applied to them but were refused admittance demanded to see the manager who told them it was more than his job was worth to admit them in contravention of the law of the land. The laid-back Sledge volunteered his desire to play in front of audiences of all colours but had no problem with toeing the government's apartheid line. For most performers any visit to South Africa to play sport or appear on a stage would increasingly become a problem during the 1970s.

The South African government responded to all criticism by standing firmly on its previously delineated lines of demarcation. In a radio broadcast on 1 June to mark the ninth anniversary of South Africa's secession from the Commonwealth, Dr Vorster told South

Africans that they were assailed by communism on three separate fronts – the international sports boycott, the permissive society and the threat to the strategic Cape sea route. What was clear to Vorster was that all the attacks that South Africa was currently experiencing were really directed against the policy of apartheid but the sportsmen were first in the line of fire. South Africa's relationship with its cricket and rugby teams was such that they were inevitably cast as sacrificial victims and, much as his government regretted that fact, he was not going to change the fundamental policy of the state to accommodate the careers of a few talented sportsmen.

> If the choice is between taking part in sport and our way of life, which we have developed in this country over generations then naturally the majority of our people will say that we have no choice in the matter whatsoever. What many outsiders don't understand [is that] in this country the whites have always stuck to themselves, the coloureds stuck to themselves, the Zulus stuck to themselves and so on.

Nobody had expected apartheid to disappear with the cancellation of the invitation to tour England by MCC but the impact of the cancellation, as Peter Hain and the Anti-Apartheid Movement always knew it would, did more to start a dialogue between the Nationalist government and its sports bodies than had ever previously taken place. White South Africans had been brought up short by the cancellation and a similar outcome to the forthcoming rugby tour of New Zealand was now a distinct possibility. They had expected trouble in the shape of demonstrations and protests outside the cricket grounds, maybe interruptions to play if police forces were stretched beyond measure, but the cancellation was a shock. The people who ran MCC were the effective leaders of Great Britain it was believed and somehow they would find a way to convince a Labour government facing a general election to support the tour.

The view of Great Britain from South Africa was badly out of focus. It was not only the days before the Internet, it was the days before South Africa permitted the introduction of television which would not begin transmission until 1976. South Africans relied for their news on newspapers and the radio which were both subject to tight state censorship laws.

It might have been supposed that with the cancellation of the tour and the announcement of the Rest of the World series, the atmosphere which had become so hate-filled would start to cool down. In his editorial for the July edition of *The Cricketer*, written a couple of weeks after the cancellation was official, E.W. Swanton initially blamed Harold Wilson for his outrageous suggestion advocating demonstrations but then he softened as he recalled his own journey from support for the tour to support for its cancellation because, 'on a balance of evils' of the damage that would be done to cricket, the danger of a white versus black division in international cricket, the disruption to the Commonwealth Games and the impossibility of enjoying watching a Test match played behind barbed wire. He had always wanted SACA to call it off so that his South African friends would not be hurt by broken English promises. They didn't, of course, and they were. He concluded sorrowfully,

> It's hard really to know which of the extremes is the more pathetic, the violent young demonstrators of the left or the elderly skinheads of the right.

Gloucestershire's South African all-rounder, Mike Procter, who had made a major impact on the performance of his new county side, inspiring them to a second-place finish in 1969, received two phone calls immediately it became apparent that he would be selected for the Rest of the World side. In them he was warned that he would have to make a full confession of his errors in having been part of a team and a country that had promoted apartheid as a public policy. One of the calls had been from somewhere in England, the other from South Africa. A petition was being sent to him which he would be expected to sign. Procter declared that he had no intention of doing anything that either of these anonymous callers had been demanding of him and that he would still be delighted to turn out for the Rest of the World side if selected. 'Both callers warned me that unless I signed the declaration I would be protested against. They did not explain what form those protests would take.' When asked to confirm that he had received similar threats, Barry Richards replied that he had not but if he did his answer would be the same as Procter's.

On the England side it wasn't straightforward either, particularly with regard to their recently recruited overseas stars. Despite the announcement by the Test and County Cricket Board that all counties had agreed willingly to release their players if selected for the new Test series, it soon became clear that Lancashire were extremely unhappy about the prospect of losing Farokh Engineer, their Indian wicketkeeper, and Clive Lloyd, their new star batsman. What rankled particularly was that they had started the season by beating Yorkshire by ten wickets in the Roses match and were going to be contenders to claim their first outright County Championship title since 1934.

Leicestershire's general manager Mike Turner told the press that he thought Lancashire's attitude was disgraceful but omitted to mention that minutes of a meeting at Lord's indicated that he was unwilling to release Ray Illingworth to captain England unless Leicestershire could reclaim him for the Sunday League matches. Their Australian fast bowler Graham McKenzie would not be released to the Rest of the World side without due financial compensation. However, the TCCB saw no reason why England players should be released back to their counties for the 40-over matches on Sunday afternoons when it had been unanimously accepted the previous season, the first year of the John Player League, that they would remain with the Test side on Sundays. Just to make some sides feel even more discriminated against, some of the Rest of the World players were to be allowed to return to their counties for these matches because they came under the jurisdiction of their own boards of control and not the TCCB. The broadcasting rights were quickly resolved. *Test Match Special* would operate under the current contractual conditions but payment for the television rights was set at a lower level than would have been the case for the traditional England v South Africa series. It would be on a par with what was paid for matches against India, Pakistan and New Zealand.

When discussions about sponsorship for the new series were under way, Turner declared himself very frustrated that sponsors had indicated that the money would go to the players and not to the counties. Indeed, had the choice of sponsor been Ford rather than

Guinness, the motor company had promised to reward the players with 12 cars. How they would be split between 18 players was not immediately obvious unless they were sold and clearly the counties would not benefit at all. Leicestershire, Turner noted, was a small club with endemic financial problems and they scraped the bottom of the barrel to pay players like Illingworth and McKenzie the most they could afford. It was outrageous that players would be getting paid twice for doing the same job. Seven years later Kerry Packer's financial inducements to players were clearly going to be pushing at a wide open door. In fact the players did better than normal because Guinness put up £2,000 to be awarded to the winning team of each Test match and an additional £3,000 for the series winners. It was a level of professional reward not known since the 18th century, when cricket was almost entirely fuelled by gambling for high stakes. The problem for England was how many games would they realistically be able to win against a Rest of the World team of all the talents?

In addition there was to be a further £7,000 distributed among the 17 counties as compensation for their loss in releasing their overseas stars to the Rest of the World side. Cedric Rhoades, the combative chairman of Lancashire, was in no way mollified by the prospect of Guinness thus greasing his palm. Unhelpfully for the TCCB he attacked the very concept of the Rest of the World matches.

> We regard them as pantomime matches and no amount of money or rigid application of it can alter this. From Lancashire's point of view the money is slight compensation for the loss of crowd pulling players like Clive Lloyd and Farokh Engineer.

The battle for the captaincy of England, indeed selection for all five of the forthcoming Test matches, had an extra significance during the summer of 1970 because it mattered less if England were beaten by the glamorous, talented Rest of the World side than it would have if they had been beaten by visitors from South Africa playing a traditional five-Test series. Therefore both players and captain could be examined for the likelihood of their selection for the tour of Australia in the winter of 1970/71. The England selectors of Don

Kenyon, Billy Sutcliffe and A.C. Smith, chaired by Alec Bedser, announced on 5 June that England would continue to be captained by Ray Illingworth rather than the previous captain Colin Cowdrey. Absurdly, the appointment was made for one Test only. If Illingworth had a decent Test summer the likelihood was that he would take the team to Australia, thus condemning Cowdrey to a fourth successive tour as vice-captain, successively to Peter May, Ted Dexter and Mike Smith. On the other hand if the Rest of the World side lived up to expectations and defeated England decisively, with Illingworth failing to make much of an impression with either bat or ball, the selectors could default to Cowdrey without recriminations or accusations of Southern bias. Illingworth had only been to Australia once, in 1962/63 under Ted Dexter's captaincy. He played in two Tests and did not set the world on fire. Had the selectors appointed Illingworth as captain for the series it would have been much harder to jettison him for the tour of Australia.

Cowdrey had played for Kent in the County Championship during May but he had been in no sort of form and it was deemed a kindness to him to leave him out in the hope that he might find that elusive touch. Four Kent players did, however, take the field at Lord's – Brian Luckhurst and Mike Denness who had both scored heavily for their county as well as the reliable Derek Underwood and Alan Knott. Other familiar names included John Snow, Basil D'Oliveira and Phil Sharpe. Geoffrey Boycott was badly out of form and John Edrich was injured so Luckhurst opened with Alan Jones, the reliable Glamorgan left-handed opener who had enjoyed a superb season in 1969 when Glamorgan had won the County Championship but with Mike Denness coming in first wicket down it meant that England would take the field with a top three who could muster only one Test cap between them. The opening attack was composed of Snow with Alan Ward, the Derbyshire fast bowler whose extra pace it was thought might prove extremely useful on the harder pitches of Australia as well as the aggressive Lancashire seamer, Ken Shuttleworth. Names that had been heavily canvassed but not ultimately selected included Dennis Amiss, Keith Fletcher and Tony Greig although Fletcher was 12th man for the first Test. The batting, without the two injured openers and missing Cowdrey, Barrington and Graveney, who had both recently come to the end of the road, looked distinctly brittle and England supporters feared they might struggle against a team of all the talents.

The Rest of the World side was selected by Garry Sobers, the captain, with Les Ames and Freddie Brown, both former England selectors. By contrast with Bedser and his colleagues, they were spoiled for choice. The team chosen to start the first Test on Wednesday 17 June was: Sobers, Eddie Barlow, Farokh Engineer, Lance Gibbs, Intikhab Alam, Rohan Kanhai, Clive Lloyd, Graham McKenzie, Graeme Pollock, Mike Procter and Barry Richards with Mushtaq Mohammed as 12th man. If Procter were to bat at nine, as seemed likely, it was a frighteningly powerful line-up. Engineer and Graeme Pollock roomed together and Engineer purrs with pleasure as he repeats a story his room-mate told him to illustrate the stupidity of racism.

> The whites were dropping catches off the non-whites' bowling and vice versa so he got them all in the dressing room and said, 'Look here, from tomorrow there are no whites and no blacks in this team. You are all green. Do you understand? You all help each other, OK? Oh and by the way when you get on the team coach the light greens should sit on one side of the aisle and the dark greens on the other.'

Amongst the players on show in county cricket who never received a call-up for any of the five Tests were Majid Khan, Asif Iqbal, Younis Ahmed, Sarfraz Narwaz, John Shepherd and Glenn Turner. The cricketing public might have been salivating to see it and hoping against hope that England might put up a decent performance but the country's attention in the first days of June was now focused partly on the general election, campaigning for which was in full swing during days of unbroken sunshine and, perhaps more important to most people, the fate of the England football team in Mexico.

The 1970 World Cup was another staging-post in the developing relationship between sport and the broadcast media, and in particular between football and television. The World Cup was estimated to create global audiences approaching 600 million and the commercial power of television in Western Europe had persuaded

FIFA to schedule its matches with maximum convenience to those audiences. It represented a significant swing of the pendulum as the power started to shift from the football authorities ever more surely towards the television companies.

World Cup coverage fought for exposure in newspapers and on radio and television with news of the general election. There seemed to be a symbiotic relationship, encouraged no doubt by Harold Wilson, between the holders of the World Cup and the Labour government, both of whom were looking to repeat the success of 1966. In the consistently warm weather of early summer, Wilson displayed the same unflappability for which Alf Ramsey constantly strove. The election was certainly not being fought on issues as Wilson took off his jacket, literally rolled up his sleeves and went on walkabouts through the friendly crowds, shaking hands with all and sundry and chatting happily. Devaluation and inflation seemed a distant memory as the nation celebrated Moore's release from custody. England laboured to a hard fought 1–0 victory over a tetchy, negative Romania in the first group game with a goal by Hurst, and in the opinion polls the Labour lead over the desperate Tories continued to rise as Ted Heath struggled to make an impact. One pressman commented that covering Heath's campaign was the equivalent of being sent out to Mexico to report on El Salvador. The Central American country was playing in the World Cup finals for the first time in its history. It exited at the group stage having lost all three games, secured no points, scored no goals and conceded nine. As election day approached, Ted Heath's Tories appeared to be heading in the same direction.

Even Jack Charlton, who had lost his place to Brian Labone, was at odds with the Tories. Apparently he had joined his local Conservative club in Leeds but had announced his intention of continuing to vote Labour as his entire family had done for generations. The Leeds Tories were greatly upset and threatened to remove Charlton's name from their list of members. Charlton, preparing to play in the match against Czechoslovakia, was unfazed by the possible expulsion, revealing that he had only joined the Conservatives in the first place because they had access to an attractive part of a river he used for fishing and as an added ideological incentive they had four good snooker tables.

After the Romania game, England were scheduled to face their sternest test since the World Cup Final in 1966 – a group stage encounter with the feared Brazilians. Brazil had demolished Czechoslovakia 4–1 in their first match and in Pelé, Jairzinho, Tostão, Gérson, Rivelino and Carlos Alberto appeared to have a core of players who successfully combined the virtues of hard work and application associated with European teams with the equally stereotypical South American skill and flair. The highly anticipated game kicked off on Sunday 7 June in scorching midday heat. England, playing in utterly alien conditions and beset by the seemingly unending travails that had plagued them since they had left Heathrow, produced arguably their finest performance for many years. This was in spite of the fact that they had enjoyed little sleep the night before the game thanks to a concerted attack of noise deliberately orchestrated by a hundred Brazil fans who had easily evaded whatever minimal security had been provided by the hotel and tried to get into the players' rooms. Ramsey complained to FIFA but it was too late and the damage had been done.

The England players demonstrated that they had learned the value of keeping the ball and not expending pointless energy under the merciless sun. Considerable pressure was placed on the full-backs, Tommy Wright replacing the injured Keith Newton and Terry Cooper to get down the wings, but in the event they were mostly involved with stemming the relentless tide of Brazilian attacks. Cooper was left for dead by Jairzinho as he hurtled down the right flank and pulled the ball back from the dead ball line for Pelé to head it down towards the left-hand side of England's goal. Banks had been covering the near post as Jairzinho crossed the ball and it seemed impossible to Pelé that he could scramble back to get a hand to the header. Pelé yelled 'Golo!' expecting to see the ball bounce up into the roof of the net. Instead, Banks made what became known as 'the save of the century', somehow turning the ball over the bar for a corner. However, for all their outstanding play and physical fortitude, England went down to a goal by Jairzinho created by a side-footed pass from Pelé.

England's World Cup was not over on 7 June despite the defeat. It was popularly believed that Moore had said to Pelé 'See you in the final' as they memorably exchanged sweat-soaked shirts. In the light of England's impressive display, supporters believed even more strongly that their team had the potential to be World Cup finalists for a second successive tournament. Four days later they just scraped past Czechoslovakia by virtue of an Allan Clarke penalty. He and Jeff Astle started the game instead of Lee and Hurst, Bell took Ball's place in midfield and Jack Charlton, looking far from the dominant central defender he had been in 1966, gave Brian Labone a rest before the Everton player's coming encounter with Gerd Müller. A draw would have been enough to have seen England into the quarter-final so, although the performance was a comedown after the previous Sunday's heroics against Brazil, everyone back home was perfectly happy to accept that the result was, in the usual managerial doublespeak, more important than the performance.

Harold Wilson continued to beam benignly on the team from his lofty position in the polls. On Thursday 11 June, a week before election day, as England qualified for the quarter-finals from the group stage, two opinion polls put Labour seven per cent clear of the Conservatives which suggested an overall Labour majority at least as large as the 96 seats they had acquired in 1966. On Saturday 13 June NOP published a poll that gave Labour an astonishing 12.5 percent lead over the rapidly wilting Tories. Wilson could sit down and watch the West Germany quarter-final knowing that his pre-election nightmare would not be realised. Crossman's diaries reveal clearly that when the Cabinet discussed the timing of the 1970 election, Wilson was very conscious of the fact that a bad World Cup for the England side might well impact adversely on the government's campaign for re-election. He thought that to go to the country in June 1970 was taking an unnecessary risk, but the Cabinet convinced him it was the right time and that the result of a football match couldn't possibly matter that much.

In *Whatever Happened to the Likely Lads?*, the 1973 BBC sitcom written by Dick Clement and Ian La Frenais (both football supporters), Terry Collier, played by James Bolam, returns to Newcastle after five years in the British Army on the Rhine and a failed marriage to Jutta, a German woman. When his best friend Bob Ferris (Rodney Bewes) asks him why the marriage disintegrated he is told that it had all been going so well until 14 June 1970. Bob is puzzled. What could have happened on 14 June, he wonders. Terry is astonished that the date isn't seared into Bob's brain the way it is in his:

> Terry: What happened? I would have thought the date was printed indelibly on the mind of every Englishman worthy of the name. England 2 West Germany 3. That's what happened.

> Bob: Oh my God, of course.

> Terry: Have you any idea what it was like to be in West Germany that night? Especially after being two up. After the second I was standing on the sideboard singing 'Rule Britannia' and 'Land of Hope and Glory'. Their faces! And then ... the shame! The humiliation! To have them all leaping up and down, eyes glazed with national socialist fervour ... I thought they were going to rush out and invade Poland again ... I just got up quite unnoticed and left ... Just got my bag and walked out of her life for ever.

> Bob: I would have done the same. It was bad enough here. I can't say I blame you, mate. I had to go to bed and lie down. For two weeks. Mind you, I think Chivers has made a difference.

It wasn't just Bob who instantly understood how Terry had felt: the ten million viewers who watched *Whatever Happened to the Likely Lads?* would have remembered the pain of 14 June 1970 and felt exactly the same way, although when the England squad landed at Heathrow on election day their reception was a commiserating one of bad luck and good wishes.

Maybe if England hadn't gone 2-0 up after 50 minutes and played the Germans off the park it wouldn't have felt so shocking. Maybe if England had been 3-0 down after 20 minutes and scored two scrappy goals in the last few minutes to offer a late burst of vain hope it would have been easier to have accepted that defeat. Maybe if Ramsey had left Charlton on the pitch, Beckenbauer would not have felt able to go on his marauding forward runs, but then the substitution of Bell for Charlton happened *after* the Beckenbauer goal. Charlton himself always said that Ramsey had done the right thing in the belief that no England team gave away three goals in 20 minutes and there was a semi-final to be played in three days' time. Bell in fact was brought down in the penalty area by Beckenbauer, but the referee refused to award what looked like a certain penalty.

All the luck that had accompanied England in 1966 deserted them with a vengeance in 1970. England had made mistakes both on and off the pitch. Off it, Ramsey had yet again failed to distinguish himself as a diplomat, alienating the hyper-sensitive Latin Americans who had not forgotten the 'animals' slur from 1966. When England in red shirts and West Germany in white had emerged on to the field for the start of the game it looked like 1966 but the atmosphere was sharply different. Difficult as it was to understand back home, England were perceived as arrogant imperialists who played boring football. Germany on the other hand were the team of plucky underdogs and the local crowd had no doubts as to which side they would support. On the field England had eased off after the second goal, stroking the ball across the pitch, trying to retain possession with their minds on the forthcoming semi-final, but in doing so let West Germany back into the quarter-final tie.

In the end it probably came down to whatever Gordon Banks ate or drank that gave him food poisoning and kept him out of the game. His replacement, Chelsea's Peter Bonetti, had played in those two pulsating Cup Finals against Leeds United at the end of April so he wasn't short of big match experience, but on the day he seemed to freeze. Unlike Banks, who gave extra comfort to his defenders, Bonetti's nerves caused Moore and Labone to be forever casting anxious backwards glances. After 68 minutes, he allowed Beckenbauer's weak shot to slip under his falling body and 14 minutes later, when Seeler stumbled but managed a back header from a Schnellinger cross to the far post, Bonetti remained flat-footed as the ball looped over him into the net. The third German goal, in extra time, was a foregone conclusion. England were out on their feet by then and the Germans were rampant. Even before Müller volleyed home to clinch victory every England supporter could see that defeat was inevitable.

For Harold Wilson the defeat must have caused some tremors, but he picked up the telephone and called Ramsey in León to congratulate the stunned manager on England's magnificent if unlucky performance. He certainly remembered the general election of 1945, when the newspapers had all predicted a Churchill victory despite the ensuing Labour landslide. The day after the calamity in

León, the Board of Trade released the latest trade figures. The visible trade balance for May showed a deficit of more than £31 million. In the election post-mortem those figures were credited with turning the tide against Labour although, like England supporters after the first German goal went in, it was still believed that the lead could not be overturned. Just as England might have had to settle for a 2-1 rather than a 2-0 victory, Labour might have to settle for a 50-seat, rather than a 100-seat, majority.

Such was the state of the parties when Brian Luckhurst and Alan Jones walked through the Long Room, out of the Lord's pavilion, down the steps and on to the turf to face the combined might of the Rest of the World on the morning of Wednesday 17 June. Nobody expected them to set off like a train – it wasn't a one-day limited overs match. They must have been hoping for 70 or 80 to be on the board by lunch with perhaps the loss of two wickets, maybe only one if fortune favoured them and Procter, Sobers, Barlow, McKenzie and Gibbs all bowled badly. They didn't reach 70. They didn't even reach 50. England took lunch with the scoreboard reading 44/7. It was perhaps England's most abysmal opening day in a home Test match since Lindwall and Miller had bowled them out for 52 in Don Bradman's last Test at The Oval in 1948.

McKenzie's first ball of the match from the Pavilion End found the edge of Alan Jones's tentative bat and lobbed over the heads of the slips, running away to the boundary. It was a most fortunate start and maybe the England openers thought their luck was in. It wasn't. From the Nursery End, with the wind at his back, the speedy Procter reduced poor Luckhurst to helpless impotence. John Arlott described the passage of play as Luckhurst hung around grimly for 50 minutes having scored exactly one run and taken a savaging from Procter as being like 'a soldier at bayonet practice on a dummy'. It is a classic Arlott metaphor, fit to rank alongside Clive Lloyd's stroke for four made with 'the air of a man knocking the top off a thistle with a walking stick'. For several overs Luckhurst failed to middle a single delivery. Jones drove at Procter more in desperation than certainty and edged the ball wide of Engineer who took off horizontally and caught it. Luckhurst battled on with his Kent colleague Denness but Procter was destroying England, although others took the wickets. At the end of his first devastating spell Procter took his sweater having bowled seven overs, taken the wicket of Jones and conceded five runs in two scoring strokes.

Eventually Luckhurst's determined resistance ended when he was caught by Richards at short leg off Sobers, who then proceeded to rip the heart out of the England innings. The ball was clearly swinging and the West Indian took full advantage, having D'Oliveira caught behind without scoring and Sharpe caught at slip for four. McKenzie dismissed Denness for 13 before Sobers resumed his demolition, having Knott caught at slip for two and John Snow, who played sensibly for nearly half an hour with his captain, edging to give Engineer his third catch of the morning. As Sobers led his team off at lunch with the scoreboard reading 44/7, the crowd stood to applaud the smiling destroyer who had already taken five wickets for eight runs. The recently retired Brian Statham was at Lord's in his capacity as an ambassador for the sponsor, Guinness. He was asked by journalists who had seen him wreak havoc from the Pavilion End when the ball seamed and swung whether he might have enjoyed bowling that morning. 'Against that lot?' smiled Lancashire's finest. 'Yes I would.'

In the England dressing room, Statham's successor as Lancashire's opening bowler, Ken Shuttleworth, due to bat at number 11, was feeling even more anxious than the dismissed batsmen. He had been playing for Lancashire against Essex the previous day and because Peter Lever had broken down after bowling 11 overs in Essex's second innings, Shuttleworth had completed 23 overs, taking 3-54, before getting in the car and driving to Lord's.

> I was bowling all day and Bondy bowled me into the ground. When I woke up on the day of the first Rest of the World Test I was stiff all over. I thought Illy would win the toss, bat all day and I could put my feet up, then we had the next day off for the general election so I wouldn't have to bowl again till some time on the Friday. Anyway Illy won the toss, batted and I think we were seven down at lunch.

There was an improvement after lunch as the England captain began the series with a spirited innings of defiance. Derek Underwood, playing forward, which was something the morning's batsmen rarely did, made a gutsy 19, taking the total from 44/7 to 94/8 before Alan Ward came out to help Illingworth see the total reach the relative respectability of 125/9 when Illingworth's fine innings came to an end. He was caught behind the wicket by Engineer off Sobers for 63. Sobers finished that England first innings with figures of 6-21 from 20 overs. Shuttleworth's first appearance in an England sweater did not last long as Ward edged McKenzie to be caught in the slips, inevitably by Sobers. Shuttleworth might have hoped to have had his feet up all that day and not have to bowl again before a new government had been installed on the Friday morning but the reality was he was pounding in to support Snow and Ward before tea on that opening day.

The Rest of the World's early batsmen were as authoritative as England's had been tentative. Barry Richards never appeared to be in the slightest trouble as the England bowlers tried to repair the damage their batsmen had wrought. Barlow and Richards, who ironically should have been playing for their country on the same ground at the same time, put on 69 before Richards, on 35 and playing with customary ease but an atypical lack of concentration, edged a ball from Ward which flew low and wide to Sharpe at slip where he caught it as he had caught hundreds of catches for Yorkshire down the years with superb skill and similar lack of drama. Kanhai was caught behind by Knott off D'Oliveira for 21 but the Rest of the World closed the day on 115/2, just 12 runs behind the England total with the combative Eddie Barlow, who had not had Richards's fortune of playing himself into form in the County Championship, unbeaten on 50. There must have been some mutterings in the Lord's pavilion that Wednesday evening as the men who had fought so hard to keep the South Africa tour alive watched Barlow and Graeme Pollock leave the field to the applause of the crowd, with another South African already back in the pavilion. What had all the fuss been about? They were to find out when the match resumed on the Friday morning.

The embattled Billy Griffith, who might have realistically supposed his difficult days were behind him when the South African tour was cancelled, now had to face the criticism that this much vaunted replacement series was proving a dud at the box office. On the first day of the match at the home of cricket, in a ground designed to hold 30,000, fewer than 8,000 spectators turned up to watch this array of the finest cricketers in the world which Griffith claimed was exactly what he had expected.

> The Wednesday start was an improvisation because of the election and we could have more election reaction tomorrow. I think the main thing many people have been waiting to see is just how this series is played. They are not interested in Festival cricket but Garry Sobers has quickly given the answer to that. I know that many are bitterly disappointed the Springboks are not here but their top players have come over and they are part of the most impressive side I have ever seen. So far as the England side is concerned this will be the hardest series of their lives and the toughest blooding for Australia.

E.W. Swanton was relieved to have laid to rest his anxieties that this replacement series would turn out to be nothing more than a festival jamboree.

> If any had supposed that this new series was going to lack anything in zest and effort as compared with the conventional Test match this opening day must have reassured them. The Rest went at their opponents as though their lives depended on it.

Unfortunately, despite the high standard of the competitive cricket, crowds were never to come flocking into the Test grounds to watch the most impressive side Billy Griffith had ever seen. There was now no England football to distract potential spectators and even the semi-finals had been played and settled with Brazil, the favourites, set to play Italy in Sunday's final after the Azzurri had scraped past West Germany 4-3 after extra time. The national attention turned to the election.

As the England goalkeeper Peter Bonetti fumbled Beckenbauer's weak strike the previous Sunday evening, senior Tories were meeting to discuss the plan of offering the leadership of the Conservative Party immediately after their election defeat was announced to the former Prime Minister Sir Alec Douglas Home, as a temporary appointment until elections could be held for a new leader. Willie Whitelaw was appointed to be the man to carry the box with the asp to Ted Heath, who seemed stiff and awkward compared to Wilson's smiling ease of manner. He appeared to be incapable of halting what they feared was a third consecutive Labour victory at the polls. On election day, as Ken Shuttleworth was recovering from his exertions, Wilson was moving through large and welcoming crowds in Trafford, Manchester, Bolton and his own constituency of Huyton in Liverpool. True there was the by now almost mandatory egg thrown at him which rather stained his light summer suit and a police horse, attempting to control the crowds near the Prime Minister and his wife, inadvertently trod on Mary Wilson's foot but when he arrived in Huyton, Wilson had no cause to fear what the next few hours might bring.

The last opinion polls varied as usual but all showed a lead for Labour at between 2% and 7%, giving Wilson an overall majority in Parliament of between 20 and 100 seats. He was relieved. The balance of payments deficit was bad news for the government and it gave the Conservatives a stick to beat them with but Labour felt Heath had overplayed his hand, accusing Labour, if it were re-elected, of needing another devaluation to steady an economy in freefall. It didn't appear to be a substantive argument and general public confidence in the economy had been high since the Budget nearly three months earlier.

Heath instead appeared to take refuge in the belief that Labour had alienated the British housewife over the past few years and that she would have her revenge at the ballot box on the morrow. Perhaps Heath had been listening to the woman who would become his Minister for Education in the cabinet he would shortly form, the Member for Finchley who could certainly have told him a thing or two about the British housewife if he had bothered to ask. Certainly she would have told him of the positive impact that stories about impending price rises might have. The *Daily Express* carried a story on its front page warning that the price of coffee, chocolate, frozen beefburgers, beer and baby food were all set to rise sharply in the immediate future. It was news like that, Margaret Thatcher knew very well, that would make people think twice about voting for Labour. It was in her opinion much more powerful than Heath's general dire warnings about trade deficits and devaluation.

Subsequent remarks by Shirley Williams confirmed that the manner in which previous Labour-voting housewives switched their support to the Conservatives in 1970, in many cases for the very first time, was a significant element in the outcome of the election.

> I think thousands, and maybe hundreds of thousands of women voted differently this time and voted Conservative.
>
> The concentration on industry, balance of payments, trade union questions does not appeal much to most women voters.
>
> But we can talk to them if we can get across that we do care about pensions and schools, poverty and ill-health. This time, in spite of the share women had in Harold Wilson's government, we did not.

Perhaps more to the point Heath was under enormous pressure from Enoch Powell and the extreme right wing of his own party. Powell was probably the most popular individual politician in the country but his popularity was born of demagoguery. He had been sacked two years previously from the shadow Cabinet after his notorious 'Rivers of Blood' speech but he exhibited no sign of retreating to the back benches quietly. Instead he made it abundantly plain to Heath and everyone else that he was trying to build support to oppose the leader of his party. In contrast to Labour where Wilson appeared in serene control, the Conservative Party appeared to be bitterly divided. Wilson even smilingly admitted on the campaign trail in Bristol that he had spent too much time in Labour marginal constituencies on the defensive and not enough in Tory marginals on the attack. It is a political maxim that parties divided by internal ideological wars do not win elections because electors do not know which side of the party will win the war. Wilson was quick to ask his hecklers whether they had been sent by Heath or Powell and continued to seek out his opponents' weakest spot. In the end the campaign proved surprisingly but thankfully free from controversy over immigration. There was certainly nothing to rival the problems at Smethwick during the 1964 election and when Tony Benn accused Powell of spreading 'obscene racialist propaganda' Wilson told him instantly to cool it. It was in neither party's interest to raise that particular temperature.

The sunshine that had shone over Britain for a few weeks continued to spread its warmth on election day. Wilson seemed to bask in it and his sunny mood was conveyed to the country. It reminded political journalists of the atmosphere surrounding Harold Macmillan's campaign in 1959 when he had swept to victory in the era of Never Had It So Good on the slogan 'Life is Better under the Conservatives'. 1970 seemed to be Labour's perfect symmetrical revenge but the reality on the ground that day was significantly different from the general expectation. The historian Peter Hennessy was a young man in his early twenties whose job it was to get out the Labour vote on a council estate in Luton and he soon realised that it was going to be a more difficult job than he had expected. The weather could certainly not be blamed. Traditionally, Labour always welcomed good weather for the day of an election because stereotypically Labour voters didn't have cars and would only come out to vote if the weather was nice. In 1970 the weather was perfect and still the Labour vote didn't turn out.

Richard Crossman was in Coventry watching with mounting anxiety as the votes were counted into neat piles. He too had experienced what Peter Hennessy had noted in Luton that Labour voters, whether out of complacency or disillusion, were simply not going to the polling stations. The Labour agent confirmed to Crossman that although he was in the lead it was turning out to be much smaller than had been confidently expected. Wilson's worst fears were being realised. Was England's defeat by West Germany on Sunday coming back to haunt Labour on Thursday? According to Crossman's diary, the expectation of victory disappeared within an hour of the first result being announced just after 11.15pm. It came from Guildford, where the Conservatives took the seat with a swing of more than five per cent.

By 1am it was obvious to everyone who was watching the results on television that the Conservatives would win quite handsomely. As the former Labour marginals fell to the rampant Tory swing only one result caused a frisson of discomfort in Bexley where Ted Heath was waiting for his own count. It came in Wolverhampton where

Enoch Powell more than doubled his majority, but most buoyant Conservatives would have attributed that to the wave of blue that was claiming red seats all over the country. In the end, the margin was 31 seats. It appeared at the time to be the most surprising of election results, which probably gave the Board of Trade announcement on the Monday morning more importance than it deserved. What is certainly true is that the polls failed to pick up the late swing from Labour to Conservative but then there has hardly been an election in recent years, when polls have allegedly become more scientific and accurate than ever before, when they actually got it right. At the time there was much discussion of the importance of the trade figures and the football result. Indeed, Roy Jenkins in his autobiography still wondered what the result might have been if the country had gone to the polls just seven days earlier.

So Harold Wilson joined Alf Ramsey not in the joint triumph of 1966 but in the shared misery of 1970. Both men lost quite unexpectedly when all the signs were that they would win. Both men were expected to retain their positions in the short term as they both had credit in the bank from previous victories. For the triumphant Conservatives it proved impossible to deliver on many of their 1970 campaign promises. The threat to revise relations with South Africa never materalised as wiser heads counselled that such a policy would align the country up alongside apartheid and make relations with the former African colonies as well as the Third World in general extremely difficult.

Having sold their house in Hampstead Garden Suburb the previous year, the Wilsons had no home of their own apart from the cottage in the Scilly Isles so when they returned to Downing Street they were relieved to learn that the new Prime Minister had given permission for them to use Chequers for a few days while they sorted themselves out. As they supervised the packing cases and watched Heath's grand piano coming into the private quarters, Eddie Barlow and Graeme Pollock were resuming their innings at Lord's. If the morning session on the first day had clearly delineated the game's direction of travel, events on the second day almost guaranteed an England defeat.

The two South Africans batted untroubled into the afternoon session before Underwood bowled Pollock with a quicker delivery.

Barlow went busily about his task of accumulating runs (Arlott imagined that he might start sweeping the pitch between overs) and reached his century in his first match for three months. Two balls after Pollock was out Barlow, on 119, pulled Illingworth to short midwicket where Underwood took an uncharacteristically athletic catch. To the dismay of the Englishmen, the two South African stars were replaced by Clive Lloyd and Garry Sobers. The latter had endured a disappointing tour with the West Indies the previous summer but any suspicions that his powers were on the wane were soon put to rest. Lloyd was beaten for pace and bowled by Ward with the new ball and Engineer quickly succumbed in the same manner but Intikhab joined his captain and that was the end of England's success for the day.

Sobers was in imperious form. He cut, drove and pulled with certainty all day and raced to 147 by close of play, having only come to the wicket at three o'clock. He was dropped once, by Luckhurst on the long leg boundary off the bowling of the ill-starred Shuttleworth who finished the day with the unflattering figures on his debut of 0-85 from 21 overs. After he had reached his century, Sobers started to indulge himself, giving the impression that he was treating it as he would a festival match, pulling Snow into the Mound Stand for a huge six. It was the sort of stroke that is now expected of Jos Buttler every over but in 1970 this was remarkable batting. The smiling Intikhab was happy to biff his way to an entertaining fifty, carrying his side to 475/6 at the close, their batsmen having scored 360 runs in the day for the loss of only four wickets. England were now 348 behind and had four more wickets to take on the Saturday before they could even start thinking about how long it would take just to make the Rest of the World bat again.

It was possible that England's dire straits were responsible for the paltry 12,000 who attended the Saturday of the Lord's Test, one of the great days in the England cricket calendar. John Woodcock in *The Times* was not impressed:

> The irony is, of course, that had England been playing a moderate Indian side at Lord's on Saturday and winning hands down the ground would have been full to overflowing. As it was there were fewer than 15,000 there to watch the best cricketers

in the world in glorious weather. The regulars who stayed away made a curious decision.

They certainly missed the start of an England fightback, even if it was too little and far too late. Sobers and Intikhab played themselves quietly in again as if determined to bat until Monday before Ward, bowling impressively fast, knocked Intikhab's leg stump out of the ground. Procter joined Sobers and the scoring rate increased until Snow finally took a wicket, bowling Procter and, shortly thereafter, induced a fierce drive from Sobers which gave Underwood a stinging catch at mid-off. Sobers had made 183 and, combined with his 6-21 in the first innings, had effectively beaten England on his own.

When Alan Jones and Brian Luckhurst went out to open the batting in the second innings with England needing 419 to make their opponents bat again, both men knew they were playing for their places not just on the Australia trip in the winter but probably for the next match, as Edrich was recovering from injury and Boycott would certainly recover his form before too long. Under such pressure usually one of two outcomes is likely: a dogged innings characterised by luck in the early stages and then a gradual unfurling of the strokes that captivated the selectors in the first place or an early catastrophe. Jones, unfortunately, opted for the latter course. Facing the first ball of the innings, a loosener from Procter, he flashed at it outside the off stump, got an edge and gave Engineer the simplest of catches. He returned miserably to the pavilion no doubt trying to console himself with the knowledge that he had played for his country, even if it was only this once, and at least he would have the cap to prove it and show to his grandchildren. Sadly, he didn't even have that. Edrich did indeed take his place in the next Test and Jones would never play for England again. In addition, the cricket authorities decided in their wisdom that facing what was probably the strongest side ever to take the field against England did not make for a Test match, official or unofficial.

Thereafter, albeit in a losing cause, the England side showed the sort of fight in adversity that was to prove significant on a difficult tour of Australia six months later. Luckhurst and Denness, after a shaky start, realised that the pitch had lost the devils that had possessed it on Wednesday morning and was playing straight and flat, although with bowling of the quality provided by the Rest of the World it was never going to be easy. Sobers picked up Denness as he glanced Intikhab to leg slip but D'Oliveira and Luckhurst started to give the disappointing crowd something to cheer. They put on 101 before Luckhurst edged Intikhab to give Engineer his sixth catch of the game. Sharpe failed to distinguish himself, falling to Sobers for the second time having scored just six runs in the match and half an hour before the close D'Oliveira, having narrowly avoided a pair after failing to pick Intikhab's googly, was well caught by Clive Lloyd off the Surrey wrist spinner for what was then England's top score of 78. As the crowd left the sun-drenched ground in the long shadows of an early evening in midsummer, England had reached the respectable score of 228/5. The last five wickets would need nearly 200 more runs to avoid an innings defeat but Saturday's play had given some assurance that the entire series was not going to be an embarrassing walkover for the Rest of the World.

There was something about Illingworth and Knott as they saw out play on that Saturday night that gave England supporters hope for the future. Illingworth had clearly got it into his head that he was never going to give up his wicket without a big fight and Knott was starting to show what that 96 not out at Karachi on the previous year's tour of Pakistan had indicated, namely that he would always make runs when England really needed them. Now, the top five batsmen had gone and defeat clearly loomed but Knott and Illingworth seemed to represent the best of England's fighting spirit. On the Monday morning they took their stand to 117 as the Rest of the World bowling attack sought the breakthrough in vain. They had come together 35 minutes before the close of play on Saturday and batted throughout Monday morning's session without offering a chance on what was now a slow, easy paced pitch.

Lunch was taken with the score on 293/5 and the two continued untroubled for half an hour into the afternoon session before Gibbs finally trapped Knott lbw for 39. In Snow, Underwood, Ward and Shuttleworth, the England tail offered little hope for the future and the big question that remained was whether or not Illingworth would reach the century his doggedness had merited. The answer to the question was unfortunately 'no'. In the nineties, the Leicestershire captain was beaten three times by Sobers' chinamen before a fourth one found the edge and Barlow snaffled the chance at slip. 323/7 quickly became 339 all out as Intikhab took the last three wickets in rapid time, giving him an impressive analysis of 6-113 off 54 overs. The England innings, although it finished with the Rest of the World victorious by an innings and 80 runs, had lasted an admirable 174 overs, indicating that the England players possessed the willingness to fight if not the skill to triumph.

The next day Arthur Coy, who was clearly still feeling the depressive after-effects of the cancellation, wrote to Donald Carr at Lord's.

> I cannot reconcile myself to the fact that soft-soaping the non-White members of the Commonwealth by interfering with the way of life in South Africa can be covered by the Council's constitution. This statement has done cricket no good whatsoever anywhere, and the general opinion is that cricket between our respective Countries is now finished.
>
> The first so-called Test against the 'Rest of the World' was a bit of a flop so it was a good job the 'Rest of the World' was not as strong as it could have been.

It isn't immediately clear how the Rest of the World side could have been stronger but it is possible that Coy is bitterly referring to the aborted full South Africa team. The selectors had to agree that from England's perspective it had been a flop of a performance and they duly made changes to the team, but Illingworth was, with extraordinary churlishness, awarded just one more match as captain. Presumably, they were still keen to be in a position to offer the 37-year-old Cowdrey the captaincy for Australia and to make their lives easier they brought the Kent captain back into the team to replace his county colleague, Denness. It was a reasonable decision given the fact that Cowdrey had made two centuries in the last two County Championship matches he had played but it looked ominous for Illingworth that over the weekend of the first Test John Woodcock had not been particularly sanguine about Illingworth's chances of retaining the captaincy for long.

> Simply as a spinner I would rather see Pocock or Wilson, partly because of their age. And as a captain, Cowdrey is no

inferior to Illingworth. Indeed, on tour, he is to be preferred. Like D'Oliveira, Illingworth has a hardy temperament: but with an eye on the future there is hardly room for them both. There seems to me to be no reason why the selectors should not decide this week on their captain for Australia; and if their answer is Cowdrey, then Illingworth for all his competence, may have to go.

If he wanted the job, Illingworth would clearly have to turn in performances for the rest of the series of the dimension he produced at Lord's. For the next match at Trent Bridge, Fletcher was promoted from 12th man, taking the place of Sharpe and, as expected, Edrich returned at the top of the order instead of the unfortunate Jones. Boycott was still unable to recover the form which everyone knew he possessed. Shuttleworth gave way so that David Brown of Warwickshire could be recalled. The Lancashire seamer felt badly done by, particularly having to bowl to the world's best batsmen on a friendly pitch the day after his exertions at Ilford.

> I was disappointed to be dropped after the first Test because I'd bowled well I thought. I had Sobers dropped during that big innings and I didn't think I'd done myself justice. In the morning the ball had swung all over the place but when John Snow and I started bowling it was a different game. You can't explain it.

Before the start of the Second Test Alan Ward's injured leg was X-rayed and damage was found just above the ankle. Tony Greig, despite a dislocated finger sustained in Sussex's Sunday League match against Surrey at The Oval, was called up to make his debut which allowed Alan Knott to bat at number eight. After the fragility displayed by the England batting at Lord's, the team that took the field at Trent Bridge was one in which Ray Illingworth must have had considerably more confidence.

A few days after the end of the Lord's Test, 15 Cambridge University students aged between 19 and 25, who had been arrested in connection with the riot at the Garden House Hotel in February, stood trial at the Hertfordshire Assizes before the notoriously severe Mr Justice Melford Stevenson. After a trial of seven days, the jury took nearly four hours to reach its decision. Seven of the defendants were acquitted, but eight were convicted, six of whom were sentenced to periods of between nine months and 18 months in prison, and two aged under 21 were sent to Borstal. One student from Brazil and a second from South Africa were also recommended for deportation. The sentences were criticised as heavy-handed, as was the judge's comment that he would have passed heavier sentences but for the 'evil influence of some senior members of the university'. It was another battle in the continuing war between the generations. The result of this one sent a shiver through middle-class law-abiding students. If it could happen to them, it could happen to us.

CHAPTER ELEVEN
JULY/AUGUST 1970

I N comparison to the months of May and June when every day, at least until after the election, seemed fraught with drama of one kind or another, July 1970 appeared an oasis of calm as the English summer ran through its traditional social and sporting calendar – Wimbledon, Ascot, Cowes, Henley, the Open Golf Championship, the First Night of the Proms – without disruption, except by the weather. True, one of the first decisions of the new Conservative government was to lift the embargo on the sale of arms to South Africa that had been imposed by the previous administration but that had been signalled well in advance of the election result and it came as no surprise to anyone.

It seemed as if all the social turmoil that had accompanied the fevered atmosphere in which the tour had been cancelled, England had failed to retain their title as world champions in Mexico and Harold Wilson and the Labour Party had lost office, had entirely disappeared and all was calm once more in England's green and pleasant land. The impact of the events of 1968, however, was still being felt. The year had seen, amongst other legislation guided through the House of Commons by the liberal, reforming Home Secretary Roy Jenkins, before he swapped jobs with Jim Callaghan at the Treasury, the passage of the bill abolishing the office of the Lord Chamberlain, the man who had been effectively the censor of whatever appeared on the stage for 230 years. Kenneth Tynan said that the abolition dragged the British theatre kicking and screaming

into the second half of the 18th century. In the wake of the new post-
Look Back in Anger theatre, the era of the so-called 'kitchen sink'
drama, it had become an embarrassing anachronism.

On 26 September 1968 the Act became law. The very next day
Hair opened at the Shaftesbury Theatre to widespread protestations
of shock and horror with its scenes of nudity and drug-taking. It
starred the then unknown young actors Elaine Paige, Paul Nicholas
and Tim Curry and was never designed to appeal to Terence
Rattigan's Aunt Edna or indeed the long-standing theatre critic
of the *Daily Telegraph*, W.A. Darlington, who hung up his quill
permanently after filing a review complaining of boredom. As soon as
the cast began to take off their clothes, a number of formally dressed
audience members walked out in protest – a fairly pointless exercise
given that the nudity was a major selling point and everyone knew
what they were going to see when they walked into the Shaftesbury
Theatre. Their traditional complaint was that because the men's hair
was as long as the women's they were unable to distinguish between
the sexes. Had they waited another five minutes before leaving they
would have had no trouble in that regard.

Hair's successor in extending what British audiences would accept
in terms of the portrayal of sexuality was *Oh! Calcutta!*, the erotic
revue that, like *Hair*, had transferred from Broadway and now opened
at the Roundhouse in north London in July 1970. It was noted by
the critics that the enjoyment and lack of embarrassment of the cast
helped the audience to accept the more insubstantial elements of the
revue's material and that the stage set's screen projections assisted
the dance numbers considerably. Irving Wardle, *The Times* drama
critic, concluded that 'In many ways it is a ghastly show: ill-written,
juvenile, and attention-seeking. But it is not a menace.' That was in
response to the worrying sign that the production had attracted the
attention of the Metropolitan Police's Obscene Publications Squad,
which sent two officers to a preview of the show. One of the officers
returned twice more to indicate to his superiors his dedication to
his duty, no doubt, paying particular scrutiny to the interpretive
dances which were performed stark naked, before recommending a
prosecution under the 1968 Theatres Act for obscenity.

The Director of Public Prosecutions then sent its panel
of experts – including two retired headmistresses – to see the

Roundhouse production and their eminently sensible judgement was that it was not obscene, which enabled it to transfer to the West End where it ran almost uninterrupted for nearly ten years despite a couple of changes of venue. Tynan was the driving force behind it, although his attempt to persuade Harold Pinter to write and direct it, which would have given it considerable theatrical gravitas, was unsuccessful. It is likely that Pinter would have been far more interested in the fate of the England team when it resumed battle with the Rest of the World in Nottingham at the start of the month.

There was some trepidation about the crowd again. Advance booking for the second Test was minimal as compared to what would have been expected for a traditional Test match against Australia, South Africa or West Indies but Nottinghamshire CCC took refuge in the fact that the previous year's Test at Trent Bridge had also attracted little interest in advance although the crowds turned up on the day. However, there was some anxiety that BBC Outside Broadcast cameras which had been present for the start of every Test match since 1951 would be absent as they were being deployed for the State Opening of Parliament. The general election still wasn't finished with messing cricket around. There was alarm that the lack of cameras would suggest to the cricketing public of the East Midlands that the cricket wasn't worth bothering about but at the same time it would help to solve the endless riddle of whether the televising of cricket benefitted attendance at cricket matches or caused them to fall.

As it transpired the crowd was disappointingly small, estimated at not much more than 1,000, but that was partly attributed to the weather because after a June of almost unbroken sunshine, July began in classic British bank holiday weather – cold and grey with intermittent bursts of rain. The start had to be delayed and the Rest of the World had only managed 40/1 by lunch. Interestingly, the successful bowling turned out to be the medium-pace swing and seam delivered by Basil D'Oliveira and the debutant, Tony Greig. It was lost on nobody present when these two in harness were bowling to Barry Richards and Eddie Barlow and then to Graeme Pollock that two players born in South Africa were bowling to two South African batsmen in a summer when the South African cricket tour had been cancelled. Greig and D'Oliveira used the conditions perfectly, each taking four wickets while David Brown and John Snow rarely managed to get the ball to deviate off the straight.

Richards reined himself in but still made a vital if uncharacteristically slow 64 before he was brilliantly caught by Knott down the leg side off Greig who, in short measure, had Kanhai caught at slip by Fletcher, bowled Garry Sobers off the inside edge before the great man had reached double figures and immediately had Engineer caught behind. At one point the much vaunted Rest of the World batting had been reduced to 126/6. The innings of the day, however, was played by Clive Lloyd who in partnership with the reliable Intikhab Alam and then with Mike Procter managed to take the score to a respectable 276 when the last wicket fell. Lloyd, who had hooked David Brown for three sixes, had clearly used his time in Lancashire well to adjust his batting to the vagaries of the English weather. Illingworth, who didn't bring himself on until the last hour of play, bowled tightly and set the field for Underwood and himself so cleverly that Lloyd remained nervously hovering on 99 for a quarter of an hour before driving Illingworth straight for four. When D'Oliveira bowled Gibbs with the last ball of the opening day to end the innings, Lloyd remained unbeaten on 114.

The second day's play took place before a crowd that had more than doubled in size from the previous day but at 2,500 it still left vast swathes of Trent Bridge seats empty. As occasionally happens in cricket, the second innings followed almost precisely the pattern of the first. Edrich and Luckhurst opened slowly but safely with few alarms and the score mounted steadily until Eddie Barlow came on a quarter of an hour before lunch with England contentedly placed on 78 for no wicket. Just as England's fast bowlers were outbowled by the swing and seam of D'Oliveira and Greig so Barlow showed McKenzie, Procter and Sobers how accurate medium-pace bowling could have devastating consequences. Luckhurst was comprehensively yorked, Cowdrey was given out caught at short square leg by Barry Richards (a decision the famous walker was initially most reluctant to accept) and then Barlow had Fletcher taken by Engineer. Instead of lunching in some comfort England went off with the score at 83/3. Immediately after lunch their prospects deteriorated still further when Barlow continued his early success by dismissing Luckhurst and D'Oliveira to give himself figures of 5-17. Greig played some typically expansive shots and raced to 14 before driving uppishly at Sobers; the ball flew off the outside edge to the gully where Gibbs took an outstanding catch. England were now 126/6, the exact situation their opponents had been in the previous day when Engineer had been dismissed by Greig.

As Lloyd was for the Rest of the World so Illingworth was for England as, for the second match in a row, he held the innings together and moved courageously towards a century only to be dismissed again in the nineties. This time he had reached 97 when in the last over of the day, and to the disappointment of the small crowd who had been absorbed by the contest, England crept into a first innings lead but lost their heroic captain when a ball by Sobers clattered into the middle and off stumps. He returned to the pavilion applauded by one and all. He had been helped initially by Knott with whom he had put on 53 and at the end by John Snow coming in at number 11 with England still 81 behind. Sobers must have been quaking in his boots as the Sussex fast bowler strode determinedly out to the middle, recalling the 128 which Snow and Higgs had put on for the last wicket against West Indies at The Oval in Brian Close's triumphant first match as captain of England. Snow and Illingworth took the score from 195/9 to 279 all out at the close. Each innings had lasted a complete day and with just three runs between the teams, it was clearly going to be a more interesting contest than the first Test had proved to be.

If the Test and County Cricket Board had entertained hopes that with the match intriguingly poised the Saturday of their Test match would bring out the Nottingham crowd to fill the ground, they were quickly disappointed. Scarcely 5,000 turned up to watch a Test match that was being fiercely contested in line with the expectations of its Guinness sponsors who had put up significant money for the winning side, at a time when players earned not much more than £1,000 a year. It was true that the International Cavaliers, stocked with British and overseas players including Cowdrey, Parks, Sobers, Benaud, Simpson and a long-retired Denis Compton, played against county sides on Sunday afternoons in 1966, 1967 and 1968 before the advent of the John Player League in 1969. The games attracted decent television audiences on BBC2 but they were regarded by both sides as festival cricket and attendances were nothing like those that the Sunday League attracted when it started. The cheque for the winning side (presumably split between all 22 players) was 100 guineas which represented a fee of £4/15/6 for each player.

In the summer of 1970, it was supposed that the cricket public which would probably have turned up in force for the scheduled England v South Africa Test seemed to have come to the conclusion that the Rest of the World Test matches were like those International Cavaliers games, somehow fake and not worth the entrance money. That was certainly the way Robin Marlar saw it. 'People recognised that the Rest of the World series was bogus and that it should have been the South Africans; that's why they didn't show up.' If they suspected that the Rest of the World players were not really motivated even by Guinness's generous sponsorship they might have had a point. Looking back on the series from the vantage point of his autobiography, Barry Richards wrote that the series,

> never had the authentic atmosphere of a country v country conflict. On our side there was a very free and easy approach; no one minded if you arrived at a ground a quarter of an hour late. England may have taken it more seriously, especially as the prize money was considerable. We felt so blessed with talent within our side that we were always going to win.

On the other hand Keith Fletcher, also writing 13 years after the series had been played, took a very different stance.

> Debates ranged for years afterwards over the official status of that series and eventually it was decided that the matches did not merit being included as Tests. To me, this was wrong. I know the England side treated them as Test matches, and there was certainly no shortage of serious intent among the World players. The natural edge of a Test was apparent in every game.

Raymond Illingworth also knew that anyone who came up against Eddie Barlow in that series knew that he could not have been playing with more purpose if he had been captaining a South Africa side in the heat of a Test match battle.

We had decent crowds but nothing like the Test matches. If it had been England v South Africa it would have been a full house. We played it absolutely seriously and I think they did as well. They did not treat them like exhibition matches. Take it easy? I tell you what … you just try playing against Eddie Barlow. He were never taking it easy. Bloody hell! Maybe for the first match because everything went their way in that one but we beat them in the second match at Trent Bridge and they took it very serious from then on.

Keith Fletcher too had enormous respect for Barlow.

The aggression that Eddie Barlow showed never bothered me. It was all part of the game as far as I was concerned. I thought he was a top player. He never swore, never verbally abused me, he was just aggressive.

Barlow had made a century in the first Test, taken 5-66 in the England first innings and now batted through the whole of the third day. Arlott described his truculent batting perfectly.

Rosy cheeked and burly, shoulders back, chin thrust forward, restlessly busy and surveying the world sharply through gold-rimmed spectacles he batted with steady purpose. If he had not twice been missed England could be now near to beating their redoubtable opponents but he survived to bat again today and he may yet decide the outcome.

Barlow finished the day on 123 not out having been dropped by Knott off D'Oliveira and by Cowdrey off Underwood. England bowled with line and length discipline and conceded only 257 in the 98 overs bowled in the day. Richards made 30 and Procter and Intikhab got into the twenties but the Rest's second innings was dominated by Barlow. When he eventually went early on Monday morning, bowled by Greig for 142, the innings folded quickly and England needed 284 runs to win what would be a remarkable victory considering the scale of the defeat they had suffered at Lord's. Barlow's century was greeted on the Saturday after tea by an exuberant West Indian spectator who raced on to the pitch to shake Barlow by the hand. In the context of what had been happening in England during the calendar year, such a sight must have warmed the cockles of many a cricket supporter's heart, wherever he had stood in relation to the tour. It was all the more depressing therefore that the West Indian was grabbed by the neck by the local constabulary, frog-marched off the playing area and forcibly ejected from the ground. That'll teach him to act as if colour had no meaning and that cricket could unite all races.

Nobody expected that England would glide effortlessly to a victory. Nearly 300 runs in the fourth innings of a match against such a bowling attack that had reduced them to rubble on the first morning at Lord's was never going to be easy but to everyone's surprise and the delight of the home side and their small coterie of supporters who were present to see it, England won the match by the convincing margin of eight wickets. It was effectively won on the Monday when England closed on 184/2, needing another 100 on the last day. All the England batsmen who came to the wicket distinguished themselves in the face of predictably hostile bowling but the weather was warm, which finally brought something resembling a crowd into the ground, the pitch was flat and the ball rarely deviated. Even when Gibbs and Sobers managed to turn it, the spin was slow enough to allow it to be played off the back foot. After the last three Rest of the World wickets fell in 35 minutes giving both D'Oliveira and Greig seven wickets in the match, the England openers Edrich and Luckhurst proceeded to lunch with appropriate caution. Although only 26 runs came in the hour and a quarter they batted, the openers had done their job of preserving their wickets and taking the shine off the ball, tasks which the England openers 50 years on appear to find almost impossible.

Edrich edged McKenzie into the hands of Barlow at slip which brought Cowdrey to the wicket and this time, to the delight of those cricket supporters who had admired the ease of his strokeplay over the previous 15 years, Cowdrey blossomed. When he reached 21, he broke Walter Hammond's record of 7,249 runs, making him at that moment the highest scorer in Test history. It wasn't one of his most sparkling innings but it resonated with the shots of a class batsman and the partnership with his Kent colleague Luckhurst yielded 120 runs, the highest of the match before Cowdrey, on 64, played all round a delivery from the ubiquitous Barlow which hit him full on the boot and had him palpably lbw. Crawford White in the *Daily Express* hoped the innings might be so well received that Cowdrey would have the captaincy restored to him, but the selectors in all fairness in the middle of the series that Illingworth was having, could not move too far too quickly. They re-appointed the Leicestershire skipper as captain for the third Test at Edgbaston even before the last rites of the second Test were read.

Any thoughts that England might find the remaining 100 runs a tricky proposition were dispelled on the morning of the fifth day when Fletcher, who had been 8 not out overnight, revealed the sort of form that Essex supporters had long known about but England spectators had rarely glimpsed. Luckhurst progressed serenely to his century, finishing on 113 not out, but the slow pace of his batting the previous day had irritated Keith Miller, who roundly criticised and called on Luckhurst to play with the freedom he had seen him display when batting for Kent. The morning of the last day, however, really belonged to Fletcher who was particularly severe on Intikhab, going to his fifty with three fours in an over off the wrist spinner. He finished undefeated on 69 and saw England home before the clock struck one. It was a highly encouraging performance by England who had shown that they were not dispirited by events at Lord's and it raised expectations that the series might yet develop into a memorable one, with crowds to match.

On the first day of the third Test in Birmingham, however, there was more anxiety about the crowds that would or would not show up. John Woodcock writing in *The Times* had been in touch with the ticket office at Edgbaston and been confronted with more bad news.

Unhappily, there is no reason to suppose that the people of Birmingham are intending to turn up in greater numbers than those of Nottingham. Although Warwickshire have probably the best appointed cricket ground in the world, it is also one of the emptiest. This is sad, especially because the Test and County Cricket Board under whose aegis the matches are being played are in desperate need of some money. The combined takings at Lord's and Trent Bridge amounted only to £28,000 to go towards the cost of staging the series including the travelling and living expenses of the three South Africans.

In fact there were to be five South Africans at Edgbaston as Peter Pollock joined his brother, Graeme, Barry Richards, Eddie Barlow and Mike Procter, thereby reuniting the South African opening pace attack that had so recently decimated the Australians on home soil. Graham McKenzie was dropped as was Farokh Engineer who had made a grand total of three runs in the two matches so far. His place behind the wicket went to the West Indian, Deryck Murray. In neither case did the replacements constitute a weakening of the impressive power of the Rest of the World side. England remained unchanged from Trent Bridge, with Dennis Amiss unable to force his way into the team on his home ground.

Illingworth won the toss in front of a crowd building up to a respectable 7,000 and elected to bat on a low, slow pitch where the ball rarely came on to the bat. Edrich and Luckhurst batted as they had done in the previous match, calmly accumulating and eschewing risk as far as it were possible. Again, approaching lunch, they appeared comfortable when both men and Cowdrey were out in rapid succession causing a small collapse from 56/0 to 66/3. Cowdrey this time lasted only two balls, trapped lbw by Sobers bowling left arm over the wicket, angling the ball towards the slips but good enough to bring it back in to leave Cowdrey helpless and make his place in the team for Australia, certainly as captain, look as uncertain as it had looked certain at the end of the previous match ten days earlier. Fletcher too went to Sobers, having collected a duck that stretched for half an hour either side of lunch. Illingworth and D'Oliveira, who seemed in command from his first ball, stopped the rot before the England captain gave Deryck Murray his third catch of the day.

Greig joined D'Oliveira and just as they had linked in harness in the previous Test as bowlers, here they put on 110 to take England to the comparative safety of 244/6. It appeared that England's two South Africans were just as good as the Rest's four or five South Africans. Both men were out before the close but not before D'Oliveira had driven, cut and pulled with fierce power, as if the ball were zipping off the WACA pitch and not keeping low at Edgbaston. He delivered an outstanding century to an England side that had looked to be in danger of wasting their admirable opening partnership. He was eventually caught and bowled by Clive Lloyd who, at the beginning of his career, was a more than useful change bowler. Greig also departed before the end, yorked by Procter for 55, but he had confirmed the impression he had given at Nottingham that here was a 23-year-old all-rounder who might give sterling service to his adopted country for many years. Alan Knott and David Brown took the score to within sight of the respectability of 300, closing on 282/7, scored off 97 overs.

Alas, the sight of 300 proved to be a mirage as the last three wickets went down in a clatter on the Friday morning as Procter clean bowled both Knott and Brown and induced a drive from Underwood which Sobers caught diving full length at mid-on. Procter's irresistible pace attack gave him figures of 5-46 from 24 overs. Snow then turned in by far his most hostile spell of the series so far. In his second over he beat Richards's outside edge twice and in his fourth he beat Barlow for speed and knocked his off stump out of the ground. To the surprise of the crowd who were expecting a strong counter attack from the Rest of the World batting, in fact it turned into an innings of attrition. Any side led by Ray Illingworth would know how to exert control but it was surprising that Richards, Kanhai and then Graeme Pollock had no answer other than to occupy the crease and wait for the bad ball.

At 80 Richards was caught at slip by Greig driving at Snow so Kanhai and Pollock ground their way through the afternoon, both batsmen on occasion being barracked for their slow play. It must have been the first time it had happened to either of them but the pitch was still low and slow and the England bowling was tight and disciplined. Pollock had displayed so far in the series none of the form worthy of the description that he was one of the best batsmen in the world which had accompanied his arrival in the country. He scratched and prodded and poked for 40 runs before Snow bowled him with the last ball before tea to claim his third wicket of the innings.

When Kanhai drove Illingworth low to Greig at mid-on the score was just 175/4 and Illingworth must have felt that England's modest first innings score might even yield a first innings lead. Such dreams quickly died as Sobers arrived at the wicket to join Clive Lloyd and the two West Indies batsmen completely changed the tenor of the day's play. When stumps were drawn 90 minutes later, the Rest of the World already had a first innings lead and both Lloyd and Sobers were approaching 70. David Brown, who went wicketless in the match remembers, 'Illy decided we weren't going to take the new ball after tea because he and Underwood were keeping things quiet but then Sobers and Lloyd just started smashing it so we took the new ball and they smashed it to smithereens. That was my last game for England.' Three overs of the second new ball went for 24 and, as the bowlers tired and the sun broke through the overcast Birmingham skies, the game shifted inexorably in favour of the visitors.

The Saturday simply confirmed the worst fears that England would have had as they left the ground at close of play on the Friday. Lloyd and Sobers began in precisely the mood they had been in the previous evening but Illingworth and his team stuck grimly to their task and tried hard not to let the talented batsmen they were bowling to get away from them. The captain eventually bowled both batsmen although Lloyd had already passed the century mark. The lower order now took over and, although nobody made a significantly large score, all of them did enough to cause their opponents damage. Procter and Murray made sixties, Intikhab 45 and even Peter Pollock was 23 not out when Sobers declared at 563/9 just after 5.30pm, allowing enough time for 17 overs of speed and spin which, to their credit, Edrich and Luckhurst resisted in a situation when it might well have been expected that England would have lost two or three vital top order wickets. Nevertheless, still 250 runs behind even with all their second innings wickets intact, England faced the prospect of having to bat for two complete days with the prospect of a draw as the best possible outcome.

Edrich went early on the Monday morning, brilliantly but not atypically caught by Sobers at backward short leg off Intikhab. Cowdrey and Luckhurst resumed their partnership and took the score to 58 before a ball from Intikhab bounced higher than the Kent opener had expected when trying to square cut it and he was caught at the wicket. Cowdrey and Fletcher batted as well together as they had in the second innings at Trent Bridge and they had put on 74 relatively untroubled runs when Fletcher pushed Gibbs into the covers and called Cowdrey for a sharp single. Cowdrey hesitated and then shouted 'No'. By this time Fletcher was halfway down the pitch and his goose was cooked as Graeme Pollock had ample time to pick up and throw to Murray. Fletcher, on 27 and going well, was run out by three feet. Cowdrey clearly felt culpable for his part in the dismissal and although he stayed for some time, scoring 71, his previously fluent innings became a thing of shreds and patches. Although D'Oliveira, replacing Fletcher, began his innings in the same dominant form he had displayed on Thursday afternoon, Cowdrey disappeared into a miasma of introspection, scratching around for his last ten runs which took nearly an hour before he swung at a loosener from Peter Pollock starting a fresh spell and helped it down the leg side into the gloves of Deryck Murray.

At one point D'Oliveira looked as though he would become the first England batsman since Denis Compton at Adelaide in 1947 to score two centuries in the same Test, but when he reached 81 he edged Sobers, bowling orthodox left arm spinners, into the hands of Barlow at slip. Illingworth and Greig continued to take the fight to the opposition but they both left before close of play, Illingworth bowled behind his legs by Gibbs and Greig caught and bowled by the irrepressible Sobers. At stumps England were 320/7 with Knott and Brown at the crease, as they had been at the close of the first day's play. England were now just 51 runs ahead with only the last three wickets remaining.

Encouragingly, England fought all the way on the last day and it took the Rest of the World until the start of the last hour of scheduled play before they finally won the match by five wickets. The last three wickets this time did not collapse in a heap. Brown stayed with Knott for over an hour in the morning and batted well for 32 until, with a rush of unjustified confidence, he hooked at Procter and got a top edge. Murray stood patiently at gully and caught the ball when it eventually descended. Underwood soon went, bowled by Sobers for a duck, but Snow once again contesting his position as a number 11, played sensibly and straight, allowing Knott to reach his fifty. When Snow was bowled by Sobers in the first over after lunch the Rest of the World needed 141 in just over three hours. As so often in matches of relatively high scores a small total in the final innings proved awkward, even for such a distinguished batting line-up.

Barlow was quickly caught behind off Snow, proving once again the unpredictability of cricket. Having taken wickets and scored heavily at Trent Bridge, he went wicketless at Edgbaston and collected a total of four runs in his two innings. Richards and Kanhai batted with a fluency neither had managed to show in the first innings but when they were both dismissed by Underwood, and Illingworth took the wickets of Sobers and Lloyd relatively cheaply, the Rest of the World had made only 107, had lost five wickets and were still 34 runs short of victory. There was an hour and three-quarters left for play and just for a brief moment the prospect of an extraordinary England victory floated in front of the eyes of their supporters. Sadly, it was a mirage; Ian Botham was still seven years away from his Test debut and 11 years away from his 5-1 in similar circumstances on the same ground. Intikhab and Procter took the Rest of the World home but England had shown great credit in defeat. They had pushed a team of better players all the way and in defeat commentators saw the prospect of a strong showing in Australia during the winter months.

One result that went Illingworth's way was the decision that was announced at lunchtime that he would not only captain England in the last two Tests of the current series but that he would logically then be in charge of the England team on its winter tour of Australia and New Zealand. There was considerable sympathy for Cowdrey who was offered the vice-captaincy as he had been under May, Dexter and Smith on previous tours. It was a measure of the Kent batsman's unhappiness that he asked for time to consider the request. It was pointed out by his supporters that he had only lost the captaincy because of his Achilles tendon rupture at the start of the 1969 season and that Illingworth had been fortunate to have captained his first six matches against an under-strength West Indies and a modest New Zealand side. After a few days, Cowdrey decided to accept the offer of the vice-captaincy which turned out to be a mistake for everyone as he lost form and heart and had quite the most miserable of all his six tours there.

Illingworth was regarded as shrewd but cautious and of course the decision highlighted the fault line that had run through English cricket since the second half of the 19th century – amateur v professional and South v North. If Cowdrey was regarded as an amateur in the tradition perhaps of Colin Ingleby-Mackenzie, always willing to risk defeat in pursuit of victory, it was a misguided supposition.

John Woodcock, the Sage of Longparish, thought that in their efforts to be fair to Illingworth the selectors had been unfair to Cowdrey but he correctly identified Illingworth as 'more shop steward than cavalier, a sergeant major not a brigadier, the personification in fact of the modern game' which was clearly not meant as a compliment. Cowdrey was a class batsman who had scored runs in Australia before and was likely to do so again. David Brown also defends Cowdrey's captaincy. 'People say he was soft but Cowdrey wasn't a soft captain. He was a good captain and I liked playing under him.' Certainly, on Illingworth's two overseas tours to West Indies in 1959/60 and Australia in 1962/63 he had made very few runs and taken almost no wickets. Off spinners rarely did well on Australia's hard pitches and the gamble was that the captain might not be worth his place in the side before the Test series was over.

Nevertheless, Illingworth led out the England side at Headingley at the end of the month, strengthened, he felt, by the inclusion in the side of a rejuvenated Boycott who had scored a big hundred against Kent and 98 against Essex in his last two first-class matches and with the comforting presence of the left-arm spinner, Don Wilson, with whom in tandem he had won many a County Championship match for Yorkshire. David Brown, who had not bowled well at Edgbaston, gave way to Chris Old, giving the Yorkshire crowd the enjoyable sight of four familiar faces in the England team. Luckhurst retained his place in preference to Edrich about whom sufficient was known that his place in the team to play in Australia was already assured.

It was a measure of the depth of talent from whom the Rest of the World could choose that they could promote Mushtaq Mohammed, who was playing county cricket for Northamptonshire, from 12th man to take the place of Peter Pollock. The South African returned to the press box from where he had emerged for the Edgbaston Test but if anyone thought that, without either Peter Pollock or Graham McKenzie, the Rest of the World's fast bowling would be materially affected they were soon confronted by Eddie Barlow at his belligerent best. His surprising lack of impact at Edgbaston was forgotten when Sobers won the toss, asked England to bat on an overcast Leeds morning and Barlow tore into the England batting.

Only Boycott with 15, Fletcher, Luckhurst and, inevitably, Illingworth managed to reach double figures as England were bowled out before the end of the first day's play for 222. Procter removed Luckhurst for 35, D'Oliveira and Greig, while at the other end Barlow took all the wickets, finishing with 7-64. Fletcher survived a nervous start, no doubt remembering his torrid debut against the Australians two years earlier at Headingley, when he had failed miserably and been mercilessly barracked by the Yorkshire crowd for scoring no runs, dropping two difficult chances and coming from the South. He made an impressive 89 second time round, putting on 118 for the fifth wicket with Illingworth (who claimed yet another fifty) before edging Barlow to Deryck Murray.

Having reached 209/5 England contrived to lose their last five wickets for the addition of just 13 runs, mostly thanks to Barlow and the first hat-trick in a Test match since Lance Gibbs performed the same feat in Adelaide ten years previously. Barlow finished off the innings with four wickets in five balls, Don Wilson being particularly miffed, having edged the ball on to his pad, whence it lobbed into the air for the England 12th man Mike Denness to take a simple catch. Denness was on the field because Richards had injured himself catching D'Oliveira and Rohan Kanhai had also gone off after bruising a thumb in attempting to stop a drive by Fletcher. Illingworth observed drily that Wilson would do anything to get himself into the records section of *Wisden*.

In place of Richards, Deryck Murray opened the Rest's first innings with Barlow and the two of them put on 67 before Greig dismissed Barlow for 37, Mushtaq for 4 and Pollock for 3. When Lloyd was bowled by Old for 35 the Rest of the World were only 152/4 with neither Kanhai nor Richards expected to bat. However, Murray was still there and, in combination with his captain, took the score to a more comfortable 220 when Murray, who had ridden his luck at times, was caught at square leg by Snow, hitting against the spin of Wilson. Sobers of course decided this would be a good time for another century which he duly completed on the Saturday morning. Kanhai came in at nine but Richards could not bat at all and the innings closed at 376/9, a first innings lead of 154.

Boycott and Luckhurst began England's second innings with a determination to wipe off the deficit before the first wicket fell. In the end they had reached 104 before Boycott drove at Barlow and sent a catch straight to Pollock at slip. Two balls later Cowdrey missed a straight ball and was bowled for 0 to add to his 1 in the first innings and the loss of the captaincy to Illingworth; it made for a miserable week. Fletcher and Luckhurst, however, continued to believe they could set the injury-hit opposition an awkward fourth innings total until just before the close Luckhurst was caught at the second attempt at short midwicket by Gibbs off Barlow. He had made 92, which, along with his century at Trent Bridge, had made England's top three for the winter tour all but certain. England spent the rest day 50 runs ahead with seven wickets left. Despite conceding that large first innings lead it wasn't over yet.

On the Monday, England, inspired by the best weather and the best attendance of the match (15,000) and of course Raymond Illingworth yet again, performed heroically. No batsman surrendered his wicket without a desperate fight. Snow, the nightwatchman and Old, giving a preview of what he was to do with Botham on the same ground in 1981, played watchfully and both gave solid support to Fletcher and Illingworth. Three wickets went down rapidly, leaving England 114 ahead with only three wickets left but Old and Illingworth put on a vital 60 and the Rest of the World, possibly with only nine batsmen, were left a tricky 223 to win. By the close of the fourth day's play England appeared to have seized the initiative. Snow, bowling as he was to do in Australia with pace and hostility, took three wickets and Illingworth two very cheap ones leaving the Rest of the World reeling on 75/5, although it would have been a concern that Sobers was still there on 11.

Not for the first time in the series England allowed the Rest of the World to wriggle free. The crowds unfortunately did not return for what promised to be an enthralling finish but those who were there clearly thought an England win was entirely possible until in Snow's second over Greig got two hands to a straightforward slip catch offered by Intikhab but dropped it. All the air seemed to go out of the tyre and Intikhab and Sobers took their partnership to an untroubled 115 before Cowdrey caught Sobers at slip for 59, but it left only a further 46 needed. However, Intikhab was caught off Wilson before lunch and Kanhai had made only four before he was caught at the wicket off Illingworth.

Procter came out to join the injured Richards with only Lance Gibbs to come. If one of these two went quickly, victory must be England's. They all thought they had the breakthrough when, before the vital partnership had scored a run, Wilson appeared to have Richards caught by Fletcher in the gully off bat and pad. The whole England side went up but the umpire was unmoved, as was Richards. Old players must wonder how many matches might have reached a different destination if they had had access to modern technology. Fifty years on Raymond Illingworth still speaks with passion of that decision.

> If it hadn't been for some bad umpiring at Headingley ... they were eight down and they should have been all out so we'd have gone to The Oval at 2-2. It was a thick edge on to the pad and Arthur Fagg didn't give it. Mind you, he also gave me out in the first innings caught behind when I was on 58 and I never touched it. The ball just brushed the top of my pad. They were two real bad decisions and they cost us the game because the second new ball was due when Richards should have been given out.

The two young South Africans then proceeded to play their shots, enjoy some good fortune, and took their side home with two wickets to spare in the middle of the fifth afternoon. It had been an absorbing game that could easily have gone the other way.

With the series now settled, England once more experimented with a view to the selection of the team for the winter. D'Oliveira and Greig were left out in favour of Amiss, who was recalled for the first time since he had made a pair on debut at Old Trafford in 1968 and Peter Lever, the 29-year-old Lancashire fast bowler. It left a frighteningly long tail of Snow, Lever, Old and Wilson but the batsmen were being entrusted to do their jobs at the top of the order. There was a decent first day attendance of about 10,000 at The Oval but Geoffrey Howard, the Surrey secretary, told the press that had the match been against the full South Africa side the likelihood was that the attendance would have been doubled. Other secretaries of the Test match grounds had made much the same observation. Over the five days of play more than 53,000 people paid to get in, no more than a respectable end to a series that had deserved far better in the way of crowds. The Rest of the World dropped Lance Gibbs, whose three wickets in the first four matches had been taken at a cost of over 100 runs each, and recalled Graham McKenzie to replace him.

Before the start of play, a minute's silence was held to remember the umpire Syd Buller who had died recently. Perhaps affected by the somewhat sombre atmosphere this created, Luckhurst was slow to react to the third ball of the match from Procter and lost his middle stump. Boycott and Cowdrey, the two class batsmen in the side, proceeded cautiously against the new ball but just when Boycott appeared set for his traditional long occupation of the crease he failed to spot Intikhab's googly and was caught by Sobers at backward short leg. Cowdrey and Fletcher batted sensibly on a slow pitch on which the ball turned only slowly and took the score to a healthy 113/2 when Fletcher was caught behind by Murray. Amiss was nervous and tentative and had made only 24 when he was bowled by a Mushtaq leg break. Cowdrey, who had passed 50 in assured mood and had looked the complete master of the attack, seemed to catch Amiss's nervousness and retreated into strokeless lethargy from which he was relieved by Sobers, who had him caught behind for 73 leaving England, with that long tail, precariously poised on 150/5. Nobody could ever understand why Cowdrey, a supremely gifted player, who rarely hit the ball in the powerful manner of May or Dexter but simply leant into it and sent it gliding through the gaps in the field to the boundary, would suddenly begin to doubt himself and retreat into his shell like this.

Not for the first or last time, England were rescued by Illingworth and Knott, who added 75 runs before the close. Early the following morning, Illingworth was caught off Intikhab but not before he had passed 50 for the sixth time in the series. Neither Old nor Wilson troubled the scorers as McKenzie took three wickets in eight balls, but Snow and Lever indulged themselves in bright stands with Knott who was 51 not out when the innings closed at 294. It was not a formidable score on a placid pitch. However, the South African openers did not get away from some tight bowling, Kanhai made only 13 and when Lever bowled Mushtaq the score was just 96/4. As so often happened during the course of this series, two of these talented batsmen seemed bound to succeed and finally, after what had been a most disappointing summer for him, it was Graeme Pollock's turn to come good. In partnership with Sobers, he brought back memories of his 125 at Nottingham in 1965. This time it was 114, most of them made in a partnership of 165 with Sobers who, like Pollock, fell to the debutant Lever, clean bowled for 79. It was a partnership, opined *Wisden*, 'which will live long in the minds of those privileged to see it'. During the last two hours of play on the Friday, Pollock and Sobers put on 135 glorious runs made with supreme artistry.

The Saturday belonged as much to Lever as it did to those two princely batsmen. He took 7-83, the best analysis of his career, having come on as third seamer to keep the batsmen quiet while Snow and Old prepared themselves to take the second new ball. In John Arlott's phrase, 'within the hour he had not merely bowled himself on to the metaphorical ship for Australia but was being offered his choice of the state rooms' – a marvellous image spoiled only by the knowledge that the England team no longer travelled by boat to Australia. Pollock was restricted to ten runs in the first 45 minutes before Lever bowled him. His command of length and direction troubled all the batsmen and only Procter, who made 51 before he was caught by Boycott, played Lever with any certainty. Sobers was bowled by a beauty that swung in late and bowled him through the gate, a ball Lever recalls with pride 50 years after having delivered it. 'He looked at me and said, "I can't play those."' England eventually conceded a first innings lead of 61, which would have been smaller had not Procter been dropped by Cowdrey off Snow and by Boycott off Lever.

Luckhurst, who had batted so well in the series and convinced the selectors that he, Boycott and Edrich would make an excellent top order, decided to make the selectors' discussion less straightforward when, to the first ball of the second innings, he was bowled by the identical inswinger from Procter that had done for him in the first. Once again, Cowdrey and Boycott steadied the ship and England were in the lead with only one wicket down before Cowdrey was bowled by Intikhab for 31. Boycott and Fletcher saw out the day with an unbroken partnership of 47 and then batted throughout the Monday morning session, taking England into a position of some strength on a pitch that was starting to turn.

Altogether Boycott and Fletcher added 154 for the third wicket, England's largest stand of the entire series, before Fletcher was caught at slip by Barlow off Sobers for 63. Fletcher's innings was skittish compared to that of Boycott, who had worked out exactly how best the Rest of the World bowlers could be combated (probably not telling anyone else, as was his wont) and followed his plans with meticulous precision. This was not Boycott the stonewaller, simply waiting for the bad ball. He took the attack to the opposition but he did so with characteristic thoughtfulness and a technique so solid it allowed him to criticise every batsman who came after him for not having one as good. Amiss, playing desperately for his place in the winter squad, stayed with Boycott to take the score to 289 before the opener reached for a half-volley from Clive Lloyd and was held at slip by Barlow for 157. This was his one innings of the series that made every England supporter glad that they had the irritating, selfish Yorkshireman to call on because whatever his deficiencies as a team-mate or in running between the wickets, nobody could doubt that he was a superb batsman.

At 289/3, with a lead of 227, England must have entertained hopes of setting their opponents a total of perhaps 350 which would have to be scored at better than a run a minute on a wearing wicket. That would make things awkward even for such a talented opposition. Bearing in mind the fierce competitiveness England had shown in all the matches since Lord's, a 3-2 series defeat would be a far truer reflection of the relative merits of the two sides than a 4-1 scoreline. Unfortunately, 289/3 quickly became 289/5 when Illingworth, who had made 476 runs in the series so far at an average of nearly 60, got a snorter next ball from Lloyd which he could only fend off as it climbed off a length and Mushtaq fell forward to catch him at short leg. Now the tail that saw Snow promoted from number 11 in the previous Test to batting at eight at The Oval proved no match for Sobers and McKenzie. The innings wilted and England were all out for 344, leaving the Rest of the World an hour on the Monday night and the whole of Tuesday to get 284 to win. Snow offered some optimism when he bowled Barlow with a vicious break back but the hopes of England supporters, that had reached their peak in the middle of the afternoon with Boycott and Fletcher still going strong, had already started to fade as Kanhai and Richards played out the rest of the Monday in relative calm, closing on 26/1 and leaving all of Tuesday to get the remaining 258 to win with nine wickets in hand.

There was a brief moment of hope before lunch on the last day when Richards and Pollock were each bowled, dancing down the pitch to hit the England spinners back over their heads but being beaten in the air. That left the Rest of the World another 200 to make with seven wickets left but Illingworth and Wilson lacked penetration. Illingworth took only one wicket in the match and Wilson two, though the latter was undoubtedly handicapped by having eight stitches inserted after cutting his bowling hand.

Lloyd joined Kanhai and this time it was Kanhai's turn to star. He had not made many runs at all in the series but he had been in prime form for Warwickshire and had scored 187 against Derbyshire the previous week. The two West Indians put on 123 at a run a minute before Lloyd was caught behind off Snow, who was bowling with the sort of hostility Illingworth would have been hoping he would display in Australia during the winter. He also removed Kanhai for exactly 100 and Mushtaq, who had not distinguished himself in either of the two matches he played, to leave England with a final sniff of victory. As the match approached its conclusion, local residents, most of them immigrants from the Caribbean, gathered on the boundary edge, determined to invade the pitch in an echo of what they had done at The Oval in the final Tests of 1963 and 1966. It was fitting that their hero, Garry Sobers, was at the crease guiding a ball from Lever away over the third man boundary to see the Rest of the World home by four wickets well before tea in a rather predictable and somewhat anti-climactic ending to what had been a superb series. Peter Lever was awarded the medal for being man of the match despite being on the losing side. The Guinness batting award for the series went to Sobers, the bowling award to

Barlow and the fielding award was shared jointly by Clive Lloyd and Alan Knott.

The following day the 16 long-awaited names of the MCC party to tour Australia and New Zealand were announced. The batsmen were Boycott, Edrich, Luckhurst, Cowdrey, Fletcher, D'Oliveira and Hampshire who had appeared in two Tests against the West Indies the previous summer, making a century on debut against the West Indies at Lord's; the quick bowlers were Snow, Ward, Lever and Shuttleworth; the spinners were Illingworth, Wilson and Underwood and the two wicketkeepers which must have caused no discussion whatsoever were Knott and Bob Taylor of Derbyshire. Of those who had played against the Rest of the World Greig, Denness, Jones, Sharp, Brown, Old and Amiss did not make the final cut. Of those perhaps only Greig could have counted himself as unfortunate, although Pat Pocock, the Surrey off-spinner, and Robin Hobbs, the Essex wrist-spinner, must have also felt disappointed. It was a team of fighters who reflected and endorsed the philosophy of the captain. They would find, when they got to Australia, that Bill Lawry's team was an easier proposition than the Rest of the World had been throughout the summer of 1970.

The Rest of the World series had originally been granted unofficial Test status like all matches between South Africa and England and South Africa and Australia since 1961 when South Africa left the Commonwealth. The result was that caps would be awarded to all the England players. That decision was later reversed, however, so that despite facing the most powerful side ever to take the field in England since the Australians in 1948 or, for those with longer memories, the Warwick Armstrong side with Gregory and Macdonald of 1921, the matches were awarded no more significance than a match against T.N. Pearce's XI or A.E.R. Gilligan's XI at the Scarborough Festival. Ironically, of course, all the South Africa Tests since 1961 should also have been relegated to similar status because the rules of the ICC stated that official Test matches could only be played between member countries of that organisation and since South Africa had left the Commonwealth in 1961 it had forfeited its place within the ICC.

The cricket season disappeared, as always, with the first nip of autumnal chill and the realisation that the long balmy summer nights were over, to be replaced by a less welcome sense of the nights starting to close in. For the players, professional and recreational, the end of the season always contained some sense in which Death had moved one infinitesimal step closer and summer's lease had all too short a date. The joy of the start of the cricket season, traditionally bathed in celestial light like the opening of Wordsworth's *Intimations on Immortality*, seems in September, when stumps are drawn for the last time, the wickets are covered and the pavilion door locked, far distant from the May of that year and even farther removed from the May of the following year.

Nevertheless, despite the turmoil that had greeted the start of the 1970 cricket season, despite the distractions of the general election and the World Cup, it had been a summer of outstanding and satisfying cricket. To the delight of all those cricket supporters who had been frustrated that for the first five months of the year politics had got in the way of what had always promised to be a feast of cricket, in the end, the cricket supporter in the summer of 1970 had been presented with a vibrant Test series and a competitive County Championship won deservedly by Kent. The 1960s had not been a great decade for Test cricket in England. The Ashes series of 1964 and 1968, with the exception of The Oval in 1968, were largely a bore. England were beaten at home twice by Australia, twice by the West Indies and once by South Africa in 1965. By contrast, the 4-1 defeat by the Rest of the World did not hurt to anything like the same degree and true cricket lovers could revel in the spectacle of the best players in the world on the same cricket pitch. With deep irony it was possible for old MCC members to sit on the tall chairs in the Long Room and look out through the large windows at cricket of the highest order being played in front of them and convince themselves that, in the wake of the cancellation, politics had indeed been thankfully separated from sport. But of course it really hadn't.

The way in which black and white players had mingled in the Rest's dressing room profoundly influenced the team's five South Africans. On his return to Johannesburg, Eddie Barlow spoke bluntly to South African journalists, reiterating that his country could only tour England again if it obeyed the latest MCC stricture of a touring party of mixed races. He told the press that in his opinion the country simply had to work towards that end or it would face indefinite sporting isolation. Would South Africa reform and rejoin the family of cricketing nations? The answer was not long in coming.

EPILOGUE

I N the winter of 1971/72 South Africa were due to tour Australia. The signals coming out of Australia were that Australians were undergoing a similar transition to that experienced by British society at the start of 1970. Years of apathy at the existence of all-white South Africa sports teams was being replaced by a gradual awakening that perhaps this wasn't really acceptable any longer.

Jack Cheetham, the president of SACA, approached his government to enquire about the possibility that the South Africa squad might contain two cricketers who were not white. His request, like so many others before, was brusquely denied. To show the cricket world that SACA was now thinking along the multi-racial lines suggested by MCC, Cheetham made a public statement to show his own good intentions. What he did not expect was the vituperative response he got from Hasan Howa, the president of the governing body for non-white cricket, who complained forcibly that the inclusion of these two men in an otherwise all-white squad would make them 'token non-whites on the team like dummies in a shop window ...[it is] apartheid in reverse: 13 players being picked on merit and two because they are not white'.

The day after Cheetham's modest inquiry was rebuffed, the government sponsored a match to be played in Cape Town between Transvaal, the Currie Cup champions, and a Rest of South Africa XI, captained by Graeme Pollock. Its purpose was to mark the tenth anniversary of the formally declared Republic of South Africa as well as a celebration of the first arrival of white men in the country. On a purely cricketing level it served as the Gentlemen v Players match used to do in England before 1963, in which a friendly match also acted as a Test trial. With Cheetham's plans of mollifying public opinion around the world – and especially in Australia – having collapsed, the players now took it upon themselves to have their say. Plans were laid the night before the game, organised by Peter Pollock. Transvaal 'won' a predetermined toss and elected to bat. Barry Richards played the first ball, delivered by Mike Procter, for a single, at which point the opening batsmen and the fielding side all left the field and returned to the pavilion. The two sides then released a statement reflecting the views of all the players on both teams. 'We cricketers feel that the time has come for an expression of our views. We fully support the South African Cricket Association's application to invite non-whites to tour Australia, if they are good enough; and further subscribe to merit being the only criterion on the cricket field.' After making the statement and ensuring their demonstration had been duly noted, the players returned to the field and continued the match.

The players believed they had made their point in a very visible but non-confrontational way, in which case they must have been somewhat surprised to be immediately both lauded and vilified. Those who really thought about it must have been somewhat conflicted as they worried about whether this was truly a political protest or a late attempt to gain grace and favour in the wider world and preserve their international careers, as they faced the stomach-churning possibility that their Test careers were already over. Continuing to play in an attempt not to upset the white authorities could certainly have been regarded as making the walking off the field an entirely trivial and futile gesture that would make no impact on anyone.

The Sports Minister Frank Waring tried to call the players' bluff by offering to back their call for multi-racial cricket, firm in the belief that they didn't actually want that at all and that what they were engaged in was a perfectly comprehensible ploy to keep MCC, ICC and the ACB all happy that they were doing something, anything, to show their support for multi-racial cricket. However, Waring was taken aback when 94 per cent of white South African cricketers who answered a newspaper poll confirmed that they were 'prepared' to play against non-whites. Hasan Howa dismissed the walk-off at Newlands as a stunt to save the tour to Australia. Ironically, the players, probably with the best of intentions, had united both opposing forces in opposition to themselves. In Australia, the government deplored the South African government's decision to exclude non-whites from its sides but, like the Labour government in Britain before the middle of May 1970, did not go so far as to ban the tour at this point.

The Vorster regime dug in and Don Bradman did his best to keep the 1971/72 tour alive by trying to act as a conciliator to both sides. He proposed to call the matches 'internationals' rather than 'Tests', accepting that Tests could only be played between full member countries of the ICC. However, Gough Whitlam's Labor Party and the labour unions made it clear that the tour was unwelcome and that they would do all they could to disrupt it legally.

It was all starting to sound worryingly like what had happened in Britain. Peter Hain flew out to Australia to give the opponents of the tour the benefit of his considerable experience. In another remarkable parallel, the cricket tour was being preceded by a rugby tour. As in Britain in 1969/70, the South African rugby team was given a rowdy and violent reception in their six-week tour of Australia between the end of June and the start of August 1971. By the following month it was clear to all, even those that supported it, that the cricket tour was unmanageable. It was another replay of what had happened in England in May 1970. Cheetham's demands and the Newlands walk-off had lit a fuse in Australia, a country that had been 85 per cent in favour of the tour nine months earlier. The tour was called off on 8 September 1971 and Australia played, surprise, surprise, against a Rest of the World XI instead.

The 1971 edition of *Wisden* included an article on the Rest of the World matches played in England in 1970, written by the editor, Norman Preston, as well as one on the cancellation of the tour for which he commissioned the statistician Irving Rosenwater rather than the obvious candidate and regular *Wisden* contributor, John Arlott. Rosenwater wrote a measured piece but his sympathies were everywhere apparent as he described the mayhem of the protests in terms of the number of arrests made and the number of policemen injured. The self-serving statements of the Cricket Council were quoted at length but the portraits of the opponents of the tour were rudimentary at best. Uncle Laurence would have done a better job, never mind John Arlott. It added little lustre to the glory of the Almanack but then *Wisden*, however admirably it was regarded as a publication of record, had always maintained a fairly conservative social stance. It had not welcomed the abolition of the amateur in 1962 and its response to the introduction of one-day cricket was distinctly lukewarm.

Although nominally an independent publication, *Wisden's* heart under Preston clearly belonged to the establishment and its attitude therefore to the South Africa controversy was entirely predictable. Robert Winder, *Wisden's* historian, wrote in 2013 that an article by Arlott in the 1971 edition instead of the one submitted by Rosenwater:

> ... would have cemented Wisden's moral authority around the world. As it was, it put a question mark over the idea that cricket even knew the meaning of the 'fair play' culture it so keenly espoused.

In 1984, the editor of *Wisden* was the cricket correspondent of *The Times*, John Woodcock. Although Woodcock had always supported the MCC line of keeping open the bridges to South Africa, he commissioned Matthew Engel of *The Guardian*, a man with a very different political outlook, to have another crack at the South Africa question. By this time the political climate had shifted still further away from the status quo ante 1970. In 1977, the Gleneagles Agreement, signed by the Presidents and Prime Ministers of all the Commonwealth countries, had mandated that all sporting contact with South Africa should cease. That same year, a multi-racial cricket authority called the South Africa Cricket Union was formed. In March 1982, a party of well known England cricketers, some, but not all, nearing the end of their international careers, contracted for the first of a series of tours of South Africa sponsored by South African Breweries. For men like Geoffrey Boycott, Dennis Amiss, Alan Knott and Derek Underwood they knew that signing up would mean the end of their Test careers. For others like Graham Gooch and John Emburey it brought a three-year ban from Test cricket when they returned home.

Keith Fletcher was kept in the dark about it as the idea took shape on the England tour of India in 1981 which he captained. Today, he has no problems justifying what they did.

> Maybe 40 county cricketers would spend every winter in South Africa, coaching at the public schools out there. They had to earn a living. I felt that way about the rebel tour of 81. I got offered £46,000 just for the winter out there but I didn't go, not for political reasons but because it was my benefit year and that was my benefit winter. My chairman would have been pretty upset if I'd told him I wouldn't be around and I was going off to South Africa. Eventually the benefit was worth £80,000 so it was financial rather than political. In 1981 Goochie and JK [*Lever*] both told me they were going before it was announced and said they'd appreciate it if I didn't say anything and of course I wouldn't and didn't. They were big mates of mine and I was the captain and they both felt they should tell me themselves rather than letting me hear it first through the press.

In 1983, a little after the conclusion of a remarkable World Cup won, against the odds, by India, a right-wing pressure group of MCC members who called themselves Freedom in Sport pestered their committee to send an official MCC team to play in South Africa in the winter of 1983/84. Their argument was the familiar one that it was unfair to English cricketers to be denied the chance to play in South Africa when English businessmen were experiencing no such prohibition as they traded with that country. Freedom in Sport was led by the Conservative MP John Carlisle and Lord Chalfont, a favourite of Mrs Thatcher. Both men must have been disappointed when the Prime Minister spoke out against the tour and confirmed the commitment of the Conservative government to the Gleneagles Agreement.

Nevertheless, Freedom in Sport easily collected the 50 signatures necessary to call a special general meeting, providing a distant echo of the more controversial meeting in 1968. MCC was therefore again obliged to conduct a postal ballot before the meeting. The result was uncannily similar to 1968. The membership supported the MCC committee by 6,604 votes to 4,344, the difference being that this time the vote was in favour of refusing to re-establish sporting links with South Africa. The special general meeting was attended by fewer than 1,000 people, less than half the capacity of Central Hall, Westminster, which had been hired in the expectation of a much larger turnout. The main speaker opposing the motion was Hubert Doggart, the former president of MCC, and he was seconded by Colin Cowdrey, who now espoused a very different political philosophy from the one he had advocated in 1968. They were supported by, among others, David Sheppard, now the Bishop of Liverpool. Although traditional supporters of South Africa like Denis Compton, Bill Edrich and Brian Johnston continued to bang the South African drum, the political and cultural atmosphere had changed in the 13 years since 1970 and they were heavily outvoted. Across the road in the House of Commons, as the debate continued, MPs were voting against the reintroduction of hanging. It was a bad night all round for the hard right.

MCC was not the same institution in 1983 that it had been in 1968. It had surrendered its traditional powers to the Test and County Cricket Board, acting under the auspices of the Cricket Council and, although England continued to play non-Test matches abroad under the name MCC, that ceased after the 1976/77 tour of India. MCC was therefore no longer the official spokesman for English cricket. If it was to send a team to South Africa it would be of a standard that would normally be sent out to fly the flag in places like Kenya or Malaysia.

There was another English rebel tour which began in January 1990 that was led by Mike Gatting, and organised in the depressing circumstances of England's 4-0 defeat by Australia in the 1989 Ashes series. Unlike the one led by Gooch eight years earlier which was played before appreciative white crowds and ignored by blacks, this one attracted violent resistance. Ali Bacher feared that Gatting would be killed when the tour reached Pietermaritzburg. Shortly after the tour began, to universal rejoicing, Nelson Mandela walked out of prison a free man and the entire structure of apartheid, which had been wobbling for some months, effectively collapsed as he did so.

Two years later, South Africa travelled once more to Australia, this time to play in the World Cup, demonstrating to all and sundry that this once pariah nation was being welcomed with open arms back into the family of cricket-playing countries. Omar Henry, Herschelle Gibbs, Paul Adams and Makhaya Ntini made their debuts for a team that, prior to 1970, would never have considered them eligible. India began a four-Test series in South Africa in November 1993 and the following year the South Africans played three Tests in Sri Lanka. While all cricket lovers rejoiced that matches involving South Africa could once again take place free from political controversy, it must have given special satisfaction to those who had campaigned to stop the tour of England in 1970 and convinced them that however aggressive the violent actions of Stop the Seventy Tour had been, the end result, 22 years later, totally justified what they did.

The events of 1970, however, did not fade entirely into oblivion. When Brian Johnston passed away in January 1994, the *TMS* feature interview *A View from the Boundary*, which was usually broadcast during the lunch interval on the Saturday of every home Test match and which had until his death been his preserve, was awarded to Jonathan Agnew, who had been the BBC cricket correspondent for three years. That summer's visitors were to be the South Africans, who would be playing a Test match at Lord's for the first time since 1965. Agnew, with commendable enthusiasm, thought it would be a good idea if his guest on the Saturday of that Test were to be Peter Hain, who had now achieved complete middle-class respectability as the 44-year-old Labour MP for Neath.

Peter Baxter was not as initially attracted to the idea as Agnew must have hoped he would have been. Baxter, who became the producer in 1973, had joined the BBC in 1966 and remembered only too well the events of 1970 and the atmosphere of turmoil in which they played out. He thought the BBC hierarchy would remember too and he treated Agnew's bold idea with considerable circumspection. He thought that if Brian Johnston were still alive and Baxter had suggested Hain as a guest, Johnston would either have rejected the idea out of hand or insisted that another broadcaster conduct the interview. For Johnston, Hain remained the scruffy 19-year-old, long-haired student who had wantonly destroyed a summer of cricket and upset all his friends.

Eventually, Baxter overcame his initial reservations and the invitation to Hain was duly dispatched and gladly accepted.

Agnew and Hain liked and respected each other immediately and the interview was successful. As play began on that Saturday, the summariser Trevor Bailey took Baxter to one side and quietly requested that the producer arrange the day's schedule so that he would not be required in the commentary box either side of the lunch interval. He was determined to avoid coming into contact with Peter Hain at all costs. It had been 24 years since the previous tour had been cancelled amidst considerable rancour and Bailey had neither forgotten nor forgiven Hain for his key part in what he obviously still thought had been a sorry state of affairs. Like Johnston, his view of Hain as a trouble maker remained unchanged by the passing years.

If the press had been inclined to follow up the story their interest quickly diminished when television cameras revealed quite clearly the picture of Michael Atherton, the England captain, taking dirt from the pocket of his trousers and rubbing it on to the ball. Like the sandpaper that nearly brought Australian cricket to its knees in 2018, the great and the good of the game responded to something essentially quite trivial, or at least arcane, with a ferocity that would be more sensibly focused on something criminal like match fixing.

The events of 1970 are now half a century distant. It can be argued that, after 1992, cricket enjoyed a happy ending and Test matches resumed with a multi-racial South Africa team playing countries the Nationalist government had previously disdained. If it was a happy ending, it has to be conceded by those who so bitterly regretted the cancellation of the tour that the long-haired, unkempt generation who noisily objected to it might have had a point. As they collect their old age state pensions, brandish their Freedom Passes at St John's Wood tube station and pay the Senior Citizens' concession rate at the ticket office outside the North Gate of Lord's they should be spared a glance of gratitude. They made the world a better place and although they caused an eagerly anticipated tour to be cancelled, they still brought about five of the most glorious Test matches any English summer has ever provided – and now completely forgotten.

APPENDIX

ENGLAND v REST OF THE

WORLD SERIES, 1970

First Test Match at Lord's, June 17-22 1970
England 127 & 339 (174 ov)
Rest of the World XI 546
ROW XI won by an innings and 80 runs

England 1st Innings

BW Luckhurst	c Richards b Sobers	1
A Jones	c †Engineer b Procter	5
MH Denness	c Barlow b McKenzie	13
BL D'Oliveira	c †Engineer b Sobers	0
PJ Sharpe	c Barlow b Sobers	4
R Illingworth (c)	c †Engineer b Sobers	63
APE Knott †	c Kanhai b Sobers	2
JA Snow	c †Engineer b Sobers	2
DL Underwood	c Lloyd b Barlow	19
A Ward	c Sobers b McKenzie	11
K Shuttleworth	not out	1
Extras 6 (lb 5, nb 1)		
Total	127 all out (55.1 Overs, RR: 2.3)	

Fall of wickets: 1-5, 2-17, 3-23, 4-23, 5-29, 6-31, 7-44, 8-94, 9-125, 10-127

Bowling	O	M	R	W	Econ
GD McKenzie	16.1	3	43	2	2.65
MJ Procter	13	6	20	1	1.53
GS Sobers	20	11	21	6	1.05
EJ Barlow	4	0	26	1	6.50
Intikhab Alam	2	0	11	0	5.50

Rest of the World XI 1st Innings

BA Richards	c Sharpe b Ward	35
EJ Barlow	c Underwood b Illingworth	119
RB Kanhai	c †Knott b D'Oliveira	21
RG Pollock	b Underwood	55
CH Lloyd	b Ward	20
GS Sobers (c)	c Underwood b Snow	183
FM Engineer †	b Ward	2
Intikhab Alam	b Ward	61
MJ Procter	b Snow	26
GD McKenzie	c Snow b Underwood	0
LR Gibbs	not out	2

Extras 22 (b 10, lb 5, nb 7)

Total 546 all out (154.5 Overs, RR: 3.52)

Fall of wickets: 1-69, 2-106, 3-237, 4-237, 5-293, 6-298, 7-496, 8-537, 9-544, 10-546

Bowling	O	M	R	W	Econ
JA Snow	27	7	109	2	4.03
A Ward	33	4	121	4	3.66
K Shuttleworth	21	2	85	0	4.04
BL D'Oliveira	18	5	45	1	2.50
DL Underwood	25.5	8	81	2	3.13
R Illingworth	30	8	83	1	2.76

England 2nd Innings

BW Luckhurst	c †Engineer b Intikhab Alam	67
A Jones	c †Engineer b Procter	0
MH Denness	c Sobers b Intikhab Alam	24
BL D'Oliveira	c Lloyd b Intikhab Alam	78
PJ Sharpe	b Sobers	2
R Illingworth (c)	c Barlow b Sobers	94

APE Knott †	lbw b Gibbs	39
JA Snow	b Intikhab Alam	10
DL Underwood	c Kanhai b Intikhab Alam	7
A Ward	st †Engineer b Intikhab Alam	0
K Shuttleworth	not out	0

Extras 18 (b 4, lb 8, nb 6)
Total   339 all out (174 Overs, RR: 1.94)
Fall of wickets: 1-0, 2-39, 3-140, 4-148, 5-196, 6-313, 7-323, 8-334, 9-338, 10-339

Bowling	O	M	R	W	Econ
GD McKenzie	15	8	25	0	1.66
MJ Procter	15	4	36	1	2.40
GS Sobers	31	13	43	2	1.38
EJ Barlow	7	2	10	0	1.42
Intikhab Alam	54	24	113	6	2.09
CH Lloyd	1	0	3	0	3.00
LR Gibbs	51	17	91	1	1.78

Match Details:
Lord's, London
Series: Rest of the World XI tour of England 1970
Toss: England, elected to bat first
Season: 1970
Match days: 17, 19, 20, 22 June 1970 (5-day match)
Umpires: Arthur Fagg and Syd Buller

Close of Play
Wed, 17 Jun – day 1 – Rest of the World 1st Innings 115/2 (EJ Barlow 50*, RG Pollock 6*)
Thu, 18 Jun – rest day
Fri, 19 Jun – day 2 – Rest of the World 1st Innings 475/6 (GS Sobers 147*, Intikhab Alam 56*)
Sat, 20 Jun – day 3 – England 2nd Innings 228/5 (R Illingworth 36*, APE Knott 12*)
Sun, 21 Jun – rest day
Mon, 22 Jun – day 4 – England 2nd Innings 339 (174 ov) – end of match

Second Test Match at Nottingham, July 2-7 1970
Rest of the World XI 276 & 286
England 279 & 284/2 (135.2 ov)
England won by 8 wickets

Rest of the World XI 1st Innings

BA Richards	c †Knott b Greig	64
EJ Barlow	c Cowdrey b D'Oliveira	11
RB Kanhai	c Fletcher b Greig	6
RG Pollock	b D'Oliveira	2
CH Lloyd	not out	114
GS Sobers (c)	b Greig	8
FM Engineer †	c †Knott b Greig	0
Intikhab Alam	c Cowdrey b D'Oliveira	12
MJ Procter	b Brown	43
GD McKenzie	c & b Brown	0
LR Gibbs	b D'Oliveira	1

Extras 15 (b 4, lb 9, nb 2)
Total 276 all out (83.4 Overs, RR: 3.29)
Fall of wickets: 1-31, 2-46, 3-55, 4-106, 5-126, 6-126, 7-172, 8-259, 9-267, 10-276

Bowling	O	M	R	W	Econ
JA Snow	20	5	58	0	2.90
DJ Brown	15	1	64	2	4.26
BL D'Oliveira	17.4	3	43	4	2.43
AW Greig	18	3	59	4	3.27
DL Underwood	9	4	25	0	2.77
R Illingworth	4	2	12	0	3.00

England 1st Innings

JH Edrich	c †Engineer b Barlow	39
BW Luckhurst	b Barlow	37
MC Cowdrey	c Richards b Barlow	1
KWR Fletcher	c †Engineer b Barlow	4
BL D'Oliveira	b Barlow	16
R Illingworth (c)	b Sobers	97
AW Greig	c Gibbs b Sobers	14
APE Knott †	c Kanhai b Intikhab Alam	21

DJ Brown	b Procter	3
DL Underwood	c Sobers b Intikhab Alam	2
JA Snow	not out	27

Extras 18 (b 1, lb 7, nb 10)
Total 279 all out (103.5 Overs, RR: 2.68)
Fall of wickets: 1-78, 2-82, 3-86, 4-106, 5-109, 6-126, 7-179, 8-191, 9-195, 10-279

Bowling	O	M	R	W	Econ
MJ Procter	17	6	42	1	2.47
GD McKenzie	21	3	60	0	2.85
GS Sobers	20.5	3	49	2	2.35
LR Gibbs	6	3	8	0	1.33
EJ Barlow	20	5	66	5	3.30
Intikhab Alam	19	3	36	2	1.89

Rest of the World XI 2nd Innings

BA Richards	b Greig	30
EJ Barlow	b Greig	142
RB Kanhai	c †Knott b D'Oliveira	6
RG Pollock	lbw b D'Oliveira	0
CH Lloyd	b Underwood	20
GS Sobers (c)	c †Knott b Greig	18
FM Engineer †	c & b Underwood	1
Intikhab Alam	c & b Brown	23
MJ Procter	c Edrich b D'Oliveira	27
GD McKenzie	not out	6
LR Gibbs	b Snow	1

Extras 12 (b 2, lb 8, nb 2)
Total 286 all out (107.2 Overs, RR: 2.66)
Fall of wickets: 1-68, 2-87, 3-87, 4-112, 5-141, 6-154, 7-220, 8-263, 9-281, 10-286

Bowling	O	M	R	W	Econ
JA Snow	19.2	2	64	1	3.31
DJ Brown	13	0	41	1	3.15
BL D'Oliveira	26	9	63	3	2.42
AW Greig	23	7	71	3	3.08
DL Underwood	26	13	35	2	1.34

England 2nd Innings (target: 284 runs)

JH Edrich	c Barlow b McKenzie	17
BW Luckhurst	not out	113
MC Cowdrey	lbw b Barlow	64
KWR Fletcher	not out	69

Extras 21 (lb 14, nb 4, w 3)

Total   284/2 (135.2 Overs, RR: 2.09)

Did not bat: BL D'Oliveira, R Illingworth (c), AW Greig, APE Knott †, DJ Brown, DL Underwood, JA Snow

Fall of wickets: 1-44, 2-164

Bowling	O	M	R	W	Econ
MJ Procter	20	9	23	0	1.15
GD McKenzie	24	8	53	1	2.20
GS Sobers	18	7	24	0	1.33
LR Gibbs	31	10	40	0	1.29
EJ Barlow	14	4	20	1	1.42
Intikhab Alam	27	9	94	0	3.48
RB Kanhai	1	0	4	0	4.00
RG Pollock	0.2	0	5	0	15.00

Match Details

Trent Bridge, Nottingham

Series Rest of the World XI tour of England 1970

Toss: Rest of the World XI, elected to bat first

Season: 1970

Match days: 2, 3, 4, 6, 7 July 1970 (5-day match)

Umpires: Arthur Fagg and Charlie Elliott

Close of Play

Thu, 2 Jul – day 1 – Rest of the World XI 1st innings 276

Fri, 3 Jul – day 2 – England 1st innings 279

Sat, 4 Jul – day 3 – Rest of the World XI 2nd innings 257/7 (EJ Barlow 123*, MJ Procter 25*)

Sun, 5 Jul – rest day

Mon, 6 Jul – day 4 – England 2nd innings 184/2 (BW Luckhurst 79*, KWR Fletcher 8*)

Tue, 7 Jul – day 5 – England 2nd innings 284/2 (135.2 ov) – end of match

Third Test Match at Birmingham, July 16-21 1970
England 294 & 409
Rest of the World XI 563/9d & 141/5 (43 ov)
ROW XI won by 5 wickets

England 1st Innings

JH Edrich	b PM Pollock	37
BW Luckhurst	c †Murray b Sobers	28
MC Cowdrey	lbw b Sobers	0
KWR Fletcher	c †Murray b Sobers	0
BL D'Oliveira	c & b Lloyd	110
R Illingworth (c)	c †Murray b Procter	15
AW Greig	b Procter	55
APE Knott †	b Procter	21
DJ Brown	b Procter	13
DL Underwood	c Sobers b Procter	1
JA Snow	not out	3

Extras 11 (lb 7, nb 4)
Total 294 all out (115.1 Overs, RR: 2.55)
Fall of wickets: 1-56, 2-56, 3-66, 4-76, 5-134, 6-244, 7-258, 8-282, 9-290, 10-294

Bowling	O	M	R	W	Econ
MJ Procter	24.1	7	46	5	1.90
PM Pollock	15	1	62	1	4.13
EJ Barlow	11	2	28	0	2.54
GS Sobers	20	11	38	3	1.90
Intikhab Alam	19	4	45	0	2.36
LR Gibbs	19	5	41	0	2.15
CH Lloyd	7	1	23	1	3.28

Rest of the World XI 1st Innings

EJ Barlow	b Snow	4
BA Richards	c Greig b Snow	47
RB Kanhai	c Greig b Illingworth	71
RG Pollock	b Snow	40
CH Lloyd	b Illingworth	101
GS Sobers (c)	b Illingworth	80
MJ Procter	b Snow	62
DL Murray †	c Fletcher b Underwood	62

Intikhab Alam	c †Knott b Illingworth	45
PM Pollock	not out	23
LR Gibbs	not out	3

Extras 25 (b 10, lb 13, nb 2)
Total 563/9d (187 Overs, RR: 3.01)
Fall of wickets: 1-7, 2-80, 3-157, 4-175, 5-350, 6-377, 7-450, 8-526, 9-538

Bowling	O	M	R	W	Econ
JA Snow	38	6	124	4	3.26
DJ Brown	14	2	65	0	4.64
AW Greig	16	0	58	0	3.62
BL D'Oliveira	24	8	58	0	2.41
DL Underwood	44	17	90	1	2.04
R Illingworth	49	13	131	4	2.67
KWR Fletcher	2	0	12	0	6.00

England 2nd Innings

JH Edrich	c Sobers b Intikhab Alam	3
BW Luckhurst	c †Murray b Intikhab Alam	35
MC Cowdrey	c †Murray b PM Pollock	71
KWR Fletcher	run out	27
BL D'Oliveira	c Barlow b Sobers	81
R Illingworth (c)	b Gibbs	43
AW Greig	c & b Sobers	22
APE Knott †	not out	50
DJ Brown	c †Murray b Procter	32
DL Underwood	b Sobers	0
JA Snow	b Sobers	21

Extras 24 (b 14, lb 10)
Total 409 all out (205.5 Overs, RR: 1.98)
Fall of wickets: 1-20, 2-58, 3-132, 4-193, 5-271, 6-279, 7-317, 8-364, 9-364, 10-409

Bowling	O	M	R	W	Econ
MJ Procter	22	10	26	1	1.18
PM Pollock	18	5	48	1	2.66
EJ Barlow	9	2	26	0	2.88
GS Sobers	51.5	20	89	4	1.71
Intikhab Alam	63	29	116	2	1.84
LR Gibbs	42	16	80	1	1.90

Rest of the World XI 2nd Innings (target: 141 runs)

BA Richards	b Underwood	32
EJ Barlow	c †Knott b Snow	0
RB Kanhai	c & b Underwood	37
CH Lloyd	b Illingworth	20
GS Sobers (c)	lbw b Illingworth	7
Intikhab Alam	not out	15
MJ Procter	not out	25
Extras 5 (b 1, lb 4)		
Total	141/5 (43 Overs, RR: 3.27)	

Did not bat: RG Pollock, DL Murray †, PM Pollock, LR Gibbs

Fall of wickets: 1-3, 2-72, 3-79, 4-100, 5-107

Bowling	O	M	R	W	Econ
JA Snow	7	2	10	1	1.42
DJ Brown	7	2	23	0	3.28
DL Underwood	15	2	52	2	3.46
R Illingworth	14	4	51	2	3.64

Match Details

Edgbaston, Birmingham

Series: Rest of the World XI tour of England 1970

Toss: England, elected to bat first

Season: 1970

Match days: 16, 17, 18, 20, 21 July 1970 (5-day match)

Umpires: Arthur Fagg and Dusty Rhodes

Close of Play

Thu, 16 Jul – day 1 – England 1st innings 282/7 (APE Knott 15*, DJ Brown 13*)

Fri, 17 Jul – day 2 – Rest of the World XI 1st innings 296/4 (CH Lloyd 62*, GS Sobers 63*)

Sat, 18 Jul – day 3 – England 2nd innings 19/0 (JH Edrich 3*, BW Luckhurst 13*)

Sun, 19 Jul – rest day

Mon, 20 Jul – day 4 – England 2nd innings 320/7 (APE Knott 16*, DJ Brown 1*)

Tue, 21 Jul – day 5 – Rest of the World XI 2nd innings 141/5 (43 ov) – end of match

Fourth Test Match at Leeds, July 30-August 4 1970
England 222 & 376
Rest of the World XI 376/9d & 226/8 (93.5 ov)
ROW XI won by 2 wickets

England 1st Innings

G Boycott	c †Murray b Barlow	15
BW Luckhurst	c Intikhab Alam b Procter	35
MC Cowdrey	c †Murray b Barlow	1
KWR Fletcher	c †Murray b Barlow	89
BL D'Oliveira	c Richards b Procter	2
R Illingworth (c)	c †Murray b Barlow	58
AW Greig	b Procter	5
APE Knott †	b Barlow	0
CM Old	b Barlow	0
D Wilson	c sub b Barlow	0
JA Snow	not out	3

Extras 14 (b 4, lb 7, nb 3)
Total 222 all out (95.4 Overs, RR: 2.32)
Fall of wickets: 1-37, 2-43, 3-81, 4-91, 5-209, 6-218, 7-219, 8-219, 9-219, 10-222

Bowling	O	M	R	W	*Econ*
MJ Procter	21	7	47	3	2.23
GS Sobers	20	11	24	0	1.20
EJ Barlow	22.4	6	64	7	2.82
LR Gibbs	5	0	16	0	3.20
Intikhab Alam	5	2	15	0	3.00
Mushtaq Mohammad	12	4	27	0	2.25
CH Lloyd	10	2	15	0	1.50

Rest of the World XI 1st Innings

EJ Barlow	c Boycott b Greig	37
DL Murray †	c Snow b Wilson	95
Mushtaq Mohammad	lbw b Greig	4
RG Pollock	c †Knott b Greig	3
CH Lloyd	b Old	35
GS Sobers (c)	c †Knott b Snow	114
MJ Procter	c †Knott b Old	27

Intikhab Alam	c †Knott b Greig	15
RB Kanhai	c & b D'Oliveira	26
LR Gibbs	not out	0

Extras 20 (lb 13, nb 6, w 1)

Total 376/9d (138.1 Overs, RR: 2.72)

Did not bat: BA Richards

Fall of wickets: 1-67, 2-84, 3-90, 4-152, 5-220, 6-280, 7-309, 8-376, 9-376

Bowling	O	M	R	W	Econ
JA Snow	28.1	7	80	1	2.84
CM Old	27	5	70	2	2.59
BL D'Oliveira	24	10	52	1	2.16
AW Greig	31	6	86	4	2.77
D Wilson	20	5	48	1	2.40
R Illingworth	8	2	20	0	2.50

England 2nd Innings

G Boycott	c Pollock b Barlow	64
BW Luckhurst	c Gibbs b Barlow	92
MC Cowdrey	b Barlow	0
KWR Fletcher	c Barlow b Lloyd	63
JA Snow	c Procter b Barlow	10
BL D'Oliveira	b Procter	21
R Illingworth (c)	b Intikhab Alam	54
AW Greig	c †Murray b Lloyd	0
APE Knott †	c Procter b Barlow	11
CM Old	c †Murray b Gibbs	37
D Wilson	not out	6

Extras 18 (b 3, lb 8, nb 6, w 1)

Total 376 all out (168.5 Overs, RR: 2.22)

Fall of wickets: 1-104, 2-108, 3-194, 4-227, 5-257, 6-267, 7-268, 8-300, 9-360, 10-376

Bowling	O	M	R	W	Econ
MJ Procter	40	14	67	1	1.67
GS Sobers	34	9	65	0	1.91
EJ Barlow	32	8	78	5	2.43
LR Gibbs	13	2	31	1	2.38
Intikhab Alam	18.5	6	28	1	1.48
Mushtaq Mohammad	14	4	44	0	3.14
CH Lloyd	17	7	45	2	2.64

Rest of the World XI 2nd Innings (target: 223 runs)

EJ Barlow	c Cowdrey b Snow	6
DL Murray †	lbw b Snow	10
Mushtaq Mohammad	lbw b Illingworth	14
CH Lloyd	c Luckhurst b Illingworth	20
RG Pollock	b Snow	8
Intikhab Alam	c D'Oliveira b Wilson	54
GS Sobers (c)	c Cowdrey b Snow	59
RB Kanhai	c †Knott b Illingworth	4
BA Richards	not out	21
MJ Procter	not out	22

Extras 8 (b 4, lb 4)
Total 226/8 (93.5 Overs, RR: 2.4)
Did not bat: LR Gibbs
Fall of wickets: 1-6, 2-25, 3-49, 4-58, 5-62, 6-177, 7-182, 8-183

Bowling	O	M	R	W	Econ
JA Snow	27.5	5	82	4	2.94
CM Old	13	5	35	0	2.69
BL D'Oliveira	11	6	17	0	1.54
AW Greig	3	0	14	0	4.66
D Wilson	18	9	29	1	1.61
R Illingworth	21	8	41	3	1.95

Match Details
Headingley, Leeds
Series: Rest of the World XI tour of England 1970
Toss: Rest of the World XI, elected to bowl first
Season: 1970
Match days: 30, 31 July, 1, 3, 4 August 1970 (5-day match)
Umpires: Arthur Fagg and Dusty Rhodes

Close of Play
Thu, 30 Jul – day 1 – Rest of the World XI 1st innings 20/0 (EJ Barlow 12*, DL Murray 6*)
Fri, 31 Jul – day 2 – Rest of the World XI 1st innings 309/7 (GS Sobers 75*)
Sat, 1 Aug – day 3 – England 2nd innings 204/3 (KWR Fletcher 41*, JA Snow 2*)

Sun, 2 Aug – rest day

Mon, 3 Aug – day 4 – Rest of the World XI 2nd innings 75/5 (Intikhab Alam 6*, GS Sobers 11*)

Tue, 4 Aug – day 5 – Rest of the World XI 2nd innings 226/8 (93.5 ov) – end of match

Fifth Test Match at The Oval, August 13-18 1970
England 294 & 344
Rest of the World XI 355 & 287/6 (87.1 ov)
ROW XI won by 4 wickets

England 1st Innings

BW Luckhurst	b Procter	0
G Boycott	c Sobers b Intikhab Alam	24
MC Cowdrey	c †Murray b Sobers	73
KWR Fletcher	c †Murray b McKenzie	25
DL Amiss	b Mushtaq Mohammad	24
R Illingworth (c)	c Barlow b Intikhab Alam	52
APE Knott †	not out	51
JA Snow	c Barlow b McKenzie	20
CM Old	b McKenzie	0
D Wilson	b McKenzie	0
P Lever	b Barlow	13

Extras 12 (b 2, lb 7, nb 3)

Total   294 all out (147.2 Overs, RR: 1.99)

Fall of wickets: 1-0, 2-62, 3-113, 4-150, 5-150, 6-236, 7-266, 8-266, 9-266, 10-294

Bowling	O	M	R	W	*Econ*
MJ Procter	20	10	22	1	1.10
GD McKenzie	24	7	51	4	2.12
EJ Barlow	16.2	2	36	1	2.20
GS Sobers	15	5	18	1	1.20
Intikhab Alam	44	14	92	2	2.09
Mushtaq Mohammad	28	10	63	1	2.25

Rest of the World XI 1st Innings

EJ Barlow	c Amiss b Lever	28
BA Richards	b Snow	14
RB Kanhai	c & b Wilson	13
RG Pollock	b Lever	114
Mushtaq Mohammad	b Lever	3
GS Sobers (c)	b Lever	79
CH Lloyd	c †Knott b Lever	2
MJ Procter	c Boycott b Lever	51

DL Murray †	b Snow		5
Intikhab Alam	c Boycott b Lever		15
GD McKenzie	not out		4

Extras 27 (lb 14, nb 13)

Total 355 all out (118.5 Overs, RR: 2.98)

Fall of wickets: 1-26, 2-46, 3-92, 4-96, 5-261, 6-267, 7-280, 8-310, 9-338, 10-355

Bowling	O	M	R	W	Econ
JA Snow	32	8	73	2	2.28
CM Old	21	4	57	0	2.71
D Wilson	18	5	58	1	3.22
P Lever	32.5	9	83	7	2.52
R Illingworth	15	3	57	0	3.80

England 2nd Innings

BW Luckhurst	b Procter	0
G Boycott	c Barlow b Lloyd	157
MC Cowdrey	b Intikhab Alam	31
KWR Fletcher	c Barlow b Sobers	63
DL Amiss	c †Murray b Lloyd	35
R Illingworth (c)	c Mushtaq Mohammad b Lloyd	0
APE Knott †	b Sobers	15
JA Snow	c Mushtaq Mohammad b Sobers	19
CM Old	b McKenzie	5
P Lever	not out	0
D Wilson	b McKenzie	1

Extras 18 (b 5, lb 10, nb 3)

Total 344 all out (150.1 Overs, RR: 2.29)

Fall of wickets: 1-0, 2-71, 3-225, 4-289, 5-289, 6-319, 7-323, 8-343, 9-343, 10-344

Bowling	O	M	R	W	Econ
MJ Procter	19	9	30	1	1.57
GD McKenzie	22.1	2	51	2	2.30
EJ Barlow	16	2	42	0	2.62
GS Sobers	42	15	81	3	1.92
Intikhab Alam	32	8	87	1	2.71
Mushtaq Mohammad	1	0	1	0	1.00
CH Lloyd	18	3	34	3	1.88

Rest of the World XI 2nd Innings (target: 284 runs)

EJ Barlow	b Snow	6
BA Richards	b Wilson	14
RB Kanhai	c Fletcher b Snow	100
RG Pollock	b Illingworth	28
CH Lloyd	c †Knott b Snow	68
GS Sobers (c)	not out	40
Mushtaq Mohammad	c Fletcher b Snow	8
MJ Procter	not out	9

Extras 14 (b 2, lb 8, nb 3, w 1)

Total   287/6 (87.1 Overs, RR: 3.29)

Did not bat: DL Murray †, Intikhab Alam, GD McKenzie
Fall of wickets: 1-7, 2-41, 3-92, 4-215, 5-241, 6-265

Bowling	*O*	*M*	*R*	*W*	*Econ*
JA Snow	23	6	81	4	3.52
CM Old	7	0	22	0	3.14
D Wilson	24	8	70	1	2.91
P Lever	10.1	2	34	0	3.34
R Illingworth	23	5	66	1	2.86

Match Details
Kennington Oval, London
Series: Rest of the World XI tour of England 1970
Toss: England, elected to bat first
Season: 1970
Match days: 13, 14, 15, 17, 18 August 1970 (5-day match)
Umpires: Arthur Fagg and Charlie Elliott

Close of Play
Thu, 13 Aug – day 1 – England 1st innings 229/5 (R Illingworth 47*, APE Knott 26*)
Fri, 14 Aug – day 2 – Rest of the World XI 1st innings 231/4 (RG Pollock 104*, GS Sobers 55*)
Sat, 15 Aug – day 3 – England 2nd innings 118/2 (G Boycott 54*, KWR Fletcher 24*)
Sun, 16 Aug – rest day
Mon, 17 Aug – day 4 – Rest of the World XI 2nd innings 26/1 (BA Richards 9*, RB Kanhai 9*)
Tue, 18 Aug – day 5 – Rest of the World XI 2nd innings 287/6 (87.1 ov) – end of match

BIBLIOGRAPHY

This book has been an attempt to place the controversy surrounding the scheduled South Africa cricket tour of 1970 in its historical context. To do that, I felt it was important to give readers a strong sense of what was happening in and around the tour almost on a daily basis in order to inform them of the pressures being exerted on both sides of the argument. What was showing in the cinema, what could be seen on the stage, what the wider political and social climate was like were all relevant to this approach and were all most easily seen through the pages of the newspapers and magazines of the day for the 12 months preceding the cancellation. The most referenced primary sources were therefore:

Daily Express
Daily Telegraph
The Cricketer
The Guardian
The Observer
The Sunday Telegraph
The Sunday Times
The Times

The interviews I conducted with the following people proved extremely helpful:

Lord Peter Hain
Mike Brearley
Peter Baxter

John Woodcock
Robin Marlar
Raymond Illingworth
Keith Fletcher
Peter Lever
Ken Shuttleworth
David Brown
Farokh Engineer
Michael Atherton
Bob Barber
Jim Cumbes
Jack Simmons

The two most valuable books which gave opposing sides of the argument were:

Bailey, Jack, *Conflicts in Cricket* (Heinemann, London 1989)
Hain, Peter, *Don't Play with Apartheid: The Background to the Stop the Seventy Tour Campaign* (Allen & Unwin, London 1971)

Other books consulted included:

Alexander, Andrew and Watkins, Alan, *The Making of the Prime Minister 1970* (Macdonald & Co. London 1970)
Arlott, John, *Basingstoke Boy* (Willow Books, London 1990)
Arlott, Tim, *John Arlott: A Memoir* (Andre Deutsch, London 1994)
Baxter, Peter, *Inside the Box: My Life with Test Match Special* (Aurum, London 2010)
Benn, Tony, *Office Without Power: Diaries 1968-1972* (Hutchinson, London 1988)
Birley, Derek, *A Social History of English Cricket* (Aurum, London 1999)
Callaghan, James, *Time and Chance* (Collins, London 1987)
Carpenter, Humphrey, *That Was Satire That Was: The Satire Boom of the 1960s* (Faber and Faber, London 2009)
Chalke, Stephen, *At the Heart of English Cricket: The life and memories of Geoffrey Howard* (Fairfield Books, Bath 2001)
Chalke, Stephen, *Summer's Crown: The Story of Cricket's County Championship* (Fairfield Books, Bath 2015)
Chalke, Stephen, *Tom Cartwright: The Flame Still Burns* (Fairfield Books, Bath 2007)

Cowdrey, Colin, *MCC: The Autobiography of a Cricketer* (Hodder & Stoughton, London 1976)

Crossman, Richard, *The Diaries of a Cabinet Minister vol.3 1968-1970* (Cape, London 1977)

Crouch, Colin, *The Student Revolt* (Bodley Head, London 1970)

Dawson, Jeff, *Back Home: England and the 1970 World Cup* (Orion, London 2001)

DeGroot, Gerard J (ed.), *Student Protest: The Sixties and After* (Longman, London 1998)

D'Oliveira, Basil, *Time to Declare: An Autobiography* (J.M. Dent & Sons, London 1980)

Duffus, Louis, *Play Abandoned* (Bailey Bros. & Swinfen, Folkestone 1969)

Fay, Stephen and Kynaston, David, *Arlott, Swanton and the Soul of English Cricket* (Bloomsbury, London 2018)

Fletcher, Keith *Captain's Innings* (Stanley Paul, London 1983)

Foot, Paul, *The Politics of Harold Wilson* (Penguin, London 1968)

Foot, Paul, *The Politics of Enoch Powell* (Penguin, London 1969)

Gordon-Walker, Patrick, *Political Diaries 1932-1971* (Historians' Press, London 1991)

Hain, Peter, *Outside In* (Biteback, London 2012)

Hain, Peter, *Ad & Wal: Values, duty and sacrifice in apartheid South Africa* (Biteback, London 2014)

Harrison, George, *I Me Mine* (Phoenix, London 2004)

Healey, Denis, *Time of My Life* (Penguin, London 1990)

Jenkins, Roy, *A Life at the Centre* (Macmillan, London 1991)

Marqusee, Mike, *Anyone But England* (Verso Books, 1994)

Maudling, Reginald, *Memoirs* (Sidgwick & Jackson, London 1978)

McKinstry, Leo, *Sir Alf* (Harper Sport, London 2006)

Murray, Bruce K., 'The Sports Boycott and Cricket: The Cancellation of the 1970 South African Tour of England', *South African Historical Journal*; vol.46 (May 2002 pp. 219-49)

Murray, Bruce K., and Merrett, Christopher, *Caught Behind: Race and Politics in Springbok Cricket* (University Kwazulu Press, 2004)

Norman, Philip, *Shout! The True Story of the Beatles* (Elm Tree, London 1981)

Oborne, Peter, *Basil D'Oliveira: Cricket and Conspiracy, the Untold Story* (Little Brown, London 2004)

Pimlott, Ben, *Harold Wilson* (Harper Collins, London 1992)

Procter, Mike, *Mike Procter and Cricket* (Pelham Books, London 1981)

Richards, Barry, *The Barry Richards Story* (Faber, London 1978)

Sandbrook, Dominic, *White Heat: A History of Britain in the Swinging Sixties* (Little Brown, London 2006)

Sandbrook, Dominic, *State of Emergency: Britain 1970-1974* (Allen Lane, London 2010)

Sheppard, David, *Parson's Pitch* (Hodder & Stoughton, London 1964)

Sheppard, David, *Steps Along Hope Street: My Life in the Church, Cricket and the Inner City* (Hodder & Stoughton, London 2002)

Sissons, Ric, *The Players: A Social History of the Professional Cricketer* (Kingswood Press, 1988)

Snow, John, *Cricket Rebel: An Autobiography* (Hamlyn, 1976)

Winder, Robert, *The Little Wonder: The Remarkable History of Wisden* (Wisden, London 2013)

INDEX